Cross-Cultural Marriage

D0947899

Please remember that this is a library book,
and that it belongs only temporarily to each
person who uses it. Be considerate. Do
not write in this, or any, library book.

Cross-Cultural Perspectives on Women

General Editors: Shirley Ardener and Jackie Waldren,
for The Centre for Cross-Cultural Research on Women, University of Oxford

ISSN: 1068-8536

Cross-Cultural Marriage

Identity and Choice

Edited by
*Rosemary Breger and
Rosanna Hill*

BERG

Oxford • New York

First published in 1998 by
Berg
Editorial offices:
150 Cowley Road, Oxford, OX4 1JJ, UK
70 Washington Square South, New York, NY 10012, USA

Berg is the imprint of Oxford International Publishers Ltd.

Library of Congress Cataloging-in-Publication Data

A catalogue record for this book is available from the Library of Congress.

British Library Cataloguing-in-Publication Data

A catalogue record for this book is available from the British Library.

ISBN 1 85973 963 6 (Cloth)
         1 85973 968 7 (Paper)

Typeset by JS Typesetting, Wellingborough, Northants.
Printed in the United Kingdom by WBC Book Manufacturers, Mid-Glamorgan.

To Peter, and to Georgie, Barney and James

Contents

Preface

Rosemary Breger and Rosanna Hill

This book arose from a workshop on Cross-Cultural Marriage, convened by the Centre for Cross-Cultural Research on Women at Queen Elizabeth House, the University of Oxford in March 1993. The chapters here cover multiple aspects of mixed marriage in diverse countries: Germany, Spain, Nepal, Guyana, Uganda, Denmark and Japan, Saudi Arabia and Pakistan, Britain, the United States and Ghana. It is worth noting that out of fifteen contributors, eleven have personal experience of marriage to a foreigner and the twelfth is a daughter of such a marriage. These experiences, even if implicit, have helped to stimulate and shape their enquiries and thus enrich this book.

The book is unusual in Social Anthropology and Sociology in that the contributions pay particular attention to the interaction between lived, personal experiences and social constraints facing cross-cultural marriages. While the areas covered and the approaches taken reflect the varied academic disciplines, research, personal backgrounds and experiences of the authors and the people with whom they have worked, the chapters share an interest in, amongst other things, the legal, social and personality factors influencing such marriage, the constraints on choice of marriage partner, the role of stereotyping the foreign Other, and how these all affect the ongoing processes of living together in daily life as a family.

This collection contains research findings as well as more preliminary or 'pilot' work that pinpoints areas meriting further investigation. Most of the contributors have used small samples for their studies, and where larger numbers of interviewees have been involved, space allows for the presentation of only a few case histories. Therefore, we are not making a claim for the representative nature of the ethnographies in the following chapters, but consider that their interest lies in the insights provided by the individual case-studies. Historically, a large proportion of social-science literature on cross-cultural marriage has come from the United States, and to a lesser extent from Britain, so that much of it was about marriages between Black and White Americans, Jews and Gentiles, or American (or British) expatriates marrying someone from the subjugated population under colonial or military conditions abroad. Because of the wide range of cultures and politico-economic situations with which this book deals, we have been able to examine a broader range of experiences than is usually presented. This enables us to consider how applicable some of the postulates and conclusions already reached about cross-cultural marriages are, thus stimulating further thought in an attempt to understand why certain issues are common and why others are not.

Cross-cultural marriage is often defined *a priori* as 'problematic'. This may preprogramme how research is structured, what information is sought and selected. While we do not shy away from looking at problematic issues, none of the contributors considers that cross-cultural marriage indicates any general form of social dis-ease, or even of assimilation. Each chapter tells its own story, within its own contexts, providing us with a rich array of case-studies. Together, these chapters allow us to examine critically the meanings and experiences of mixed marriage, and the strategies people develop in order to cope.

When considering contributions, we were faced with more questions than could be answered about the nature of 'mixed' or 'cross-cultural' relationships. One major issue centred, of course, around immigration laws, and the restriction of entry visas and residence permits to legally recognized marriages between women and men. States do not permit the entry of foreign partners who are not formally married. Since there had to be a cut-off point somewhere, the contributions in this volume are concerned with people who are legally married, and do not include less formalized relationships. The only exception to this arises in Shibata's chapter, where, although the case-study she discusses is of a formally married couple, her samples were drawn from a wider population that included both formalized and non-formalized unions.

Furthermore, given that the issues looked at and experienced are gendered (as well as having race, class and regional aspects), there is a bias here towards women's views. This is not only because all the chapters are written by women, except for one, which is written by a wife and husband team (Alex-Assensoh and Assensoh), but also because in the following chapters most informants were female and so the case-studies portray primarily women's experiences and concerns.

Eight papers were presented at the Workshop, and seven of those are published here. The eighth, 'Mixed Marriages and their Impact on Child Rearing', by Dr M. Nasirullah, which focused primarily on a therapy group for mixed-race families, was thought to be outside the scope of the present volume. The chapters by Alex-Assensoh and Assensoh, Maxwell, Semafumu and Shibata were added to the collection at a later date.

Because the contributions here look at both the social and the personal issues involved in such marriages, this book could be of great interest to professionals in the field of marriage guidance and child welfare. Western societies are becoming increasingly multicultural, so that there is a genuine professional and political need to understand such issues, and to bring this understanding to the attention of the non-academic professional world where it could be put to use helping people and, ideally, informing policy decisions. This book could be highly relevant in helping the growing number of people in cross-cultural marriages understand the problems they may face, but also in pointing out the enriching potential they have to offer mainstream society. The themes pursued here could also be of great interest to social scientists working in the fields of gender, kinship and ethnicity: we hope that discussions here might provide stimulation for further research into this fascinating topic.

Acknowledgements

Firstly, we should like to thank all our contributors for their interesting chapters, and their patience and support in the long drawn-out birth of this book. Secondly, our thanks to all those who have read and commented on the various draft versions of the chapters that follow, especially our series editors, Shirley Ardener and Dr Jackie Waldren. And lastly, to our families and friends who have supported us and borne with us.

Notes on Contributors

Yvette Alex-Assensoh, an American political scientist, earned her Ph.D. degree in Political Science from The Ohio State University in Columbus, Ohio. Currently she is serving as an Assistant Professor in the Department of Political Science on the Bloomington campus of Indiana University. For the 1993–4 academic year she served as a Postdoctoral Fellow at the University of North Carolina at Chapel Hill, USA. Dr Alex-Assensoh, who is completing manuscripts for New York University Press (co-edited volume) and Garland Publishers of New York, has published in numerous scholarly and popular journals, including *Journal of Third World Studies* and *Urban Affairs Review*, on whose Editorial Board she serves.

A.B. Assensoh, born in Ghana, holds a Ph.D. degree in History from New York University, and is an Associate Professor in the Department of Afro-American Studies at Indiana University, Bloomington, USA. In 1987 he was a Visiting Fellow at the Centre for Cross-Cultural Research on Women at the University of Oxford. The author of several books on African history and Black politics, Dr Assensoh has also published extensively in scholarly and popular journals. For about a decade he has served on the Editorial Board of *Journal of Third World Studies*.

Rosemary Breger was born in Zimbabwe, and has lived there and in South Africa, Germany and Britain. She is married to a German who grew up in Namibia. Her personal experiences as a migrant foreigner have influenced her academic interest in migration, ethnicity and stereotyping, on which she has undertaken research in both Cape Town (for an MA in Social Anthropology) and Germany (for a doctoral degree in Sociology). Her doctoral research looked at German media discourses on Japan, and how the resident Japanese community in Düsseldorf reacted to these; her most recent publications are on this work. She is currently an Associate Research Fellow of the Centre for Cross-Cultural Research on Women at Queen Elizabeth House, University of Oxford, and lectures in adult community education.

Rosanna Hill studied Anthropology at University College London and is now a freelance researcher and community education lecturer living in Oxford. She has a keen interest in marriage and the family, and works with a wide cross-section of families teaching parenting and relationship skills.

Jane Khatib-Chahidi is a social anthropologist, freelance writer and researcher, living in Oxford. She has published several articles on her original research areas of Iran and Shi'ite Islam, interests largely inspired by her marriage to an Iranian, and several years of living in Iran before 1979. More recently she has written about women in the Turkish Republic of Northern Cyprus, a country she regards as her second home.

Tamara Kohn is a lecturer in Anthropology at the University of Durham. She has conducted field research in the Scottish Hebrides, East Nepal and north-east England. Her work has focused on the experiences of incomers, intermarriage, tourism, and the creation of identity. Such interlinked foci are no doubt in some small part stimulated by her own experiences through 'mixed marriage' and travel. Raised in Chicago and then the San Francisco area, she studied Anthropology at UC Berkeley, the University of Pennsylvania and Oxford. Recent publications which discuss intermarriage include 'Incomers and Fieldworkers: a comparative study of social experience', in K. Hastrup and P. Hervik (eds), 1994, *Social Experience and Anthropological Knowledge*, London: Routledge.

Meenakshi Krishna was born in 1950, and brought up in an extended family in India. She studied Mathematics (MA, Oxford) and Philosophy (M.Phil., Yale) and returned to India in 1976 for the birth of her son. Her work experience has included being an Executive Director, Agfa Gevaert India Ltd; Partner/Director, Omni Management Consultancy; and member of the managing committee of Mobile Crèches, Bombay. She is now involved in managerial and consultancy practice, dividing her time between Bombay and London. She is interested in the relationship between culture, society, psyche and technology, and in the distance between conventional organization theory and the multicultural aspects of managerial practice.

Audrey Maxwell was born in 1934 in the Judge's Bungalow in the Dutch Fort of Galle, Ceylon (Sri Lanka), of mixed-race parents. Her father T.W. Roberts (Ceylon Colonial Civil Service) was from Barbados and also had mixed antecedants (Afro-Caribbean and Welsh), as did her mother (Dutch and Portuguese Sinhalese). After obtaining a BA from the University of Ceylon, she taught for a year, then travelled to England and continued working as a teacher in schools in London. Later, continuing her education at University College, London, and the University of Sussex, she obtained postgraduate qualifications in Anthropology. She has worked as a researcher in community development, race relations and community medicine, as a refugee relief worker in Sudan, and has taught and done voluntary work in Oxford and abroad.

Renée Paton was born and raised in New York. She studied Psychology at the City College of New York (BA) and took an MA in Clinical Psychology from the same university. In 1972 she obtained a Ph.D. from the City University of New York, researching on aggression and fantasy. She has worked as a clinical psychologist with adolescents and young adults in England, the United States and Israel. She joined Oxford Polytechnic in 1974 and is currently a senior lecturer in Social Psychology at Oxford Brookes University. Cross-cultural marriage has been a characteristic of her family over the last three generations.

Kirsten Refsing was born in Denmark in 1948 and received her Ph.D. in Japanology from the University of Copenhagen. Since then she has taught at universities in Denmark and Japan, and is currently a Professor at the University of Hong Kong. She also spent a year as a full-time consultant for the National Museum of Denmark. Following her dissertation on the Ainu language, published by Aarhus University Press in 1986, she has published a number of articles on Japanese and Ainu culture and language and has recently edited a ten-volume series for the Curzon Press entitled *The Ainu Library: Early European Writings on the Ainu Language.* She was married to a Japanese man for twelve years.

Sanyu Semafumu is a Senior Lecturer in Law at Coventry University. Educated mainly in Uganda, she taught at Makerere University, and also practised law with a keen interest in legal aid and legal education as a means of empowerment for lay women. Her main research interests are in law, gender and development, and issues of difference and access to law. Married with two children, she comes to the subject of cross-cultural marriage having experienced it at first-hand, as her husband is Antiguan.

Yoshiko Shibata is an Associate Professor at Kobe University in Japan, where she teaches Latin American and Caribbean Culture. She has done extensive fieldwork overseas, specializing in the Caribbean area and Latin America, and spent two years studying at the University of the West Indies in Jamaica. She has been a visiting scholar in the UK at the Institute of Social and Cultural Anthropology in Oxford, and at Warwick University. Her two books and many other publications are mostly on the Caribbean. Her personal experience of a 'mixed marriage' (her husband is English) has contributed to her interest in the subject of intermarriage in Guyana.

Mary Sissons Joshi was born in 1947 in London of Australian parents. She read Psychology at Sheffield (BA) and Oxford (D.Phil.), and held teaching appointments at the University of Cambridge in Social and Political Sciences (1973–6) and the University of Sussex in the School of African and Asian Studies (1976–85). In

1976 she visited India on a British Council Lecturing scheme, and has been there every year since then. In 1983–4, the Nuffield Foundation financed her research on Hindu diabetic patients' perceptions of illness. In 1988, after two years as a research officer with Oxfordshire Social Services, she joined Oxford Brookes University as Senior Lecturer in Psychology. Her published research is mainly in cross-cultural psychology and in risk perception and preventive medicine.

Jackie Waldren is a part-time lecturer and tutor in Social Anthropology at the University of Oxford and Oxford Brookes University. She took her first degree at University of California at Los Angeles, and her M.St. and D.Phil. at Oxford where she is a Research Associate at the Centre for Cross-Cultural Research on Women and a Member of Linacre College. Her current research is on the impact of tourism and development on gender and sexuality in Spanish-speaking countries. Her latest publications include *Insiders and Outsiders: Paradise and Reality in Mallorca* (1996), *Tourists and Tourism: Identifying with People and Places* (co-editor, 1997), and *Anthropological Perspectives on Development* (co-editor, 1998). She combines teaching in Oxford with co-directorship of the Deià Archaeological Museum and Research Centre in Mallorca where she has lived for over thirty years. Three of her five daughters are married to Spanish men.

Mai Yamani, a Saudi Arabian born in Cairo, has lived, studied and worked in several other countries including the United States, where she obtained her first degree in Social Anthropology, and England, where she obtained an MA and her Ph.D. in Social Anthropology from the University of Oxford. She has lectured at the King Abdul Aziz University, Jeddah, and was the Academic Advisor to the Centre for Contemporary Arab Studies at Georgetown University, Washington. Her interests include social, cultural and human rights' issues in the Arab states, particularly the Gulf Cooperation Council States, and women and Islam. Amongst her most recent publications is *Feminism and Islam: Legal and Literary Perspectives*, which she edited. She also writes frequent articles on social affairs for the Arabic newspaper *Al-Hayat* and the magazine *Al Rajul*. She is currently Associate Research Fellow of the Middle East Programme, Royal Institute of International Affairs, London.

1

Introducing Mixed Marriages

Rosemary Breger and Rosanna Hill

A Parable on the Nature of Difference

A Jewish woman from Scotland had three sons. She was delighted when, in the
1960s, the third one got engaged because at last one of her sons was going to
marry a Jewish girl. The wives of the other two were both Christians (one
Scottish and one English) and she felt that two cross-cultural marriages in the
family were more than enough. She would welcome with open arms this latest
daughter-in-law from New York, whom she felt would understand and share
her son's cultural background. However, once the couple was married and living
in a tiny two-room flat in England, things did not go so smoothly. First the
Scottish mother-in-law came to stay and it was not long before she was asking
her son, 'What sort of woman have you married? She doesn't even know how
to serve afternoon tea and cakes!' The daughter-in-law dutifully undertook to
get to grips with the intricacies of British meals, guided by her mother-in-law.
She had mastered the system when her own mother came on a visit from New
York, only to be shocked and horrified to find her daughter serving her husband
a cup of tea and chocolate biscuits when he came in from work. 'A man must
be fed properly at the end of the day. What sort of wife are you to serve your
husband candy when he comes in from work?' The new bride felt lost somewhere in between the two older women, but in this case she had enough
confidence in herself and in her marriage to let the mothers fight it out between
themselves.

Through the rituals around food and eating, this true anecdote serves to highlight
some of the intriguing problems and conundrums that arise from the subject of
cross-cultural marriage: for example, what makes a marriage cross-cultural, especially to the people most intimately concerned? What are the differences between
expectations and reality, for the couple who marry and also for their relatives? In
what ways do visions of exotic foreigners seduce or repel? How do people, women
in particular, cope with the lived experience of these differences – as an enrichment,

a palette offering diversity and freedom to change, or as a feeling of cultural dispossession and alienation? How do people negotiate any perceived gulf between Self and Other, or even Self constructed as Other in a foreign society?

Overview of the Contributions

The questions outlined above, among many others, are addressed in the chapters that follow. We were particularly interested in examining the interface between lived personal experiences and broader social factors in cross-cultural marriages. Earlier anthropological and sociological work on marriage, written mostly by men, has already given us men's ideas on marriage, often rationalizing the experience through functionalist-type rules, laws and affiliation patterns, such as the work of Malinowski (1927), Evans-Pritchard (1951) and Radcliffe-Brown (eg. 1952; see also Goody 1971 for a collection of writings). Even later anthropological work, such as by Needham (1962), Lévi-Strauss (1966) and Fox (1967), tended to centre on marriage rules and rationalized exchanges, while sociology tended to look at explaining changing family or household patterns (e.g. Young and Willmott 1957, 1975; Goode 1963; Bott 1971; Laslett 1972), neglecting the actual people involved. One of the breakthroughs of some feminist work on the family since the mid-1970s has been, firstly, the recognition paid to the structuring role of gender in all aspects of life (cf. Ardener 1975), and also its focus on individuals' very different lived experiences of marriage and family life, showing how experiences differ according to gender and age, and building up from there to general models (eg. Friedan 1963; Oakley 1974; Thorne 1982; see also the overview in Abbott and Wallace 1990). It therefore presents a challenge to incorporate into the study of marriage the interaction between wider social processes and the individual's personal lived experiences, such as the idea of individual romance, the attraction to a foreign partner that surmounts custom and hostility, what Kohn in this volume calls 'the reckless anti-strategy of love'.

Most of the chapters here tend to look primarily at women's experiences. One reason for this is that all but one of the contributors are women, and their informants are mostly women, so that the experiences related reflect the gendered nature of informants' worlds. There are, of course, many areas where these experiences are similar in form, but different in content, to those of the husbands involved, and our book does not entirely neglect male concerns.

The experiences related below show that there are features common to almost all cross-cultural marriages, despite the very different cultural situations described, so that many core issues weave in and out of the experiences related in all the following chapters. Briefly and simplistically, these central threads within ongoing, changing lives revolve around three main, related fields of action: firstly, what 'out'-marriage means; secondly, who does or does not marry out, and why; and thirdly, what happens within such marriages. The following chapters examine in various ways the entwined factors influencing choice of spouse; identities and perceived differences, romanticized or otherwise; differing definitions and expectations of marriage and family; and how people in such families perceive and cope with mismatched expectations and cultural diversity. They relate the resourcefulness with which daily situations are acted on, affecting the lives and lifestyles of those involved in mixed marriages. These themes provide a rough chronology of events according to which the chapters in this volume are ordered. In this way, each chapter contributes to parallel discussions in other chapters. At the expense of oversimplification and some repetition later in the Introduction, the following paragraphs give a broad overview of the chapters in order to help the reader find her or his way around the book.

Central to all our discussions are perceptions of difference – what makes a marriage mixed not only for outsider professionals, but also for the people in it. It is therefore appropriate to start this collection with Waldren's chapter, 'Crossing Over: Mixing, Matching and Marriage in Mallorca', which discusses in particular what 'marrying out' means to the people involved. She shows how ideas of what constitutes 'mixed' marriage have changed following national and regional socio-political changes in Spain over the last two hundred years.

The second chapter, 'Chance, Choice and Circumstance: A Study of Women in Cross-Cultural Marriages', is a preliminary study of what sort of person marries out, and why some people should choose an outsider as spouse. Khatib-Chahidi, Hill and Paton found that as a group, outmarrying women resembled each other more than would be expected by chance.

From looking at what 'out'-marriage means, and who does it, it seems appropriate to examine how choices of spouse are constrained by a variety of factors, some social, some formally legalized. A central agent in this process is the formation and propagation of both positive and negative stereotypes of the foreign Other, a topic discussed at length in most chapters. In 'The Seduction of the Exotic: Notes on Mixed Marriage in East Nepal', Kohn discusses how seductive, romanticized stereotypes of a foreign Other predispose young women to marry out of their cultural group. She criticizes the long convention in anthropology in which marriage with exotic outsiders is explained only in structural and functional terms, without considering the choices and perceptions of difference held by those involved in the act of courtship (particularly those of young women).

In 'Crossing Racialized Boundaries: Intermarriage between "Africans" and "Indians" in Contemporary Guyana' Shibata continues this discussion, but looking at the role of negative stereotypes this time. She illustrates how the propagation of negative discourses about each group and their accompanying stereotypes are deeply embedded in the political and economic history of the area, and are therefore highly emotionally charged, especially those concerning the out-marriage of 'Indian' women. She documents through her poignant case-study that although these stereotypes change over time, they nevertheless may have a tragic impact on the lives of people involved in 'Indian'–'African' mixed marriages.

But of course, stereotypes are not the only factor restricting choice of spouse. The state, and its laws regarding what constitutes a marriage, who can marry whom, and its immigration policies also play a great, but often overlooked, role in limiting choice of spouse. Public discourses about different groups of foreigners may also find their way into how immigration officials interpret discretionary laws. Alex-Assensoh and Assensoh discuss how immigration laws and both positive and negative stereotypes affect marriages between African-Americans and Africans from Ghana, in 'The Politics of Cross-Cultural Marriage: An Examination of a Ghanaian/African-American Case'. They document how perceptions of differences between African-Americans and Black Ghanaians tend to be reduced to racialized oversimplifications, in the assumption that Blacks from all over the world are more similar to each other than to American Whites merely on the basis of colour. In some cases, this blinds partners or extended family to the extent of cultural differences in marriages between African-Americans and Africans.

In 'Freedom of Choice or Pandora's Box: Legal Pluralism and the Regulation of Cross-Cultural Marriages in Uganda' Semafumu continues the discussion of the role of the state in marriage patterns in her findings on plural marriage forms between various ethnic and religious groups. Uganda, as many other African countries, has a plurality of marriage forms, reflecting the multicultural nature of its citizens, each with its own distinct regulations regarding polygamy, inheritance and communal property. She shows how some women deliberately subvert the law and marry illegally under several of these laws to maximize the social acceptabilities of their mixed marriages as well as to guarantee their personal interests.

Breger also considers the role of the state in restricting cross-national marriages, using case-studies from Germany, in 'Love and the State: Women, Mixed Marriages and the Law in Germany'. She shows how the state can restrict entry and residence visas and work permits of some foreign spouses, or even refuse mixed couples permission to marry in Germany. The state's unwillingness to give foreign spouses civil or political rights is related to definitions of national identity and citizenship embedded in long-standing negative discourses towards foreigners that are also apparent in the media.

The following chapters relate how mixed families structure their daily lives. In a mixed marriage, there may be various degrees of awareness of difference, with some differences being celebrated, whilst others may become points of conflict. This awareness and evaluation of difference is not only on the part of the immediate family, but also on the part of the larger extended family, and the community in which it lives. Family bonds can be strengthened if there is something larger, beyond the awareness of difference, to unite the family. Yamani, in 'Cross-Cultural Marriage within Islam: Ideals and Reality', looks at the role of religion in unifying a cross-national marriage. She documents how moving to a new locality, away from extended kin influence and public intolerance of outsiders, can help maintain the marriage. Where a mixed couple lives seems to play a significant role in the flexibility they have in negotiating around their different cultural expectations, and escaping many negative effects of public and private ethnic stereotyping. But this is an option generally open only to the relatively wealthy.

But in many cases, those involved in a mixed marriage may not at first be aware of quite how divergent their beliefs and practices are, which results in mismatched expectations and a growing sense of frustration. Sissons Joshi and Krishna, in 'English and North American Daughters-in-Law in the Hindu Joint Family', analyse the intimate workings of life within a patrilaterally extended family. They note how differences in everyday rituals revolving around, for example, attention, conversation, the use of space and privacy, and food are strongly related to familial structures of power and hierarchy, role expectations, and culturally divergent notions of personhood. These often conflict with the expectations and experiences of the incoming daughters-in-law. Within a close extended kin group, it can be very difficult for dissenting voices to be heard, especially the voices of the traditionally powerless: the new, incoming bride.

Refsing looks at mismatched gender role expectations, addressing the issue of how gender identity is negotiated between partners from two cultures with very different perceptions of gender roles, in 'Gender Identity and Gender Role Patterns in Cross-Cultural Marriages: The Japanese–Danish Case'. Her work shows how the wider socio-economic environment strongly influences the adaptability of gender roles. She shows that where these role expectations are completely mismatched, then there is a greater likelihood of these marriages to break down.

The final chapter, 'Not all Issues are Black or White: Some Voices from the Offspring of Cross-Cultural Marriages', refocuses the reader on the vexed question of identity, by looking at the diversity and choice of identities available to children of mixed marriages. Maxwell, herself a child of very mixed parentage and grand-parentage, lets the reader hear their voices as they relate their experiences. Common to them all is how their feelings of belonging and identity change not only as they grow up and move through significant life-cycle phases, but also closely reflect changing relationships at and outside home.

Mixed Marriage

Defining Marriage and Family

At the heart – both literally and figuratively – of cross-cultural marriages there is the issue of what is defined as a valid, legally and socially legitimate marriage.

This of course also relates to the gendered roles, norms, and access to resources within the marriage. Even within Europe, in medieval England, the Church faced great difficulties in defining marriage (Leyser 1996: 106). Given that our contributions include such a variety of cultures, a central theme is concerned with different definitions of marriage and family, and the involvement of and responsibilities towards extended kin, since in many cultures marriage is not seen as a joining together of two individuals, but as a union between two families continuously reinforced through mutual obligations.

As with any institution or, indeed, any word, finding a cross-cultural definition is always problematic, and editing this volume has reminded us of the dangers of ethnocentricity when talking about 'marriage'. As Leach (1982) points out, in English alone the word has at least four general meanings. The first has to do with the legal aspect, dealing with rights, legitimacy of children and so forth. The second describes the actual, practical household, the routine of marriage. The third concerns the ceremonial aspect, the wedding and other ceremonies which may precede or follow it, and fourthly there is the joining of families, the affinal relationships which are formed on marriage. For some people a religious dimension may encompass one or more of these definitions. All these aspects are considered in the following chapters.

We would add to these another meaning not usually explored by anthropologists, but which would perhaps spring easily to mind in late twentieth-century Europe and North America: that is the psychological or emotional aspect of marriage which is concerned with a relationship between two individuals. When, today in Britain, we talk about a couple having 'a good marriage', we are likely to mean that they are happy and well-suited emotionally, perhaps that they communicate well with each other. However, the case-studies in this book demonstrate that 'a good marriage' means very different things to different people.

For example, in her Guyanese case-study, Shibata describes Pearl's marriage to Krishna. Pearl has 'mixed blood' ('African' and 'Indian'), though she normally identifies herself as Black, and her husband is classified as 'Indian'. Guyana has a long history of racial conflict between 'Africans' and 'Indians' and intermarriage has always been difficult. Pearl and Krishna met at a Jehovah's Witness meeting, and later married, despite some cultural differences and opposition from families. Their marriage was a strong one, buoyed up by their shared Christian beliefs, but it is unlikely that Krishna's family would have described it as 'a good marriage'. Pearl's mother-in-law Parvati deeply resented her, made attempts to poison her, and, the couple suspect, had some hand in the mysterious death of their youngest (and darkest skinned) son. Shibata describes the racist stereotypes used in Guyana to enforce politico-cultural categories which are supposedly racially distinctive, but which, after many years of blurring 'by acculturation and interracial sexual relationships', have more to do with economic, political and religious interests.

Parvati's belief in these stereotypes inhibits her from accepting her Black daughter-in-law.

Yamani's example of a marriage between two Sunni Muslims from different countries makes it clear that in the reckoning of the bride's elite Saudi Arabian family 'a good marriage' would mean one which linked their family, through their daughter, with another family of high status, one with 'purity of blood' whose lineage they respected. For them, the wealth of the groom's extended family was less important than its lineage, and the groom's personal attributes and social achievements came even further down the list of priorities. Yamani explains that in Saudi Arabia 'A person's worth is socially evaluated on the basis of the extended family. The individual without a family background that meets such criteria counts for nothing; outside the context of his ... family, the individual has no social identity.' The groom in this case came from Pakistan; he was not an Arab, his family was unknown, and the bride's family were thrown into confusion as they had no way of placing him or assessing his worth. This was not, however, a problem for the bride, for the couple had met at an English university and it was enough for them that they were both Muslims and loved each other.

In both these cases the marriage desired – and achieved – by the couple concerned was not thought to be desirable by at least one of the families involved. Thus what constitutes 'a good marriage' in local terms, or what is important in a marriage, varies not only from one society to another, or from one ethnic group to another, but also within smaller groups, even within families and across generations.

Defining 'Mixed': Self and Other

'Mixed' or 'cross-cultural' marriages here are taken to mean marriages between two people from different linguistic, religious, or ethnic groups or nations. However, the perplexities of what constitutes a different culture begin a great deal nearer 'home', as the anecdote at the beginning of this chapter illustrates. Deborah Tannen (1986), as others before her, indicates the scale of the problem of definition in her comment that, given the gendered nature of all our experiences, there is in fact a cultural divide between the sexes within the same class and culture. So, too, is this true to varying extents of different classes or even regions within the same society. Thus, all marriages could be said to be cross-cultural in some way.

Therefore, a central recurrent theme in this volume concerns discussions about the nature and significance of collective, gendered definitions, including stereotypes, of Self, Other, and Self as Other. There can be no concept of Self without a concept of Other, that which Self is not. Although it often appears that a group of people has a clear idea of who belongs and who does not, on closer inspection the dividing line proves to be extremely fluid; moreover, definitions can alter markedly over time, as the work here by Waldren, Maxwell, and Alex-Assensoh and Assensoh shows. The chapters below indicate the importance of the contexts in which definitions are made, the degree of flexibility of such definitions, and how they may change. The definition of memberships is always both relational and situational; in other words, who is an insider can be defined only against who is an outsider, and this is necessarily embedded in the changing political and socio-economic relationships between these groups (Barth 1969; Cerroni-Long 1984; Breger 1990). Other and Other's culture becomes the symbolic marker of boundaries and of difference.

Definitions of who constitutes outsiders are also open to change: they vary depending on who – in class, regional, national, generational or gendered terms – is doing the defining, and whether personal or collective definitions are being used. The context of the definition, which can be economic, social, political, or religious, also helps structure the definition of who belongs and who does not (Dower 1986). For example, elites in a society may define their sense of belonging only in terms of their class position when it comes to protecting their assets, but in times of war, they will call on a common national bond, that may include persons of one type of religion (such as Christians), but exclude others (such as Jews). This means that not all groups of outsiders appear equally 'strange'; some groups seem more familiar, their presence is more tolerated, their cultural practices perhaps even admired. This leads to a hierarchy of acceptable 'foreign-ness' (Thränhardt 1985; Breger 1992).

Waldren discusses below how, in Mallorca, definitions of collective Self and Other, central to the concept of 'mixed', have changed from the nineteenth century to the present, and thus affecting choice and acceptability of marriage partners. Changing social and economic relations on the island and increased contact with foreigners after the Second World War were accompanied by a fascination with differences. This included an increasing number of mixed marriages to 'exotic' Others – non-Spaniards, sometimes from different class and religious backgrounds. Non-Catholics had to leave the country to be married in a civil ceremony before 1975. However, with the rapid development in Spain over the past twenty years, cultural pluralism has increased both regionally and nationally, civil marriage and divorce are allowed and practised, and the focus of mixed marriages seems to be on the partners identifying their similarities rather than their differences.

In some cases, a group's perception of its difference from other groups may seem to ignore a wide range of similarities it might share with them (as is often pointed out in the discussions on Japanese discourses of national identity, eg. Miller 1982; Mouer and Sugimoto 1986; Dale 1988). Conversely, two people from different cultures may actually have more in common than they have differences, especially if they share a similar urban, highly educated, professional background (cf. Spickard 1989; Cottrell 1990).

The complex and interrelated notions of Self and Other are active at various social levels, a wider group definition of 'Us', and a related, individual, personal definition of 'Me'. The personal notion of Self is embedded in wider definitions of a collective, group concept of Self, itself set within a broader matrix of political and economic relationships.

On an intimate, personal level, this involves a gendered idea of personhood, and, in a mixed marriage, the willingness to accept the 'Otherness' of the partner. On the level of personal social interaction, the gendered Self must fit into an existing family structure in a particular kinship tradition, and into prevailing moral discourses about her identity and roles. In addition, freedom to negotiate change, and, more to the point, to get away with it, are closely bound up with larger group stereotypes of Self and Other, not only in informal discourses, but also expressed in hitherto perhaps unchallenged customs and laws. Mixed marriages are often treated with suspicion precisely because they call into question the boundaries between Self and Other.

The Imagined Ethnic Community

It is often taken for granted by the people concerned that 'tradition' has always been, and should always continue, 'tradition' does not, or should not change; and if changes occur, they are to be mourned. In this way, cultural practices may often be simplified and stereotyped, by both insiders and outsiders, as unchanging, morally charged indicators of the 'essence' of the group, especially in times of national or group mobilization (for example, during political campaigns, media panics, war, cf. Bachu 1993). For mixed marriages, the underlying assumption is that it is quite clear what the cultural practices of the partners are, and how they differ: people of culture 'A' do this, those of culture 'B' do that.

In this way, the 'ethnic culture' is 'homogenized', that is, it is assumed that the cultural conventions, including religion, language, norms and expectations, are not only the same for people of a particular ethnic identity, but are also completely accepted and practised by them all, that there is one 'pure', easily identifiable set of ethnic 'traditions', religion and speech (see Breger, this volume, on the creation of a sense of 'national culture' in Germany; also Hobsbawm and Ranger 1983). This tends to lead to an implicit, uncritical assumption that 'ethnic culture' is easily identifiable, without much internal variation between regions or class, that there is somehow or somewhere a golden set of rules for ethnic practices. There is an associated assumption, which may or may not be true, that people of the same ethnic identity form a cohesive group, an interacting, self-aware community. While these beliefs might suit politicians, especially minority-rights ones (see MacDonald 1994), it brushes over the fact that there is generally divergence of cultural practices, speech forms, and so on, from region to region, and class to class, let alone from one century to the next, or that there may be several concurrently existing very different sets of practice whose practitioners may reject the practices of others within the large 'ethnic' grouping. These issues have long been discussed, perhaps most famously by Steadman (1969) and Said (1978), in their discussions of what, and who, constitutes 'the East' and 'the West', and how this is achieved.

Furthermore, Johnson and Warren (1994) criticize anthropologists for creating and perpetuating the idea that people from a particular culture who live abroad necessarily form an 'ethnic community', with all the implications of interactivity, and that they adhere to a clear set of cultural practices. They suggest this arises historically from anthropological preoccupation with self-contained small-scale societies, which has lead anthropologists to over-rate the cultural and social cohesion and closed nature of tribes, villages, and more recently, ethnic groups in urban areas. While this criticism is rather too sweeping, and studies have changed focus since they wrote (e.g. MacDonald 1994; Essed 1995; Brah 1996, who all emphasize the diversity, change and conflicts within gendered perceptions of collective identity through the group's relationships to other ethnic groups, the dominant culture and other political processes), its general message should still be heeded.

However, it needs to be stressed, especially in the context of mixed marriages and ingroup notions of what constitutes difference, that even within the ethnic community identities can be plural, cross-cutting, conflicting and contested, with different ideologies supporting them (Hobsbawm and Ranger 1983; Cottrell 1990; Garcia 1992; Burton 1994; MacDonald 1994; Spiering 1996). There are a range and diversity of norms and customs within an ethnic community, as there are outside of it, some of which form for a time a central 'core' of dominant practices, and others which form a changing continuum of decreasing acceptability, a 'periphery' of more, or less, tolerated divergences (see, for example, MacDonald 1994). These customs, practices and ideologies undergo change as they interact both with each other, and with the socio-political and economic environments around them, not just of the dominant society, but also with those of other ethnic groups, in what Brah (1996) has called 'the broad relationality of diasporic space'.

Significant, too, is how rigidly these notions of difference are enforced formally and informally, publicly and privately. Mixed marriages need not necessarily be literally beyond the pale of ethnic acceptabilities; they might fall somewhere within the periphery of semi-tolerated divergence.

Awareness of Difference

Hardach-Pincke (1988), in her work on German–Japanese marriages, shows that within such marriages awareness of cultural differences changes, depending on the couple's place in the life cycle and their socio-economic situation. She shows in her sample how the couple's awareness of cultural differences gradually becomes individualized, that is, differences are put down to the individual personalities and not to cultural variation. The extreme case is when such cultural differences are completely denied, which she notes seems to occur especially in mixed marriages where the partners have undergone similar socialization processes and share the same values, as, for example, in marriages between highly educated professionals. She concludes that Otherness is therefore no longer perceived in the partner, but is externalized and seen only in the outside culture.

When collective definitions of Self or Other tend to concentrate on the differences between groups, they thereby necessarily ignore or play down any similarities. This sort of focus thus helps maintain the idea that ethnic groups generally have little in common with each other, by focusing on cultural items, such as dress, beliefs, rituals, food – all of which of course do change in time – making these seem to be of great importance in defining groups. This of course then neglects issues like how access to resources is controlled, both within and without the group, as well as neglecting the power relationships between an ethnic group, other ethnic groups, and the majority culture (Brah 1996).

Johnson and Warren, in *Inside the Mixed Marriage* (1994), also criticize an apparent fascination with 'difference', especially in the USA, where scholarly work on ethnicity and cross-cultural processes tends to concentrate on racial (physical) and ethnic (cultural) differences, thus ignoring conflict relationships both within and between groups. Rex, too, has long criticized British anthropology of ethnicity for being simplistically apolitical (see, for example, Rex and Mason 1986).

There is thus a danger that a preoccupation with race, ethnicity, Other – that is, with difference – blurs the fact that there are so many other facets affecting cross-cultural encounters, such as education, personality, class or legislation. Alex-Assensoh and Assensoh, in this volume, also comment on the blindfolding effect of 'racializing' difference in the USA, that is, ascribing differences primarily to race. They note that therefore African-Americans often perceive themselves and are perceived by others to share a common cultural background with Black people from Africa rather than with their fellow Americans: their phenotypical similarity becomes the marker of identification.

Marrying Out

Choosing a Foreign Spouse: Stereotyping

Stereotypes, by their crude over-generalizations which include all of a group, simplify and ignore social diversity. They thus create archetypes. As Said (1978), Steadman (1969) and Dower (1986) all comment, group characteristics are presented as if they are universal to the group, often as specific group or national 'characters' that are inherent, 'natural', and therefore unchangeable. These characteristics are very often couched in terms of an implicit moralizing dichotomy which draws boundaries between 'Them' and 'Us' (Breger 1990). But these boundaries are not merely passively descriptive; they incorporate a value judgement of the group that is embedded in the power differential between the various groups within that society (Dudley and Novak 1972; Foucault 1974; Brah 1996). Stereotypes are thus highly emotionally charged.

On the one hand, this encourages people to choose a spouse from within their own circle. On the other hand, positive or negative stereotypes of the outsider group into which someone has married can influence how extended kin, the local community, even the authorities react; in other words, stereotypes can affect the social acceptability of an exogamous marriage. The role of stereotypes in pre-structuring from which groups spouses may be chosen is explored below in various ways by Waldren, Shibata, Breger and Kohn.

Spickard (1989) discusses how negative stereotypes of each other act to 'filter out' potential spouse choices between African-American women and White men in the USA: the majority of mixed marriages between these groups are between White women and African-American men. African-American women have a stereotype of White men closely associated with a past of slavery, political insecurity, and sexual harassment in which these women were the victims of White men, whereas White men have a stereotype of African-American women as overly dominant, controlling, too strong, demasculizing. He describes how, on the other hand, White women tend to stereotype African-American men positively in strongly sexual and musically creative images, while Black men tend to stereotype White women as caring, sensitive, and relationship-oriented.

Alex-Assensoh and Assensoh discuss how these issues affect African-American marriages with Africans from Ghana, both in the personal sphere and via state immigration laws. Like Breger and Yamani, they show how state legislation constrains marriage choice to foreigners considered too different, and how this feeds into public discourses on such foreigners as by definition inimicable to 'national identity'.

Personal Choices

Khatib-Chahidi, Hill and Paton's research also attempts to throw some light on the matter of choice, but within a more personal context. Their informants were asked to recall how they had felt at the time (sometimes many years earlier) about marrying a foreigner. Interestingly, most of the women remembered their feelings of confidence at finding the 'right man' and a marked lack of concern about his 'foreignness'. Very few of them bothered to find out about their future spouse's culture, his family or country before marriage, as this did not seem important to them. Khatib-Chahidi et al. suggest that some of their informants chose to marry out to escape from a highly restrictive home life, while for others from liberal families outmarriage was a logical extension of a life which involved travel, foreign friends and an openness to outsiders and new experiences.

Control and the Role of the State in Partner Choice

The role of tolerance or intolerance to outsiders in different cultures is examined in many chapters at various levels: individual reactions, active network pressures, and the power and will of the modern state firstly to restrict the choice and then the liberties of foreign spouses. It is often assumed that the constraints affecting choice of marriage partner and the success of a marriage tend to be mostly informal in modern democratic countries. However, a wide range of formal constraints plays a significant role not only in defining what the state expects and tolerates in a marriage relationship, and thus in defining categories of acceptable marriage partners, but also in controlling citizens' rights to marry non-nationals, as Breger's work here on German marriage to foreigners shows, and Alex-Assensoh and Assensoh discuss with respect to marriages between African-Americans and Ghanaians. Generally, the more atypical the marriage partners are perceived to be, the more stringent the state control. States give or withhold permission to marry (as Yamani shows, Saudi Arabia does not permit its citizens to marry non-Saudis without special dispensation), give residence and work permits, control access to jobs, to citizenship rights, and may, under certain circumstances, revoke all the above rights in case of divorce, including access to children.

Furthermore, states exhibit degrees of tolerance and intolerance towards various groups of foreigners, which change in time according to changing political and economic relationships between the respective countries. The idea that those who do not share the majority's culture are considered at best to be outsiders, at worst, a threat to the national polity, is anchored in laws and collective self-definitions. Media discourses representing foreigners negatively perpetuate and reinforce such stereotypes (Thränhardt 1985; Breger, this volume).

Who Marries Out

In looking at cross-cultural marriages, one should also consider what opportunities there are for people from different backgrounds to meet each other. Thus opportunities for outmarriage form a central theme in this book: what influences them, how choices are constructed and constrained both informally (as discussed by Kohn, Khatib-Chahidi et al., Shibata and Yamani), as well as formally by the state and laws limiting or even forbidding marriage to non-nationals in some countries (as discussed by Yamani, Breger, Waldren and Semafumu).

It is sometimes popularly maintained that the end of the twentieth century has seen an unprecedented rise in the numbers of mixed marriages, because of the vast scale of population movements caused by refugees, wars, famine, work migration, tourism and so forth, which thus bring more peoples than ever before into contact with each other. Where people have an education, this too is a transportable resource, unlike property, and enables movement away from the natal community (should the receiving nation state be disposed to accept foreign qualifications, see Breger, this volume). However, just because people migrate to another area or country does not necessarily mean that they are able or want to form close relationships with other groups. There are many studies which show how migrant groups often have restricted access to relationships with host-society groups, either through their own excluding practices (cf. Spickard 1989; Abdulrahim 1993, see below), or, more often, through those of the dominant group (cf. Hitchcox 1993). Perhaps it would be more accurate to note that at different points in their histories, some groups have been more open to mixed marriages than others, and toleration swings not only in allowing which foreign Other may be chosen as a spouse, but also in tolerating the very principle of outmarriage.

Other work has shown that the length of time migrants have lived within a new society is closely related to the degree with which they marry out; that is, first-generation migrants tend to have low out-marriage rates, but more of their children will marry out, while the third generation will have a high out-marriage rate (Lee and Yamanaka 1990). While statistics tend to support this model, what this empirically-based description does not indicate, however, is why some groups are chosen as potential spouses, whereas others are not. What factors create or lessen the social distance between groups?

Spickard's own work (1989) corroborates this generational aspect of the rate of outmarriage, but with some interesting exceptions. He notes that this does not hold at all for Black Americans, where the rate of outmarriage has remained low across generations. He relates this, amongst other things, to the deliberate political choice of Black people not to marry out, as the rise of Black Consciousness since the 1960s has aimed to give Blacks a higher sense of self-worth and to politicize their affiliations. This political awareness is particularly strong amongst the educated middle classes, which in other groups are precisely those who marry out more often. Alex-Assensoh and Assensoh discuss the political nature of some mate choices in their chapter in this volume. This example also indicates the shortcomings of considering cross-cultural marriages as signifying assimilation into the dominant society.

In many anthropological descriptions of marriage patterns, it is often implied or even stated that marriage of women out of the group may be more strictly controlled than that of men. Barbara (1989) observes that in political situations where minorities are oppressed by majorities, as for example Algerians in France, minority women become 'forbidden persons', that is, they are restricted by their own menfolk in relationships with majority men. He suggests this is because this is the last arena in which minorities still have some control over their private lives. Buijs (1993) notes that where men are uprooted and powerless, deprived of their ability to fulfil their accepted gender roles, there is empirical evidence (provided by other chapters in that book) that they will increasingly try to control and circumscribe their women, even using increased violence. Abdulrahim (1993) illustrates this process for Palestinian refugees in Berlin, where the unemployment of men previously active and important in politics leads to strong feelings of disempowerment. The men react by reconstructing an ideal of female seclusion, and the separation of space according to gender that they had not practised even in Palestinian refugee camps. So they reconstruct group identity, specifically around male honour and female shame, involving their increased control of female movement and behaviour, which in particular aims to restrict their contact with German men and the possibility of such an alliance.

This is linked to the notion of a 'gendered ethnic centre' which revolves around ingroup ideologies of ethnic femininity and their linked stereotypes based on women's domestic reproductive roles. These define women in terms of highly emotional symbolic roles associated with the essence of family, childhood, love, such as 'the mothers of our people'. They often also incorporate a sexual morality, implying that 'our' women are 'chaste', 'their' women not necessarily; and that 'our' women are vulnerable to the aggressive sexuality of 'their' men, (but not from 'ours') (see Breger, below for further discussion). Such ideologies can then become highly effective, politically motivating symbols differentiating 'us' from 'them', proclaiming a moral superiority in belonging to the 'inside' or 'us' (Burton 1994; MacDonald 1994). This is often found reflected in grass-roots and media discourses about mixed marriages, and thus may influence how others respond to such a marriage. While this notion of a gendered ethnic centre is useful, it does not, however, always seem to influence women's actual marriage choices.

Where there are reliable statistics, this model of 'forbidden women' becomes more problematic. Such figures reveal that many more women from the dominant groups in the USA, Germany and France (and possibly other European states for which we do not have the figures) marry out than do men, roughly 60 per cent of all outmarriers being women (cf. figures in Spickard 1989; Barbara 1989; Wolf-Almanasreh 1991). This has also been shown to hold true, however, for some very low-status minority groups, such as Japanese women migrants in the USA, even at the turn of the century when such women were outnumbered up to ten to one by Japanese men (Spickard), or Chinese women migrants to the USA (Lee Sung 1990).

One of the most influential sociological models regarding outmarriage came from the work of the Chicago School on the process of assimilation. They believed that incoming migrants to the United States would gradually become assimilated to form a new identity as Americans. It was based on Park's (1950) and Gordon's (1964) models of the United States as a melting pot where marriage between different groups of immigrants would become progressively more common to form literally a new American people and new culture, a 'melting pot' of all immigrant nations. Gordon emphasized the gradual, multiple nature of assimilation, in a process starting with immigrants' acceptance of the host society's core customs and culture in the process of acculturation, followed by their assimilation into the host society's workforce in the key phase he called structural assimilation, then by marrying into the majority society, after which they would identify themselves as Americans, take on American attitudes and behaviour, and finally attain civic assimilation. Mixed marriages were taken as the most convincing sign of increasing social integration by immigrant groups to the United States.

This politically optimistic model was criticized for its assumption of a predictable one-way movement of simplistically homogenized cultural practices and values, migrants always supposedly giving up their cultural practices to adopt 'American' ones, which ignored power structures and relationships of domination and coercion (but see Lal 1986, for a defence of Park and the Chicago school). It also notably ignores the question of to what extent immigrants adopt which practices and attitudes, and in which contexts they do so, and at which level they are incorporated into economic, political and social relationships. It downplays people's active and creative involvement, and the multidirectional flow of ideas, practices and mores (cf. Price 1969; Archer 1986).

This early work was modified by such researchers as Ruby Kennedy (1944; 1952), who maintained that mixed marriage in the USA did not simply take place across all boundaries, but occurred within a 'triple melting pot' defined by the three main religions of Catholicism, Protestantism, and Judaism. Hereby, immigrants from different cultures married each other within their religious group, but there was little marriage between these religious groups (cf. Spickard 1989).

Some early theorists (such as Hoge and Ferry in the 1940s and 1950s, cited in Spickard 1989), especially social psychologists, as well as diverse community leaders, warned that mixed marriages were symptomatic of community disintegration, or even that choosing to marry out was a symptom of deviance. Merton (1941; see also Muhsam 1990) embroidered this line of thought in his sexist model of compensatory hypogamy (marriage between people of different status groups), which looked at how female social 'failures', such as 'ugly', 'unwanted' White women, would marry out and socially down in a compensatory exchange: she gets the husband she so desperately wants, possibly with higher qualifications, and he gets a higher status wife. The mixed family and their children, according to Merton, are defined socially by the lower status. The problems with this model, besides its sexism, is that it assumes firstly, that all women want to get married; that women are chosen and men choose; there is no reason given as to why a man of high standing within his own group would want to marry someone of low standing within her own, especially if the couple were not going to be accepted into her group; and finally, whose definition of beauty is being used, anyway? Is he therefore implying that White American men marry only for beauty, while all others marry only to maximize their own social positions?

Other models (such as that proposed by Imamura 1990) continue this assumption of social dis-ease by concentrating on marginalization experienced by foreign spouses. While this undoubtedly often occurs, it is not the whole story. In addition, it predefines such marriages as problematic. These models come primarily from studies of marriages in the United States or Europe, or those of their citizens' mixed marriages abroad under military or colonial conditions.

There is another interesting set of issues that might affect the decision to marry out or not, revolving around what Cohen (1974) called the 'formal organization of ethnicity', meaning a conscious organization of identity and commitment within political and economic relationships. The work of Bonacich and Modell (1980), Aldrich et al. (1985), and many others, similarly looks at the impact of residentially segregated ethnic enclaves on the formation of small protected ethnic markets, and how it is in the best interests of ethnic entrepreneurs to encourage feelings of ethnic solidarity; they thereby create a captive market. These people then have a doubly – economic and emotional – vested interest in maintaining the belief in, and participation in an ethnic community. Spickard takes these ideas further in attempting to relate them to who within an ethnic group might marry out, and who might be defensive against the idea of accepting a mixed marriage. In his work on Jewish out-marriages in the USA, he notes that what he calls 'the degree of articulated Jewish identity', and the 'tightness', the degree of interaction within the group affected decisions to marry out, and the acceptability of it:

> Generally, it was those people who were most emancipated from their ethnic heritage who chose to intermarry. This meant that those upper-class Jewish, Japanese and Black Americans whose wealth did not depend on their ethnic fellows intermarried more frequently than those who derived their living from the ethnic community (Spickard 1989: 348).

Furthermore, it is often assumed that many of the old barriers to intermarriage are slowly eroding. For example, the decrease in the importance of religion in regulating lives, that is, the growth of the process of secularization, in Europe and North America is cited in secularization models as a reason why more people may marry out (see, for example, Spickard 1989; Donnan on mixed marriages in Ireland, 1990; Judd 1990; Larson and Munro 1990; Kalmijn 1991). In secularization models, educational and professional similarity has been seen to be increasingly important in the sorts of cross-cultural marriages that occur now, towards the end of the twentieth century. This has lead to the current debate in work in America and Europe as to the relative importance of religion (Kennedy 1944; 1952) or class and education (Spickard 1989; Larson and Munro 1990; Kalmijn 1991) in choosing potential spouses. Work on secularization has shown that, in America and Europe nowadays, people of either very low status, or middle status, the highly educated, tend to marry out of their groups, but not the elite. Kalmijn (1991: 800), while supporting secularization models, in fact notes that a major problem in all American work on the significance of secularization or religious affiliation in mate choice is profoundly affected by the lack of records on religion in official marriage statistics.

In addition, with the slow rise in women's rights especially in Europe and North America, women have more freedom in marriage choices within certain parameters of acceptability (as discussed in theories which look at the concept of 'social distance'). However, what cannot be neglected is that in many situations one way of constraining choice, or even enforcing endogamy (marriage within the group), may easily be replaced by another. Just because there may no longer be any legal barriers to spouse choice does not mean to say that informal barriers are not effective, such as negative discourses on foreigners which may influence not only how the local community reacts to the marriage, as Shibata shows here, but also may influence officials who have discretion in granting visas and entry permits, as Breger, and Alex-Assensoh and Assensoh show. Therefore to say that secularization as well as the growth of women's rights have freed some constraints to partner choice is only part of the issue: we must always look to see if other constraints have then been imposed, or become active, instead.

The intermarriers described in this volume, however, come from a very wide range of class, educational, religious and cultural contexts, ranging from tribal peoples in Nepal to those involved in marriages between Muslims from different countries. We are exploring a wider range of samples than is often met with in American or European-based secularization or triple-melting pot models. The types of cross-cultural unions we look at take place for a variety of reasons: our contributors demonstrate that in some marriages, religious affiliation is still of core importance, as for many Muslims, whereas in others, such as between Muslims and Christians in Uganda, or Christians and Buddhists in Denmark and Japan, it is not. Educational background is comparatively equally low for people from different hill-tribes in Nepal, but unmatched in the case of some German men marrying women from Asia. There is then a multiplicity of reasons why people in various social contexts choose to marry out.

What many of our contributors did find occurring, though, was the significance of various boundary-ranking measures, that is, indicators of perceived 'social distance', in influencing the decisions about which other groups could provide potential spouses, and which groups were simply not considered. For example, Breger shows that a German man might consider marrying a Polish, Austrian or French woman, but under no circumstances consider marriage to a Black Algerian refugee, because of the various hierarchies of acceptability of foreignness combined with the political and economic status of the group to which the woman belonged (cf. Wolf-Almanasreh 1991). Yamani discusses such a hierarchy of preference in detail for Saudi–Pakistani marriage. Kohn looks at the role of positive images of exotic Otherness in the choice of spouse made by women in a Nepalese hill-tribe. Waldren examines the historical changes in Mallorca in definitions of what constitutes 'mixed' marriage and its acceptability.

Personality and Marrying Out

Khatib-Chahidi, Hill and Paton (this volume) also examine the question of who marries out, but from a more psychological approach. The women they interviewed had to have met and decided to marry their future husbands whilst living in their own countries. The interviews were concerned with finding out about the earlier life experiences of the women and discovering how they had felt about themselves, their families, their social contexts and their future spouses at the time of marriage. The researchers highlight common themes which emerged, such as feelings of marginality (both positive and negative) which many women reported experiencing prior to meeting their future husbands. They also describe a personality test which they administered to their informants whose results supported the impression gained from their interviews that their sample of women were, amongst other things, particularly unconventional, adventurous and experimenting. Although this work is just a pilot study involving a small, non-random group of informants, some of whom had already been married a good many years, it throws up questions about marginality and the personalities of women who marry out which merit further investigation.

Within the Mixed Marriage: The Heart of the Matter

Culture and Belonging

By definition, culturally mixed marriages present those involved with a wider palette of cultural practices than culturally homogenous marriages, including such issues as gender roles, child-rearing, mores, language and general lifestyle by which to shape their lives. Sometimes, there may be little awareness of difference, or indeed the differences may be minimal (cf. Cottrell 1990). On the other hand, in the process of everyday life, differences can become clearer, forming a highly charged minefield of conflict, or a source of enriching diversity, or even both. Sometimes there may be conscious awareness of difference from the start, with deliberate negotiation and choice by the families on which customs they prefer. How freely and how consciously customs are adopted and adapted also depend on whether the 'mixed family' is living under the influence of extended kin, or within an ethnic community where following perceived 'traditions' is considered important. Furthermore, the attitude, especially as reflected in the educational system under which mixed children will be educated, and laws of the country in which the family lives might influence the acceptability or propagation of some customs. For example, this can be through legal restrictions on customs such as polygyny (marrying more than one wife), or the school system with possible hidden moral agendas regarding the acceptability of foreign customs, and language learning.

Coping with the alternative customs, roles, norms, ideologies offered to those in a mixed marriage can enable creative incorporation and choice as Yamani and Maxwell indicate. The couple in Yamani's example reconstructed a micro-identity through negotiating what customs and rituals from both parental cultures to include in the new family, an ongoing process of what might be called 'cultural *bricolage*' bound together by a common deep religious belief. The geographical distance from both natal countries greatly reduced kin influence. More to the point, it enabled the family to choose those parts of each cultural tradition they personally wanted to keep, unencumbered by the pressure of home public discourses of collective Self and tolerated intolerance. Maxwell's case-studies talked of the enrichment such choices offered them.

Including an outsider into the fold may, however, act to re-enforce adherence to cultural practices and in this way reify them, as Shibata shows in her analysis of intermarriages in Guyana, where Black daughters-in-law may be judged by Indian mothers-in-law by their ability to cook Indian food in a special way. Indeed, the foreigner may actively embrace certain romanticized aspects of her/his partner's life, thereby reconstructing them and upholding them with more emotional conviction than the partner does, as Waldren notes in describing the enthusiasm with which some foreigners pursue their vision of 'traditional rural community living' in Mallorca.

Differing definitions of what constitutes a marriage in terms of the gendered roles and expectations within it, and the degree of involvement of and duties towards extended kin may cause confusion, or be perceived as enriching. It follows that when two cultures come together in the intimate relationship of a marriage, the participants (the spouses and/or their extended families) can experience a disturbing mismatch of expectations. Romano (1988) discusses from the viewpoint of cross-cultural counselling the problems that can consequently arise. Within the marriage, concepts of personhood, space and privacy, language use, communication patterns, and child-rearing practices can be major points of misunderstanding. This mismatch is well illustrated in most of the contributions in this book.

Refsing, for example, looks at the mismatch caused by the different discourses on gender identity currently dominant in Denmark and Japan. In Denmark, there is a tendency towards more equal sharing of domestic duties and employment, reflected in current gender identities. In Japan, to the contrary, there is still a strong association of women with their somewhat secluded domestic roles, and of men as providers. Therefore, in Denmark where Japanese men find themselves unem-ployed because of adverse employment conditions, whilst their Danish wives find jobs, their sense of gender identity as providers comes under strong attack. Danish women in Japan who cannot find jobs similarly suffer an identity crisis.

A prime example of mismatched expectations is when someone from a culture in which marriage is seen as the formalizing of an emotional relationship between two individuals chooses a spouse from a culture where marriage primarily means the joining of two families. Sissons Joshi and Krishna write at length about the problems that can arise from such a situation in their study of English and North American women who married into Hindu joint families. Many of their informants 'found it hard to adjust to the degree of control which their Indian mothers-in-law expected to exercise over the joint household' and expressed feelings of anger, confusion and powerlessness at having to defer to these older women and also to males of their own age. Very often control was taken away from them in areas which, on marriage, they had expected to make their own decisions, or at least to consult with their husbands; neither of these options was open to them. Opportunities for private discussions with their spouses were rare, and sometimes the mothers-in-law's instructions pervaded the most intimate spaces of their marriages: one 'complained how it was only after ten years of marriage that she was "permitted" by her mother-in-law to buy a night-dress and not follow the . . . custom of sleeping in a sari'. Some of the potency of Sissons Joshi and Krishna's chapter comes from the voices of the disempowered expressing their disappointment; as one woman they interviewed said, 'It wasn't my idea of marriage.'

In the case of Ghanaian/African-American marriages described by Alex-Assensoh and Assensoh, there may also be a mismatch between the expectations of the extended family in Africa and those of the individual spouse in the USA. Here there can be conflict or confusion about expectations of support for the extended family. An African-American wife might find it difficult to contemplate supporting her Ghanaian husband's relatives in Africa whom she had never met, whilst his extended family might be fearful of their son failing to meet his obligations to them if he married a woman (albeit an African-American) in the United States. Yamani, in this volume, suggests that these duties to the extended kin can be so onerous and expensive that some men from Saudi Arabia may prefer to marry foreigners so as to release them from the burden of taking on the heavy responsibilities of entertaining and caring for a local wife's family.

Language: More than just Words

In a mixed marriage where the partners do not share the same mother tongue, the language in which they decide to communicate at home can be symbolic of the extent to which each partner is prepared to forego her or his cultural background and incorporate new elements. In Yamani's example, where Urdu and Arabic are the languages in question, the family actually spoke a third language equally foreign to both parents, but in which both were fluent. Waldren observes how intermarried couples in Mallorca often used several languages: '. . . each parent had a different native language, they communicated in what was for some of them a third language (English) and would speak to their children in either parent's language or in English or Spanish'. She also notes that there was a gender element to ease of acceptance into rural Mallorquin society, in that male foreigners could often achieve communication through communal actions (working alongside local men) rather than through the words which their female counterparts needed to understand in order to communicate with and comprehend local women.

There may also be elements of control and dependence in the choice of language, when one partner refuses to learn the other's language. Breger documents a case-study where this happened to a so-called bought bride from Asia. The German husband had no knowledge of her language, while she could speak some English, but no German. Communication in such a relationship proved to be extremely difficult, and all decisions and dealings with the outside world were necessarily undertaken by the German husband. The wife could not find any but the most menial jobs where the necessity of understanding was limited, which further increased her economic dependence on him. Similarly, in her work on Danish–Japanese marriages, Refsing illustrates how lack of new linguistic skills sometimes constrains employment opportunities for both men and women: besides affecting gendered expectations, this must affect the power relations within a marriage.

Language also involves patterns and expectations of communication: who is allowed to say what to whom, according to gender and generation hierarchies, and how this should be said. A good example of this can be found in Humphrey's work (1978) on the prescribed roles of young wives in rural, pre-1950s Mongolia, where she describes the highly complex speech patterns and vocabulary the women developed in order to circumvent complex linguistic taboos placed upon them by their husbands' agnatic kin. Sissons Joshi and Krishna (this volume) describe how many issues of family life that are conventionally considered to be primarily husband-wife decisions in middle-class America and England became forbidden topics of conversation when in India. One informant had always discussed business affairs with her husband in an open and critical way when living in the USA, but she had felt increasingly perplexed when she discovered that in India she was not permitted this freedom. Discussion of such matters was not allowed 'either in front of her in-laws or even with her husband who now deferred to his parents' views and authority'. Living within his extended patrilateral household a husband would seem to change and close up. Other women noted that on returning to India their teenage children were reprimanded for expressing views about social and political matters in front of their elders, whereas this kind of expression had been encouraged when living in the USA. Some issues were simply not the province of children, even adult children, and others were certainly not the province of women.

It was not acceptable to broach particular subjects directly with the main protagonist; expected paths of communication required talking with similarly statused people.

In contrast to the seemingly harsh disempowerment of a new bride by her husband's kin, described here by Sissons Joshi and Krishna and by Humphrey (1978: 94), '. . . fathers-in-law do sometimes test their daughters-in-law by trying to catch them out, or by setting up further arbitrary word taboos which are not already included in the forbidden list of names', Kohn's work on Nepal (this volume) presents a less hostile attitude. When a non-Yakha speaking bride marries into a Yakha household, 'Generally, members of the new family attempt to ease the incomer into the household by including her in their conversation . . .' using Nepali, the lingua franca, and '. . . an incomer who is unable to learn to speak Yakha with any fluency is not summarily dismissed as a lost cause . . .' Although she admits that here, too, the bride's experience is usually a lonely and difficult one, and that the reason for the attempted communication is often so that household chores can be carried out smoothly, there is a stronger sense of (linguistic) incorporation, acceptance and adaptability in this case.

The theme of who can express what to whom, is intriguingly expanded in Refsing's case-study where a Danish husband congratulated his Japanese wife on the way she had learnt to show her anger. This touches on problems which can arise in mixed marriages from different expectations about the degree to which 'openness' and displaying emotions are tolerated (see also Sissons Joshi and Krishna).

Children of Mixed Marriages

Part of this central theme of identity within a mixed cultural environment must concern the choices that confront the children of such marriages. Maxwell shows in her chapter that for such children, where a plurality of identities exists, not only is there personal conflict in their choice of identity, but also often an outspoken and open discrimination against some choices from the community in which they live. Benson (1981) and Alibhai-Brown and Montague (1992) also noted that because of the politics of race, the communities' reactions to the mixed couple may be disabling and coercive regarding the latter's potential choices of identity. Mixed couples and their children may be abused by groups on both sides, harassed, or even molested for 'betraying' their 'culture' or 'race'. Watson (1977) talked about such children as 'between two cultures', and also noted the problems they experienced. Maxwell notes that mixed children's choices of identity are seldom 'hard and fast' forever, but can change with the rhythms of life-cycle progressions and the socio-political environments in which the person lives. Children of mixed marriages, like their parents, may therefore choose to incorporate features from any or all cultural sides to which they are heirs: bi- or multi-culturality need not necessarily be an encumbrance unless the person is forced to choose between one or the other. It is a salutary lesson in unravelling the processes of personal identity, ethnic or otherwise, to remember that feelings of belonging change according to social, economic and political contexts.

Resources

The handling of resources in any marriage can lead to argument and confusion, but within a cross-cultural marriage there is arguably more room for misunderstanding. Several of the following chapters discuss problems connected with the management of financial resources within a marriage: these include issues such as unemployment, work permits and which partner earns more (see Breger, Refsing and Semafumu, this volume); obligations to one partner's extended family (see Alex-Assensoh and Assensoh, Sissons Joshi and Krishna) or other wives (see Semafumu); or even, as Kohn describes, obligations to a wife's imported spirit which could lead to expensive sacrifices of precious livestock. However, taken collectively the 'stories' in this book are not, on the whole, talking about the impoverished. We are fully aware of the extra burden that social and/or financial hardship might place on cross-cultural marriages, and there is a place for further research on these conditions.

The movement of property has always been closely linked with marriage. In thirteenth-century England 'Before betrothal, it was customary for the financial settlement to be agreed between the families of the bride and groom. A woman was expected to bring to her marriage a dowry which . . . represented her share of her family's inheritance. There was an expectation . . . that she in turn would be endowed with rights (dower rights) in her groom's lands' (Leyser 1996: 107). Despite the fact that in late twentieth-century England the vestiges of this practice may be apparent only in the exchange of wedding rings (Leach 1982), marriage is inherently also an economic event, usually involving the passage of goods, land and/or money between different groups. Anthropologists have often studied this from the point of view of the groups concerned, looking at the benefits gained by the clans, lineages or families who gave or received bride-wealth or dower, and women too have often been seen as objects of exchange (see, for example, Lévi-Strauss 1966), whose choices and voices were muted. This discussion has been extended by feminist theorists who look at the economic benefit to both husbands and family, and employers of the unpaid role of wives in the domestic reproduction and 'servicing' (feeding, caring, cleaning) of the labour force (Oakley 1974; Walby 1986).

However, in her study of two Tibeto-Burman peoples in this volume Kohn shows that one of the reasons Yakha women in East Nepal choose to marry Limbu men, is because 'Limbu husbands give much more gold to their wives than Yakha men', demonstrating that women are more than mere pawns in a system of exchange between male members of different clans: these young women are choosing their own partners. She is also allowing us to hear the voices and opinions of the women themselves concerning an economic dimension of their marriages: this gold is for them, not for their male elders. Thirdly, while Kohn admits that 'The interest women have in gold is, on the one hand, a material one', what is really new and challenging about her contribution is that she shows us how the women's interest in the Limbu men's gold is not *just* mercenary. She suggests that for these young girls there is an exciting aestheticism intrinsic in gold, there is romance in 'the act of giving gold and bestowing beauty on new wives'.

Being accepted as a member, or not, of a group also profoundly affects a person's access to the resources of the group: these start on a national level with the various rewards and obligations of citizenship, and continue down to whatever resources the group itself has, including potential spouses. Some chapters in this volume (especially those by Semafumu, Breger, and Alex-Assensoh and Assensoh) include this aspect of identity in relation to the acceptability of outsiders as spouses, but this book is not the place to elaborate on these issues in great detail. The reader is referred to the lively debate elsewhere about what constitutes citizenship, who is incorporated within its fold (Marshall 1963; Turner 1990), and how access to its concomitant rights and duties varies along the overlapping parameters of gender (e.g. Ward et al. 1992; Walby 1994; Lutz et al. 1995), ethnic identity and 'foreign-ness' (e.g. Rex and Mason 1986; Harrison 1991; Garcia 1992; Cohen 1993), and age, or place in the life cycle (Turner 1991).

Resourcefulness

Although exogamy is strongly affected by formal and informal group rules, practices and stereotypes, the people involved are not passive: despite opposition, they may pursue their own interests, create their own identities, and in so doing, they challenge or subvert rules and contribute towards social change. Even leaving aside specific financial problems, managing and negotiating other cultural resources within mixed marriages calls for compromise and commitment, as these chapters show. Several authors describe situations where couples have fought hard to marry, suffering disapproval and pessimism from family and friends, and have adopted a zealous approach to making the marriage work. Semafumu summarizes the views of her interviewees as follows: 'The women saw the various areas of difference from their partners both as a challenge to be overcome, and as an important reason for the continued success of their marriages, in that people expected them to fail, which made the couple even more determined to prove them wrong.' Shibata, Alex-Assensoh and Assensoh, and Khatib-Chahidi et al. came across similar attitudes in their research (see also Alibhai-Brown and Montague 1992). It is moreover interesting to note that the women in Khatib-Chahidi et al.'s sample are all still with their husbands, 'in marriages that have stood the test of time, ranging from five to forty years, an average of twenty years'. We are tempted to conclude that in some cases the cross-cultural marriages that do manage to survive the problems which may be thrust upon them are particularly strong, and this strength comes in part from the determination described here to make the marriage work despite outside pressures.

Semafumu discusses how, in Uganda, an understanding of the multiple legal options of marriage contract (reflecting the country's cultural diversity) will influence Ugandan women's choice of both marriage form and partner. She shows how her sample of educated women is aware of the advantages and constraints that each legal form offers them. The informants often choose, illegally, to marry under several laws in order to maximize the social acceptability of a mixed marriage, the economic implications of ownership of and access to family resources and assets, the duties towards and claims of extended kin, inheritance, and so on, and to control possible polygyny. That is, these women use their knowledge of the laws to subvert the law and maximize their own self-interests.

Breger discovered that a common reaction of mixed couples to a perpetual background of disapproval was to reject mainstream German culture in favour of energetic participation in the ethnic group of the foreign partner. This was always presented by her informants as a deliberate choice of creating a new identity which accepted certain sorts of differences. However, there was not always easy accept-ance by the ethnic group concerned. In such cases, people often joined the religion of their foreign partner, especially in the case of proselytizing sects of Islam and Buddhism.

Counselling and Divorce in Mixed Marriages

The approach of members of the dominant cultures in Europe and America to cross-cultural marriage counselling has been severely criticized for assuming that marriage breakdown is automatically linked to cultural difference, where the cultures concerned are rather simplistically imagined to be homogeneous (see the discussion above). Speight et al. (1991), as others, note that the professionals doing counselling or the research tend to be White members of the dominant group, who may or may not be aware of how their own culturally based ideas may feed into their work. Speight et al. maintain that it is often assumed that the problems which might arise in a mixed marriage are necessarily associated with the racial or cultural characteristics of the Other, an Other coming from a group which holds a lower position in the socio-political hierarchy (see also Johnson and Warren 1994). Cottrell (1990) also criticizes studies of divorce rates in mixed marriages for concentrating on cultural difference while neglecting to place these in any broader political and economic contexts. As Speight et al. maintain, 'the use of the term cross-cultural implies a comparison between two groups (i.e. the "standard group" and the "culturally different group"). To truly adopt a broader view of what constitutes cross-cultural counselling, language and terminology must reflect this perspective' (1991: 8).

They suggest a new model for counsellors to use, incorporating the theory that 'All counselling is multicultural in nature . . . This re-definition does not naively imply that cultural differences are not important; rather, [it] encourages us to look concurrently at our individual uniqueness and our commonalities' (1991: 11). They therefore define three overlapping areas to be taken into account: human universality, cultural specificity and individual uniqueness.

It might be useful to borrow this model to look at cross-cultural marriages. Until recently, anthropologists have tended to look at cultural specificities in their search for human universalities recognizable in repeated patterns of social organization, but there was little place in their studies for individual uniqueness. When studying marriage this last aspect cannot be omitted (cf. especially Kohn's chapter, this volume). As Johnson and Warren point out, 'While society is solely concerned with mixed marriages as they relate to intergroup relations, the marriages themselves are between individuals. This is the interpersonal dimension, which quite obviously for the partners is by far the most important aspect of the marriage' (1994: 7).

Differences in 'cultural baggage' do not seem to be a major point of contention in mixed marriages, although of course they can act as effective symbols of domination or resentment (see Barth 1969 on the reification of cultural baggage; Romano 1988). Yamani notes how stereotypes of cultural achievement, within the historical and religious histories of Islam, may be used in arguments between Saudi and Pakistani couples to justify their own or denigrate the partner's actions or ethos.

There are of course many problems afflicting these sorts of marriages, and divorce must often be the outcome. However, although it is often suggested that exogamous marriages tend to end in divorce more frequently than endogamous marriages, statistics on this are hard to find, especially if there is no obvious clue in registry records that the marriage was indeed exogamous. There are no internationally available statistics on mixed marriages contracted in one country, nor on what happens to the couple if they leave and live elsewhere, whether they stay together or not (Wolf-Almanasreh 1991: 23–9). Where such statistics are present, the way they are calculated will considerably alter the end result of the ratios both of intermarriages and of divorces (see, for example, Lee and Yamanaka's work 1990).

Lee Sung (1990) shows how such statistics are misleading when it is not clear to what base population they refer, that is whether intermarriages are based on the total population figures of either group, or whether they are based on the total number of marriages in either group, or simply the total number of marriages. She gives the example of four Chinese people, two of whom marry out, whereas the other two marry each other. Based on the number of marriages, two of the three marriages are then exogamous, whereas only one is within the group: two-thirds marry out, one-third marry within their group. However, based on the total population of four people, two people marry out, whereas two marry in, giving the figure of half the marriages being exogamous, half endogamous. Her own figures on Chinese exogamy in the USA found that, in contrast to other studies, in fact there was no statistically significant difference between the divorce rates of endogamously and exogamously married couples, although a slightly higher number of outmarriers did divorce than inmarriers. Wolf-Amanasreh comes to a similar conclusion, with slightly fewer divorces for mixed marriages than for German–German marriages, but warns about the difficulty of calculating accurately without reliable data.

Conclusion

The main front-page article in *The Guardian* newspaper (a liberal national daily paper in Britain) on Monday, 27 January 1997 criticized the then Prime Minister John Major for vetoing a European Union move to create a centre from which to monitor racism in Europe (which has, however, since been set up). The centre was proposed in the wake of increasing right-wing extremist lobbying, and outright racial violence throughout Europe, with evidence that such national groups were beginning to work together across Europe. Britain's decision came a week after the attempt by European-wide neo-Nazi groups under the leadership of the British Combat 18 faction to send letter bombs to people in mixed marriages in Britain. Luckily, this plot was foiled. But it indicates not only the horror of racism still active and brutal, but also the daily courage necessary for such couples and their children to face the smaller-scale, casual racism and discrimination – not only from majority White people, but also from the minority groups, such as Blacks, Indians and Chinese in Britain – that abounds in everyday life.

Living in a mixed marriage can be an intimate performance of juggling identities and the ideologies associated with them, a dance sometimes threatening to perform as well as to behold. It is sometimes enriching, but always also calls into question deeply held assumptions about the nature of one's own identities, and those of one's reference groups. But in a modern world faced with the bleak horror of violent ethnic-nationalist conflict, is it not essential to examine very carefully precisely what these boundaries signify, and the political and personal racism they may justify?

References

Abbott, P. and Wallace, C. (1990), *An Introduction to Sociology. Feminist Perspectives*, London: Routledge.

Abdulrahim, D. (1993), 'Defining Gender in a Second Exile: Palestinian Women in West Berlin', in G. Buijs (ed.), *Migrant Women: Crossing Boundaries and Changing Identities*, Berg: Oxford.

Aldrich, H., Cater, J., Jones, T., McEvoy, D. and Velleman, P. (1985), 'Ethnic Residential Concentration and the Protected Market Hypothesis', in *Social Forces*, 63, no.4, pp.996–1009.

Alibhai-Brown, Y. and Montague, A. (1992), *The Colour of Love. Mixed Race Relationships*, London: Virago Press.

Archer, M. (1986), 'The Myth of Cultural Integration', *Br. J. Sociology*, 37, no.3, pp.333–53.

Ardener, S. (ed.) (1975, 1977), *Perceiving Women*, London: Dent.

Bachu, P. (1993), 'Identities Constructed and Reconstructed: Representations of Asian Women in Britain', in G. Buijs (ed.), *Migrant Women. Crossing Boundaries and Changing Identities*, Oxford: Berg.

Barbara, A. (1989), *Marriage across Frontiers*, transl. D. Kennard, Clevedon: Multilingual Matters.

Barth, F. (ed.) (1969), *Ethnic Groups and Boundaries. The Social Organisation of Culture Difference*, Bergen: Universitetsforlaget.

Benson, S. (1981), *Ambiguous Ethnicity: Interracial Families in London*, Cambridge: Cambridge University Press.

Bonacich, E. and Modell, J. (1980), *The Economic Basis of Ethnic Solidarity. Small Businesses in the Japanese-American Community*, Berkeley: University of California Press.

Bott, E. (1971), *Family and Social Network*, London: Tavistock.

Brah, A. (1996), 'Thinking through Gendered Diasporas', paper presented at the workshop 'Gender, Diasporas and Changing Societies: A Workshop', convened by the Centre for Cross-Cultural Research on Women (University of Oxford) and the Centre for Research in Ethnic Relations (Warwick University), held at Queen Elizabeth House, University of Oxford, 30 November 1996.

Breger, R. (1990), *Myth and Stereotype. Images of Japan in the German Press and in Japanese Self-Presentation*, Frankfurt: Peter Lang.

——, (1992), 'The Discourse on Japan in the German Press: Images of Economic Competition', in R. Goodman and K. Refsing (eds), *Ideology and Practice in Modern Japan*, London: Routledge.

Buijs, G. (ed.) (1993), *Migrant Women. Crossing Boundaries and Changing Identities*, Oxford: Berg.

Burton, P. (1994), 'Women and Second-Language Use: An Introduction', in P. Burton et al. (eds), *Bilingual Women. Anthropological Approaches to Second Language Use*, Oxford: Berg.

——, Dyson, K. and Ardener, S. (eds) (1994), *Bilingual Women. Anthropological Approaches to Second Language Use*, Oxford: Berg.

Cerroni-Long, E.L. (1984), 'Marrying Out: Socio-Cultural and Psychological Implications of Intermarriage', in *Journal of Comparative Family Studies*, XVI, no.1, pp.25–46.

Cohen, A. (1974), *Urban Ethnicity*, ASA, 12, London: Tavistock.

Cohen, R. (1993), 'International Labour Migration in the Post-War Period – "Now you need them, now you don't"', in M. O'Donnell (ed.), *New Introductory Reader in Sociology*, Nelson: Walton on Thames.

Cottrell, A. Baker (1990), 'Cross-National Marriages: A Review of the Literature', *Journal of Comparative Family Studies*, XXI, no.2, pp.151–69.

Dale, P. (1988, 1986), *The Myth of Japanese Uniqueness*, London: Routledge.

Donnan, H. (1990), 'Mixed Marriage in Comparative Perspective: Gender and Power in Northern Ireland and Pakistan', *Journal of Comparative Family Studies*, XXI, no.2, pp.207–26.

Dower, J. (1986), *War Without Mercy. Race and Power in the Pacific War*, London: Faber and Faber.

Dudley, E. and Novak, M. (eds) (1972), *The Wild Man Within. An Image in Western Thought from the Renaissance to Romanticism*, Pittsburgh: University of Pittsburgh Press.

Essed, P. (1995), 'Gender, Migration and Cross-Ethnic Coalition Building', in H. Lutz et al. (eds), *Crossfires: Nationalism, Racism and Gender in Europe*, London: Pluto.

Evans-Pritchard, E.E. (1951), *Kinship and Marriage amongst the Nuer*, Oxford: Clarendon Press.

Foucault, M. (1974, 1969), *The Archaeology of Knowledge*, London: Tavistock.

Fox, R. (1967), *Kinship and Marriage*, Harmondsworth: Penguin.

Friedan, B. (1963), *The Feminine Mystique*, Harmondsworth: Penguin.

Garcia, S. (1992), 'Europe's Fragmented Identities and the Frontiers of Citizenship', London: Royal Institute of International Affairs, Discussion Papers, no.45.

Goode, W.J. (1963), *World Revolution and Family Patterns*, New York: Free Press.

Goody, J. (ed.) (1971), *Kinship. Selected Readings*, Harmondsworth: Penguin.

Gordon, M. (1964), *Assimilation in American Life. The Role of Race, Religion, and National Origins*, New York: Oxford University Press.

Hardach-Pincke, I. (1988), *Interkulturelle Lebenswelten. Deutsch-Japanische Ehen in Japan*, 590, Frankfurt: Campus Forschung.

Harrison, M.L. (1991), 'Citizenship, Consumption and Rights: A Comment on B.S. Turner's Theory of Citizenship', in *Sociology*, 25, no. 2, pp.209–13.

Hitchcox, L. (1993), 'Vietnamese Refugees in Hong Kong: Behaviour and Control' in G. Buijs (ed.), *Migrant Women. Crossing Boundaries and Changing Identities*, Oxford: Berg.

Hobsbawm, E. and Ranger, T. (eds) (1983), *The Invention of Tradition*, Cambridge: Cambridge University Press.

Humphrey, C. (1978), 'Women, Taboo and the Suppression of Attention', in S. Ardener (ed.), *Defining Females*, London: Croom Helm.

Imamura, A. (1990), 'Strangers in a Strange Land: Coping with Marginality in International Marriage', *Journal of Comparative Family Studies*, XXI, no.2, pp.171–91.

Johnson, W. and Warren, M. (eds) (1994), *Inside the Mixed Marriage. Accounts of Changing Attitudes, Patterns, and Perceptions of Cross-Cultural and Interracial Marriages*, Lanham: University Press of America.

Judd, E. (1990), 'Intermarriage and the Maintenance of Inter-Ethnic Identity', *Journal of Comparative Family Studies*, XXI, no.2, pp.251–68.

Kalmijn, M. (1991), 'Shifting Boundaries: Trends in Religious and Educational Homogamy', *American Sociological Revue*, 56, pp.786–800.

Kennedy, R.J.R. (1944), 'Single or Triple Melting Pot? Intermarriage Trends in New Haven, 1870–1940', *American Journal of Sociology*, 49, pp.331–9.

——, (1952), 'Single or Triple Melting Pot? Intermarriage in New Haven, 1870–1950', *American Journal of Sociology*, 58, pp.56–9.

Lal, B. (1986), 'The "Chicago School" of American Sociology, Symbolic Interactionism and Race Relations Theory', in J. Rex and D. Mason (eds), *Theories of Race and Ethnic Relations*, Cambridge: Cambridge University Press.

Larson, L. and Munro, B. (1990), 'Religious Intermarriage in Canada in the 1980s', *Journal of Comparative Family Studies*, XXI, no.2, pp.239–50.

Laslett, P. (ed.) (1972), *Household and Family in Past Time*, Cambridge Group for the History of Population and Social Structure, Cambridge: Cambridge University Press.

Leach, E. (1982), *Social Anthropology*, New York: Oxford University Press.

Lee, S. and Yamanaka, K. (1990), 'Patterns of Asian American Intermarriage and Marital Assimilation', *Journal of Comparative Family Studies*, XXI, no.2, pp.287–305.

Lee Sung, B. (1990), 'Chinese American Intermarriage', *Journal of Comparative Family Studies*, XXI, no.3, pp.337–52.

Lévi-Strauss, C. (1966), *The Elementary Structures of Kinship*, Boston: Eyre and Spotiswood.

Leyser, H. (1996), *Medieval Women: A Social History of Women in England 450–1500*, London: Orion.

Lutz, H., Phoenix, A. and Yuval-Davis, N. (eds) (1995), *Crossfires: Nationalism, Racism and Gender in Europe*, London: Pluto Press.

MacDonald, M. (1994), 'Women and Linguistic Innovation in Brittany', in P. Burton, K.K. Dyson and S. Ardener (eds) (1994), *Bilingual Women. Anthropological Approaches to Second Language Use*, Oxford: Berg.

Malinowski, B. (1927), *Sex and Repression in Savage Society*, London: Routledge and Kegan Paul.

Marshall, T.H. (1963), *Sociology at the Crossroads*, London: Heinemann Educational Books.

Merton, R. (1941), 'Intermarriage and the Social Structure', *Psychiatry*, no.4, pp.361–74.

Miller, R. (1982), *Japan's Modern Myth: The Language and Beyond*, New York: Weatherhill.

Mouer, R. and Sugimoto, Y. (1986), *Images of Japanese Society. A Study in the Social Construction of Reality*, London: KPI.

Muhsam, H. (1990), 'Social Distance and Asymmetry in Intermarriage Patterns', *Journal of Comparative Family Studies*, XXI, no.3, pp.307–24.

Needham, R. (1962), *Structure and Sentiment*, Chicago: University of Chicago Press.

Oakley, A. (1974), *Housewife*, London: Allen Lane.

Park, R. (1950), *The Collected Papers of Robert Ezra Park*, Free Press: New York.

Price, C. (1969), 'The Study of Assimilation', in J.A. Jackson (ed.), *Migration*, Sociological Studies II, Cambridge: Cambridge University Press.

Radcliffe-Brown, A.R. (1969, 1952), *Structure and Function in Primitive Society*, London: Cohen and West.

Rex, J. and Mason, D. (eds) (1986), *Theories of Race and Ethnic Relations*, Comparative Ethnic and Race Relations, Cambridge: Cambridge University Press.

Romano, D. (1988), *Intercultural Marriage, Promises and Pitfalls*, Yarmouth: Intercultural Press.

Said, E. (1978), *Orientalism*, London: Routledge and Kegan Paul.

Speight, S., Myers, L., Cox, C. and Highlen, P. (1991), 'A Redefinition of Multicultural Counselling', in *Journal of Counselling and Development*, 70, pp.8–16.

Spickard, P. (1989), *Mixed Blood. Intermarriage and Ethnic Identity in Twentieth-Century America*, Madison: University of Wisconsin Press.

Spiering, M. (1996), 'National Identity and European Unity', in M. Wintle (ed.), *Culture and Identity in Europe*, Perspectives on Europe, Contemporary Interdisciplinary Research, Aldershot: Avebury.

Steadman, J. (1969), *The Myth of Asia*, New York: MacMillan.

Tannen, D. (1986), *That's not what I Meant*, New York: Ballantine.

Thorne, B. (1982), 'Feminist Rethinking of the Family: An Overview', in B. Thorne and M. Yalom (eds), *Rethinking the Family: Some Feminist Questions*, New York: Longman.

Thränhardt, D. (1985), 'mythos des fremden – deutsche angst und deutsche lust', *kultuRRevolution*, 10, pp.35–8.

Turner, B. (1990), 'Outline of a Theory of Citizenship', *Sociology*, 24, no.2, pp.189–217.

——, (1991), 'Further Specification of the Citizenship Concept: A Reply to M.L. Harrison', *Sociology*, 25, no.2, pp.215–18.

Walby, S. (1986), 'Gender, Class and Stratification. Towards a New Approach', in R. Crompton and M. Mann (eds), *Gender and Stratification*, Cambridge: Polity Press.

——, (1994), 'Is Citizenship Gendered?', *Sociology*, 28, pp.379–95.

Ward, A., Gregory, J., and Yuval-Davis, N. (eds) (1992), *Women and Citizenship in Europe. Borders, Rights and Duties*, European Forum of Socialist Feminists, London: Trentham Books and EFSF.

Watson, J. (1977), *Between two Cultures*, Oxford: Blackwell.

Wolf-Almanasreh, R. (1991), *Mein Partner oder Partnerin kommt aus einem anderen Land. Inter-kulturelle Ehen, Familien und Partnerschaften. Ein Wegweiser für die Selbsthilfe*, 2nd ed., IAF, Verband bi-nationaler Familien und Partnerschaften, Frankfurt: Interessengemeinschaften der mit Ausländer verheirateten Frauen e.V.

Young, M. and Willmott, P. (1962, 1957), *Family and Kinship in East London*, Harmondsworth: Penguin.

——, (1975, 1973), *The Symmetrical Family*, Harmondsworth: Penguin.

2

Crossing Over: Mixing, Matching and Marriage in Mallorca

Jackie Waldren

Introduction

In this chapter I look at the changing perceptions of 'mixed marriage' on the island of Mallorca and in parts of the Spanish mainland over the past century. Marriage cannot be understood at any time without some insights into the concomitant political, social and religious climates of the periods under discussion. In a country like Spain where the Catholic Church was omnipresent and omnipotent until 1975, marriage represented a covenant that combined Church, state, individuals and families. According to the Church, any marriage that did not conform to these criteria was a 'mixed marriage'. There were degrees in the meanings of 'mixed marriage' in Biblical terms. The first degree meant a disparity of denomination between a baptized Catholic and a person baptized as a member of another Christian denomination. The second degree was between a baptized Catholic and a non-baptized person. This situation could be altered only by periods of complicated study to learn the Catholic meanings of marriage, including obligations toward Church and family, baptism and education of children. A non-baptized spouse would have to gain sanctification through study and marriage to a sanctified partner. The Church was pleased to receive converts. 'Differences' were erased before marriage could take place.

The marriage contract entailed mutual obligations that were to be recognized by both parties and included commitment to the Church, regulated inheritance of private property and the reproduction of the Catholic family. Preparation for marriage entailed couples learning to control sexual desire and internalizing the Church's teachings that 'Sex is not for pleasure or vice but to place a son in the sacred service of the church' (Janer 1980: 14). For centuries prior to the 1930s the Church combined with various regimes to maintain control over sex, social life and history.[1] Studies of sex and family life are poorly documented for these periods, however, according to José Alvarez:

We know by means of overall figures from medical and health records, that female prostitution was widespread as a means of sexual initiation for males and an escape from, or tolerated addition to, later married life but we have very little detailed information here. Nor do we know much about the lived experience of family life. Here, the occasional autobiography reveals grim scenes of traditional patriarchal tyranny, often expressed through violence towards women and, of course, towards sons whose upbringing was geared to their being 'tamed' . . . The Penal Code sanctioned violence against an adulterous wife by her husband and stipulated that in such cases the punishment for murder shall be exile, while attempted murder or causing bodily harm were not punishable offences (1995: 88).

The meaning of 'mixed marriage' in Spain has altered considerably over time. The major changes seem to fall into three main stages: first 1800 to 1936, second 1936 to 1975, and third, 1975 to the present. During the first period and most of the second, society was composed of a conservative land-owning oligarchy and a subjugated peasantry, with rigid religious and social controls. Until 1973, marriage in Spain was possible only within the Catholic Church, apart from a short period during the Republic of 1931–6 when secularizing initiatives included separation of the Church and state, the extension of non-religious state schooling, and the provision of civil alternatives to Church marriage and Church burial. Since the death of Franco in 1975, rapid introduction of social and economic development has led to various changes in marriage patterns and laws concerning the protection of women in cases of violence. Divorce has also become legalized despite the Church's continued objections.

Today it is possible to marry in civil ceremonies or in churches of other denominations. This 'choice' to marry whomever and however one pleases means that concepts of 'the person or individual', the perceptions of Self and Others as well as the social, religious and legal definitions of citizenship, culture, marriage, violence, insiders and outsiders have altered dramatically during this period (see Waldren 1996). When we speak of 'mixed marriages', to what practices and to whom are we referring? My findings suggest that the meaning of 'mixed marriage' has been continuously negotiated according to the social and economic circumstances of each period.

1800–1936: Class, Locality and Identity

Nation and Church generated representations of ideal unions, with women considered sacred, while they legitimated the control of female sexuality, in the name of 'tradition' and the perpetuation of the *patria* (native land) and the *patrimonio* (cultural heritage). A person's identity was conferred by birth within a religiously legitimated marriage, recognized by baptism with a Christian name.

Full membership in a community was based on becoming the head of a household through marriage or inheritance.[2] Gender roles were clearly related to the reproduction and continuity of this household and its role as an integral part of the combined families recognized in each union. Spanish nationality and citizen's rights were transmitted through the father and women did not become the legal equals of men until 1931. Citizenship could be earned by marriage or through application for naturalization after long-term residence.

Marriage was of critical importance as far as it concerned the reproduction of the social system or the continuity of a particular social relationship over time. Individual interests were secondary to the reproduction and continuation of the patrimony (in this case the nation, the family and its property). Inheritance was a major factor in the movement of peoples, in the structure of marriage patterns and in gender roles. Records for the seventeenth through the nineteenth centuries show that marriages contracted for the children of large estate owners were alliances with other propertied families on the island. These marriages resulted in combined properties which were even larger and had greater potential. The marriage partners were born into an ascribed social class and their marriages were perceived as matches which brought together all that was best in blood, spirit, property and persons (Waldren 1996: 58–62).

Since inheritance was by primogeniture, most of the new estates built up during this period were for second- and third-born children of estate owners who were given less valuable lands. Dowry (*doté*) in most parts of Spain is a form of pre-inheritance, an advance on the younger son's or daughter's share in the family properties and moveable assets.

> A larger or smaller dowry indicated the place of each woman in the marital circuit of the island and condensed the elements (prestige-honour) and the economics (transmission of wealth) on which the order of alliances between houses is based. A social picture emerges in which each individual represents the role assigned him or her by his or her position as a member of a family of a certain social standing (Bestard 1991: 132).

Only when financial difficulties occurred did these estate owners allow their younger daughters to marry affluent Palma businessmen, who, until that time, had been considered outsiders. The closely interrelated social and economic arrangements that preceded marriages continuously imposed themselves on the marriage partners. Marriage was not just a contract between two people, but rather an economic, religious, social pact between persons, families, properties, generations, and the reproduction of those factors over and over again. A mixed marriage at this time meant that the partners were from neighbouring villages, or towns, but it would have been most difficult and hardly likely for any further differences to have been accommodated in the tightly contained system of land-ownership and tenure.

Among those people subsumed under the broad heading of 'peasant', which included tenant farmers, owners of small properties, regularly employed agricultural workers, fishermen and day labourers, the majority of marriages took place between members of the same village, with preferences shown for close neighbours. Most partners traced some kin ties even if these were quite dispersed over time. Marriage to another of the same class and background from an adjoining or more distant village or town on the island was considered a 'mixed marriage' in that the persons were from different villages, and this difference was invested with significance.

Nicknames still used today refer to the in-marrying spouse's place of origin, *La Poblera* (a woman from the town of La Pobla), *El Sollerich* (a man from the town of Soller) and so forth. Despite long periods of courting and regular socializing between villages, those who married from one village to another or even one neighbourhood to another have told me stories about how difficult it was for them to cross over, to settle into their new 'family', often composed of husband's or wife's parents, aunts and uncles, in a different neighbourhood or a different village. The person's identity in the new setting was based on difference rather than similarity. An entire oral history of the village and its members can be derived from studying nicknames, house names, and forms of address used in the present (Waldren 1988). Thus names become metaphors for social relations, revealing a process of cultural reproduction. The importance of belonging to generations of local or island kin is continuously restated, but it can be understood only by those who share the idiom.

Peasants and rich alike insist they chose their own mates but it was clear that social life was so structured that one was always made aware of proper potential marriage partners: the choice was very much guided. Courting was initiated while out walking (*paseando*) on the village streets, after church or at social gatherings in the city with age-mates and friends. As Zonabend found in France: 'The choice of spouse clearly shows the preponderant role of women in arranging of a marriage, in keeping a prudent outlook in marriage matters. Matchmaking mothers, female intermediaries, quarrelsome future mothers-in-law . . . make or break a marriage' (1984: 99–102).

We see in all these different interpretations of 'mixed marriage' that belonging to and identifying oneself as a member of a family, village, town, nation is determined by each member being socialized into local and larger cultures through a set of criteria which he/she is encouraged to reproduce generation after generation: these include language, customs, belief, behaviour, politics and spatial connotations. The internalization of these values allows one not only to participate in that grouping, but also to perceive differences between Self and Other, insider and outsider. In identifying the Other, differences are categorized in terms of gender, race, class, religion, locality or nationality (see Sissons Joshi and Krishna, this volume). One's own group values are highlighted by encountering those of the Other. When we discuss mixing we are considering various concepts of belonging: inclusion/exclusion, insiders/outsiders, local/foreign, we/they, and so forth.

In Mallorca, each person had varying perceptions of belonging which spread out along a continuum from nuclear to extended family, neighbourhood, village, other mountain or plains villages, to towns, Catalunya, and finally as a member of the Spanish people and nation. An individual's perceptions are a product of his or her personal experience in specific contexts.

Mallorquins migrated to the New World during the last century and to France and other areas of northern Europe this century. Among the peasant group, young men who neither owned nor were to inherit property migrated to the New World between 1860 and 1890. Only having had access to a limited sphere of experience, they associated all evils, illness, immorality and the unknown with the women in the new country, while 'home' took on the image of purity and salvation. In all but one case in the village I studied, the men returned to claim local wives rather than 'mix' socially with the women they encountered abroad. Many returned abroad soon after marrying, leaving their new wives at home under the protection of both their families, and sent most of their earnings back for a future home in their natal village.

In Spanish and Catalan there are two different terms for outsiders: *forasters* and *estrangers*. Each implies a distance away from the centre or inside. *Forasters* are Spaniards who were born outside the village or island: on the mainland, or in what were once other Spanish territories. A *foraster* shares a national heritage and rights and obligations as a member of the Spanish State. Catalans are close to Mallorquins geographically and linguistically, but due to long-standing political and economic animosities they are less tolerated than other Spaniards. When the term *estranger* is used, it refers to a stranger, a foreigner, someone from outside Spain. An *estranger*-foreigner-outsider has no official status. Being an *estranger* is sometimes useful in that one is not subject to pressures of political, religious or social conformity, but it also deprives one of a sense of belonging.

Those *estrangers* who travelled through and the few who settled in Mallorca during the nineteenth century were strangers in the full sense of the word: unknown, unfamiliar, alien. George Sand and the composer Frederick Chopin came to Mallorca in 1838 hoping to cure Chopin's consumption while enjoying the beauty of the island landscapes. Sand's attitudes, her eccentric dress and her independence seem to have challenged everything sacred to Mallorquin society at the time. She in turn, disillusioned by her search for the rustic ideals romanticized by Rousseau, wrote scathingly of the inhabitants of the island. The local values of modesty, marriage and chastity were greatly reinforced via the contrast to the example of this sophisticated Parisian woman seen as living 'in sin' with her ill lover.

The Archduke Luis Salvador of Austria (non-heir apparent to the Hapsburg dynasty) acquired a number of large estates on the northwest coast of the island. The many well-known foreign artists and writers who visited him between 1867 and 1913 were models of social decorum, although the Archduke himself was seen as a strange mixture of nobility and animal nature, preferring to sleep on the floor rather than the bed, and eating with his hands in company. His regular use, as lord of the manor, of the *droit de seigneur* led to arranged marriages between the children of employees on his various estates who benefited materially from his involvement with one or both parents in their youth.[3] His relationship with a young local woman, Catalina Homar, from a land-owning family reinforced the local negative perceptions of mixed relationships. A few years into their relationship, Catalina was confined to quarters with leprosy (some say it was syphilis) which she had contracted on their voyages to Africa. The Archduke built her a house deep in the coastal forests of his estates, isolating her from the contagion she might spread to others. Such an event and the many myths that developed from it only reinforced the endogamous ideology of the islanders.

Like the Archduke, foreigners who arrived in Mallorca during the first two stages were automatically placed in the category of elite land-owners: educated, well-mannered, well-dressed men with 'smooth hands' (the local criterion of a gentleman – one who does no manual labour). The sort of people who were able to travel to this area in the past were clearly of the leisured classes. The existing social structure included hierarchical relationships as a normal part of life and these 'gentlemanly' strangers were easily accommodated alongside those to whom the locals were accustomed to proffering their services. Visitors to the island in the nineteenth century represented the 'feared', unknown outside, but they could be 'tamed' and made 'understandable' to some extent by being placed in the existing social categories of gentleman and artist, which allowed the locals to define them as eccentric, interesting and useful, thus containing them within the local stereotypes surrounding these categories.

Foreigners did not threaten local values or the local way of life. As Simmel wrote:

> We confront the stranger, with whom we share neither characteristics nor broader interests, objectively; we hold our personalities in reserve; and thus a particular difference does not involve us in our totalities. On the other hand we meet the person who is very different from us only on certain points within a particular contact or with coincidence of particular interests, and hence the spread of conflict is limited to those points only (1953: 44).

The vast cultural differences that attracted foreigners to Mallorca during the past centuries also served to protect the local people from any intimate contact with them. Locals and foreigners perceived the village from different perspectives. The locals' view of their village was of a socially defined space and time, involving generations of kin, religious activities and a landscape that demanded toil and sweat. The foreigner, on the other hand, held an idealized, distanced view of landscape combined with romantic images of paradise. The gains to each were different but reciprocal.

By the 1930s, foreign travellers were bringing new and different values and ideas onto the island and political activists and 'anarchists' on the mainland were introducing progressive ideals and practices. Cleminson suggests that

> Spanish anarchism criticized the moral codes of the middle classes and rural peasants for their insistence on compulsory marriage and for their attitudes towards sex. This alternative moral system was seen as a mechanism for the subversion of existing power structures. Many anarchists rejected marriage by the Church as unnatural and restricting, perpetuating inequalities and the power of one sex over another. Anarchists lived as couples without being married which in a society based on rigid concepts of 'propriety' and 'decency' was considered an overt attack on the Catholic Church and its established norms. Subversive also, and viewed with constant disapproval by the Church was the use of contraceptives, whether employed as a method of preventing venereal diseases or as a form of contraception, thus separating pleasure from procreation . . . In marriage, the power of men over women in capitalist society was replicated, creating authoritarian ministates in the worker's hearth (1995: 119).

1936–1975: Tourism and the Lure of the Romanticized Other

Spain modernized rapidly after the devastation of the Civil War and made great efforts to re-establish contacts with the European allies. Many of the intelligentsia chose exile rather than to live under Franco's totalitarian regime. During and after the Civil War large numbers of young men and women from Mallorca (again, usually those who were not direct heirs to land or houses) went to France to be trained, joining relatives who had gone there during the previous generation's migrations. If a suitable Mallorquin woman was not available in this foreign kin-based situation, the man, like the migrants to the New World in the previous century, would return to Mallorca 'to fetch a wife'. A marriage between two Mallorquins was still considered preferable to that with a French person. The French, in turn, also showed a marked concern with marrying within their own community, '. . . bringing together the young people who made up the "matrimonial area", the "marriage world" – neighbours, relations and more or less remote cousins' (Zonabend 1984: 89).

In the 1950s, young people were encouraged to come to Spain from abroad to learn about the language and culture of the country. In turn, Spaniards increasingly applied to study throughout Europe. Access to new cultures broadened social relations, while increased knowledge relaxed fears of 'the Other', at least for the young and highly educated. In many areas of Spain, relationships developed between foreign male college students and Spanish girls. A young man could not marry in without providing credentials to the family of his fiancée, and if not a Catholic, he would be asked to convert. These mixed marriages were subject to such scrutiny before they took place that once they were sanctioned the couple was welcomed in both natal homes. However, women who came to Spain as students or English teachers had more difficulty in being accepted. Spanish women were still highly chaperoned at this time, so foreign women who travelled and lived alone were looked on with suspicion. Parents of their male friends often perceived them as morally lax and unsuitable, and men saw them as easily available sexually. Nonetheless, some did pass inspection if they maintained decorum and met the right kind of people to introduce them to locals.

Many professors of Spanish language and literature in British and American universities today are partners of this type of mixed marriage. Any mixed marriage at this time implied that the bride and groom shared similar status based on education, and it was assumed that only those from the 'better' social classes had access to travel. This was sometimes an illusion, and some young Spanish brides found themselves isolated, lonely and enclosed within the small confines of a flat without heating or hot water in a strange and unwelcoming country, dependent on their husbands for every necessity. The religious, sacramental aspect of their Catholic marriages helped them to stick it out and often situations improved. However, some preferred to return home alone, despite family and village criticism such as, 'A Catholic wife's place is with her husband.'

The sixties was a period of cosmopolitan life in the capital cities and especially in the resort areas on the islands. Mixed marriages became more acceptable for those Mallorquins who were identifying with change and 'modernity'. The Balearics offered the northerners sun, sea, sand and romance. Foreign women had more relaxed moral codes than Spanish women in this period. Mallorquin men were able to broaden their horizons geographically and sexually.

Among one particular group of business families in Mallorca the marriage of their sons and daughters to those of British business families allowed them to overcome a stigma that had thwarted their complete integration into Mallorquin society for centuries. Even four hundred years after conversion to Catholicism and continued financial success, those referred to as *Chuetas*, the name given to Jewish converts in the sixteenth century, were seen as unacceptable marriage partners for the children of noble, landowning or affluent business families. Foreign spouses gave them a new identity as members of an international society. They spoke English at home, as it was more highly valued. They raised their children with English nannies (as some of the nobles in the past had done), and sent them abroad to be educated.

Mass tourism narrowed the social separation between locals and foreigners even more. Foreigners came from all backgrounds and places. Rapid tourist development throughout the island and migration from outlying villages and the mainland to the cities and newly developing resorts opened up the world view of young people in many areas of Spain. Regular wages, social security and health care, controlled working hours and access to a varied social life helped to narrow the economic and social gap that had kept the worlds apart. Tourists were just ordinary people temporarily on holiday. There was a decreasing concern for status and an emphasis on sharing differences, especially on the part of young men.

In the eyes and imaginations of the cool, fair northern girls, the warm, dark, handsome Spaniard was imbued with all the characteristics of the mysterious Mediterranean: exotic, masculine, passionate, emotional, sexy (see Kohn, this volume, on the allure of the exotic). Tourists lived their holiday lives in public, forming many cross-cultural or mixed liaisons of shorter or longer duration. Widening one's horizons and experiences was part of the ethos of being 'unfettered' and 'free' – while on holiday. Their everyday and nightly actions, expenditures and lifestyle were completely alien to those of most Mallorquins. It was a time for the pursuit of personal pleasure among the foreigners, and the Spanish men who provided the workforce and the social life quickly learned to participate. Nevertheless, the *laissez-faire* attitudes of the tourist community stood in stark contrast to the restrictive moral and economic aspects of local life away from the tourist areas. Boundaries between locals and foreigners were still carefully maintained: local girls did not frequent the cafés or discos and foreign men had little or no access to local women of any age.

Consequently, the mixed marriages that resulted in Mallorca were mostly between Spanish men and foreign women: during the sixties, marriages took place between Spanish waiters, taxi drivers, tour coach drivers, mechanics, nightclub personnel and performers (in other words, those who interacted regularly with tourists) and girls from most of the developed European countries. If the girl was not Catholic they would go to Gibraltar or back to her home country for a civil marriage. Spanish nationality was given automatically at marriage. This was not so much mixing as crossing over (class, nationality, status, knowledge, experience), entering into relationships that opened up a wider panorama of experience and opportunity.

The lingua franca of most couples was English but in time, and depending on where they lived, each learned the other's language. These couples moved back and forth between one another's countries and usually settled in Mallorca while work was plentiful. They lived in rented flats, away from the pressures of families, and went out every night working or socializing with many other mixed couples. The birth of children often altered these arrangements; many women began to find themselves staying at home with small children with no kin of their own and a husband who worked nights in the tourist industry and was of little or no help at home. Quite a few Scandinavian women returned to their natal homes and, finding both state and parental support more conducive to living with small children, they chose not to return to their Mallorquin husbands. Grandparents who had adapted to their foreign daughters-in-law felt abandoned and reminded their sons of all the warnings they had been given about 'marrying your own kind'. It reinforced the Mallorquin saying: 'Allowing a child to marry a foreigner is the same as losing your child.' They believed the attractions of 'the Other' to be like the devil – tempting and winning, but in the end only leading to harm.

The village of Deià, on the northwest coast of Mallorca, was well known for the many foreign artists and writers that had visited it and the expatriates who had settled there early in this century. Despite this long-term contact with foreigners, until 1965, there were only three cross-cultural or mixed marriages in the village. One local girl, the fisherman's daughter, was courted by a German man for six years before he succeeded in gaining her acceptance and her family's permission to marry. They were wed in 1960 and the family begrudgingly allowed her to be taken off to Germany. The village school teacher, a woman from the neighbouring island of Cabrera, quietly married a resident German-American artist in Gibralter. After living abroad for various periods, the couples returned to settle in Mallorca. The women preferred Mallorca because they were surrounded by an extended family and long-term friends. The men in these mixed marriages also preferred to live and work in Mallorca where many opportunities were available for them to use their languages and find work. A few years later Lucia, the daughter of Robert Graves, married a Catalan musician after her graduation from Oxford University. Today they live apart, she is in London and he is in Madrid.

For outsiders who married into rural or large extended Mallorquin families, ease of acceptance centred on their ability to adjust to the ways of their new family. Language comprehension was sometimes not as important as behaviour, an easy nature, and the ability to fit in. Many foreign women noted that their mothers-in-law never ceased explaining things to them, and if the girl looked perplexed the mother-in-law just spoke louder and louder until the girl was forced to feign understanding. Foreign men seem to have had an easier time as comprehension often took place through action rather than words. Men shared in maintenance chores or went to the café together. Foreign women, however, found themselves surrounded by women chatting about everyday affairs, and were frustrated by their inability to communicate in Catalan. Domestic space and amenities were limited in Mallorquin rural houses in the sixties. Many houses lacked running water, cooking was on charcoal, water had to be drawn from a well and clothes washed at a stand by the stream. I moved to Deià at this time, and it was a challenging experience to adapt to these far simpler conditions. A young foreign woman from a home that had always had running water, cookers and heating, had to learn completely new skills.

In most cases of mixed marriage between a local and a foreigner, parents readily accepted cultural differences if the in-marrying person was superior socially or economically. However, in a few cases, there were parents who rejected, disowned, even disinherited their sons for marrying foreign girls. Among such cases that I encountered, the birth of a grandchild brought the families together again.

1975–1996: Regional Identities and Re-assessing Outsiders

Just prior to Franco's death in 1975 Spanish bishops opted for separation of the Catholic Church and the state (1973). From this time onward, civil marriages were allowed and churches of other denominations were permitted to hold services. There was a huge rise in marriages in villages and towns after this with many non-Spanish mixed couples legalizing their long-time unions in local city halls. Expatriates who had been together for years, had children in the local schools and had been perceived as families by the village, went along to the city hall after completing some very complicated paper work and were married by the justice of the peace – whom they knew as Francisco, the local carpenter. The locals saw this as a positive sign of their own influence on their neighbours' way of life. Foreigners were legitimating their unions and that of their children in the eyes of society.

The end of the seventies and the early eighties saw the emergence of a new form of social democracy and a constitution that created seventeen autonomous regions. Rediscovering, reinterpreting and reinventing regional identities led people to turn inward once again, to search for unique differences and to re-identify those who had helped or hindered their progress toward this new position of regional autonomy. Language became an important element in social cohesion and group identity, so those who did not speak Catalan or Mallorquí were grouped together as outsiders. Spanish, the national language, was to be joined by Catalan for public use. British, French, American, German had any other foreign residents, once valuable assets to the community, became outsiders and were criticized for imposing 'western values' on local identity.

This heightened awareness of regional identity was evident when the local school chose to be one of the first on the island to change to Catalan as its primary language, relegating Castillian Spanish to just a few hours a week. Some of the parents voiced their concern over the difficulties they felt might occur for the large number of children from diverse backgrounds in the school. Foreign parents' involvement in school decisions had been respected in the past, but on this issue they were told 'if they did not agree with the changes they could leave the school'. There were thirty-five children in the school, about one-third of whom were from mixed marriages. These mixtures included:

Women/Men
Deianenc/Welsh
Deianenc/German
Italian/Dutch
English/American
American/German
Spanish/English

Among the mixed couples, each parent had a different native language, they communicated in what was for some of them a third language (English) and would speak to their children in either parent's language or in English or Spanish. In many cases, the children were soon speaking Mallorquí, a language their parents did not understand.

The impact of the resurgence of regional language and identity on marriage and residence patterns can be seen in four marriages that have occurred between locals and foreigners since 1985. Two British men who married local women have tried to adapt as fully as possible to the characteristics they perceive as 'real' Mallorquin culture: learning the language, working on the land, building rustic dwellings for 'simple' living, avoiding too much modern technology, and so forth, albeit on a temporary basis interspersed with teaching and travelling. While they romanticize the past, their fathers-in-law continue to joke, affectionately but honestly, about how hard they worked to get off the land to give their children a better life, only to see the sons-in-law, whom they perceived as above themselves, actively seeking the drudgery they endeavoured to leave behind. Moreover, most of the foreigners, not having grown up on the land, never really get the hang of it. There are, however, a few foreign men who have learned the traditional stone terracing techniques and they are conscientiously restoring walls that few locals have the energy to maintain.

In contrast to some foreign husbands who try to recreate a romanticized and no longer strictly true image of local men and their relationship to the land, the local girls are assuming more independent roles and endeavouring to alter the conventional standards which kept girls at home, under the watchful eye of parents and family members, until they married. One local girl left home and moved into her German boyfriend's house when her father refused to allow him to come to visit her at her family house. After a week, the parents, embarrassed at the effect her actions had on their reputation in the village, begged her to return, agreeing to welcome him to their home and to discuss their engagement. They were married the following year. A few years later, the birth of twin daughters with pale blue eyes and blond hair made the family very proud and the grandparents were often seen caring for the girls while the parents were at work.

By the 1980s, the political climate of Spain had adjusted to the devolution of power to regional governments and Europeans with the means to live well were welcome additions to villages and towns. The prosperity of the 1980s was evident in the new visitors and residents in Deià. The pop musicians, business people and nouveaux riches from Düsseldorf, Paris, London and the USA were different sorts of outsiders from those who had come to Deià in previous decades. Their designer clothes, fast sports cars and free spending impressed the local youth. Forty per cent of the village men and women between sixteen and thirty-five worked in the hotels, restaurants and boutiques that catered to this affluent crowd. This close contact has had a dynamic effect on village life, personal ambitions, incomes, the cost of living and social relations.

Young Deià villagers, be they locals or the children of long-term foreign residents, identify directly with these new visitors and their activities. They share similar interests in music, clothes, leisure and social life. They work together in the hotels, plan activities together and support one another's projects. A Mallorquin girl married a Swedish contractor in 1990. He bought her a village house and a BMW car and she administers his businesses, which are all in her name. She feels she has the best of both worlds and, like other local women today, she is taking a more active part in business, politics and local life. Today's women are conscious of their identities as both Mallorquins and as women, and have gained a sense of autonomy through the advantages opened up during the past decade. The concept of mixed marriage is once again seen in the light of the changing values within the village. Difference lends attraction to some relationships, while others find their similarities outweigh any potentially problematic differences.

The reaction of the children of cross-cultural marriages reflects the variety of responses to mixed marriages. Some of these children want to return to their foreign parents' home countries, feeling that they have somehow lost out on part of their cultural heritage, and thereby part of their identity, and only by returning will they fully understand themselves and their parents. On the other hand, others have identified so much with local life that they have formed relationships with Mallorquin men or women and found jobs within the village and are hoping to find permanent housing when the time is right.

What is perceived today as mixed marriage is quite different from that in the previous periods. For example, two of my daughters have married men from the neighbouring town. They resisted the typing of their marriages as mixed or cross-cultural. They and their husbands were quite adamant about being of the 'same culture'. They were born in Mallorca, are completely tri-lingual, know everything about everybody in the village and live comfortably in a world they find absolutely familiar. The fact that their parents are foreigners and that they themselves spent many years studying in the UK does not affect the way they feel about belonging. They and their local friends work together, socialize together, travel widely, pursue winter sports and participate in the multicultural activities that are available in Mallorca today.

Unlike the spouses of the British–Mallorquin, the German–Mallorquin, and the Swedish–Mallorquin couples who are often reminded that they are *estrangers*, foreign children who have grown up in the village identify themselves as 'locals' and they are perceived as locals when it is to the benefit of neighbours, bureaucracy, and when all runs smoothly. I think they are straddling a fence, sometimes more on one side than the other, but never fully on one or the other. But even children of parents from two neighbouring villages are said to have 'one foot in each camp'. Among local families there are hierarchies based on ownership of land, education, family social and political positions, forms of employment and many other variables that make people feel more, or less, part of the village. It is apparent that many circumstances affect a person's own sense of belonging, as well as a community's recognition of that person as one of its members (Waldren 1996). When we discuss the perceptions of mixing, matching or crossing over, I think we need to consider whose terms we are using, ours or theirs, emic or etic? I think we must see these terms as basically situational. Categories are important but they do not get in the way of on-going relationships – most of the time.

The main point is that after centuries of closed marriage circuits in Mallorca, it has become possible to accommodate 'mixed' and cross-cultural marriages. To accommodate means to bring within, to include. The process is slow and requires individual commitment and confidence on the part of both parties who enter into the union. The reasons for this, I am suggesting, derive from the fact that indigenous views of social identity have expanded to include a wider sphere of potential relationships. In 1996, social pressures to conform are less rigid and concepts of 'personhood'and social identity are more personal. Young people identify with similarities between one another rather than with the differences their families feared in the past. This does not mean that they are giving up their traditional culture. They are re-interpreting it to meet the needs of the present. They have created new 'boundaries of commonality within which meaning is shared'(Cohen 1982: 9).

Spaniards have been experiencing rapid development and change over the past twenty years which has encouraged cultural pluralism both regionally and inter-nationally. Traditions have been adapted and often re-invented to meet the demands of the present. Drawing on examples from one small village on Mallorca, I have tried to show the impact of outside and inside events on the process of change. We began with matched marriages based on similarities of belief, status, kinship and fear of difference. This was followed by fascination with differences, with the Other, a period of striking out, of widening horizons of mixing and crossing-over, and we have arrived at the end, or at a new beginning, with mixed cross-cultural matches, or is it matched cross-cultural mixes?

Notes

1. 'In 1900, 65 per cent of the Spanish working population was involved in agriculture. By 1930 this had fallen to 46 per cent. A similar portion lived in rural or semi-rural population centres (those of under 10,000 inhabitants). 59 per cent were illiterate in 1900, 32 per cent in 1930' (Alvarez 1995: 82). This was a world subject to Church teachings and excluded from the political sphere.
2. Community membership was given to all Spanish nationals when they reached the age of twenty-three. However, men, as household heads, were considered to be the representatives of their houses at council meetings. Men who lived with their in-laws often had to wait many years before assuming active participation in village affairs. Women became household heads if they were widowed and had no sons.
3. Rumour has it that the Archduke was bi-sexual, that his liaisons with men and women were always rewarded with generous gifts and if a woman became pregnant he would make sure that a marriage was arranged and that the couple had a place to live.

References

Abram, S., Waldren, J. and Macleod, D. (eds) (1997), *Tourists and Tourism: Identifying with People and Places*. Oxford: Berg Publishers.

Alvarez, J. (1995), 'Rural and Urban Popular Cultures', in H. Graham and J. Labanyi (eds), *Spanish Cultural Studies*, Oxford: Oxford University Press.

Bestard, J. (1991), *What's in a Relative?*, Oxford: Berg Publishers.

Cleminson, R. (1995), 'Politics of Spanish Anarchism', in H. Graham and J. Labanyi (eds), *Spanish Cultural Studies*, Oxford: Oxford University Press.

Cohen, A. (ed.), (1982), *Belonging: Identity and Social Organisation in British Rural Culture*, Manchester: Manchester University Press.

Janer, G. (1980), *Sexe i Cultura a Mallorca: El Cançoner*, Mallorca: Editorial Moll.

Radhakrishnan, R. (1992), 'Nationalism, Gender and the Narrative of Identity', in A. Parker, M. Russo, D. Sommer, and P. Yaeger (eds), *Nationalisms and Sexualities*, London: Routledge.

Simmel, G. (1953), *Conflict in Modern Culture and Other Essays*, New York: Free Press.

Waldren, J. (1988), 'House Names as Metaphors for Social Relations', in *Oxford Journal of Social Anthropology (JASO)*, 19, no.2, pp.166–9.

——, (1996), *Insiders and Outsiders: Paradise and Reality in Mallorca*, Oxford: Berghahn Books.

Zonabend, F. (1984), *The Enduring Memory: Time and History in a French Village*, Manchester: Manchester University Press.

3

Chance, Choice and Circumstance: A Study of Women in Cross-Cultural Marriages

Jane Khatib-Chahidi, Rosanna Hill and Renée Paton

Introduction

This chapter presents the preliminary findings of a pilot study into mate selection in international[1] mixed marriage which addresses the question of 'Who inter-marries?' Is it purely a matter of chance meeting and romantic love as many of us like to believe: an inherently random choice, as Lykken and Tellegen (1993) suggest? Or, do individuals select their spouses, consciously or unconsciously, according to certain predetermined criteria? As the norm in relationships is homogamy (see amongst others, Rubin 1970, 1973), where like tends to marry like, why do a minority of individuals choose their mate from outside their social group? Do such individuals share similar characteristics: family background, life experience, personality, or a combination of such variables? Or, do their marriages merely reflect propinquity as the trend in modern life for travel has widened 'the field of eligibles' beyond national boundaries?

Mate selection is one of the most researched aspects of marriage (for surveys see Adams 1979; Surra 1990; Atwood 1993; Buss 1994). However, as Cottrell (1990) commented on research into international marriage in general, there appear to be few studies directed to mate selection in this type of intermarriage. While post-Second World War studies of war-bride or colonizer marriages provide some interesting insights into these types of international intermarriage (see, for example, Spickard 1989: 123–58), much of the research seems to emphasize the problems these marriages may encounter, in circumstances very different from those today (Cottrell 1990: 159).

We recognized that the research already done into marriage, and intermarriage – interracial, interethnic or interfaith – within one country may have relevance for international mixed marriages, but we did not want to take its results for granted. It seemed to us that marrying a foreigner was rather a different matter from marrying

49

a member of another ethnic group in one's own country, if only because it would involve migration and resettlement of at least one of the partners. Neither did we accept, as many suggested to us, that international intermarriage was necessarily a consequence of people working, studying or travelling away from their home country. That at least one of the parties in such marriages is abroad at the time they met is a necessary but not sufficient condition for them to marry: for the few who meet foreigners and choose to marry them, the vast majority, despite foreign travel and prolonged residence abroad, prefer their own compatriots as marriage partners.

Our opportunistic sample reflected these considerations: it consisted of twenty women, in existing mixed marriages, who had met and decided to marry their future foreign spouse in their own country.[2] We obtained basic biographical data on all the women and also on their husbands. We interviewed nineteen of them using in-depth but unstructured techniques; we wanted our subjects to tell us what *they* believed had been formative experiences in their lives before marriage. Eighteen of our subjects who had English as their mother tongue, or were sufficiently bilingual in English, were asked to complete a personality test.

Sample Profile (N=20)

Our sample of twenty women[3] showed several characteristics previously found in other studies of people in mixed marriages. Earlier research, such as that by Whyte (1990) and Blau (1977), has shown that people who 'marry out' tend to be either highly educated, professional middle class or working class, to marry later than the average age of their particular group (Surra 1990) and to come from families with previous cross-cultural marriages (Cottrell 1990). They also tend to marry those of similar status to themselves (see amongst others, Blau 1977: 49; Whyte 1990: 122).

The age at marriage of the women in our sample was late (average and median, twenty-seven years). This is of greater note than the bald figure would indicate since it should be borne in mind that half of them married in the 1960s and 1970s when age at marriage was younger than now (see Surra 1990: 845, who gives 23.6 median age for the United States of America in 1988 as an all-time high). Four women were between two and five years older than their husbands. The age at marriage may be related to the educational level and social class of our sample.

Fifteen women were university educated; four had doctoral degrees, and several more had other post-graduate qualifications. The husbands tended to be of similar educational standard although, unusually, there were seven instances of wives with higher educational qualifications than their husbands. In only three of the twenty couples did the husband have an appreciably higher educational level and occupational status than his wife. The women who had paid employment and the husbands of our sample were in predominantly Class 1 occupations (professional and executive).

The twenty women, aged from twenty-five to fifty-five years (average forty-four years), were nationals of nine countries: Britain, USA, Turkey, Cyprus, Austria, France, Iran, Spain and Russia. Their husbands came from eleven different countries: Britain, USA, France, Cyprus, Turkey, Iran, Jordan, Sudan, India, Iraq, Egypt and Liberia.

Ten women had foreign antecedents as judged by the nationality of their parents and the place of birth of their grandparents, i.e. at least one of the parents or grandparents was born in a different country or had been the citizen of a different state from their children for some part of their lives (see also Maxwell on mixed families, this volume). This was also true for five of the husbands. Seven women were first or second generation residents of their respective countries. This factor proved highly relevant, and is in line with previous research findings that participants in cross-national marriages are often children of mixed marriages themselves, living either in immigrant subcultures or in a third culture (Cottrell 1990: 163).

Only one woman had been married before, although four of the husbands had been previously married (all to foreigners). This contrasts with previous findings on ethnic intermarriage which report high rates of previously married people (see, amongst others, Kuo and Hassan 1976: 558 for Singapore; Lee Sung 1990 for Chinese Americans).

Sixteen couples had married across both religious and national boundaries. Only three women and three men actually practised their professed religion; in only one case was this a couple. Four women professed no religious belief. One couple converted to Islam and one woman joined her husband's religion, also Islam. Previous research has shown that those who intermarry are less likely to have strong religious convictions and less likely to practise their faith (see Resnik 1933; Spickard 1989: 131) and this seemed to be borne out by our small sample. We should note, however, that this is not always the case and, as Yamani illustrates in this volume, religion can sometimes function as a means of integrating a cross-cultural union, uniting two people from different cultures and different language groups. In our case, lack of religious commitment may suggest that our subjects (and their spouses) were less rooted in their own cultures.

One further point which emerged during the interviews was that at least six subjects came from natal family backgrounds which seemed lower in the socio-economic scale than those of their husbands, but through their education and achievements they had changed social class. Blau (1977: 37) comments that socially mobile people are 'in some sense marginal men and women'. This is perhaps relevant to the issue of marginality which we discuss below.

Finally, none of the sample came from broken homes.

Why This Man – The Women's Story (N=19)

How They Met: Education and Language
It seems likely that several chance elements played some role in how our subjects met their future husbands in the first place. The most common factor was education: ten of the future husbands were in their wife's country for their higher education, most of them at post-graduate level. Two other men were there working as university teachers.

Thirteen of the wives interviewed had first met their husbands in situations related to study: seven women were students at university, six of whom married fellow students; one woman was teaching in the university where her future husband was a student; three women were working in a university (one in the library, and two in administration) where their future husbands were studying. In one instance, an adventitious meeting occurred at an airport when the woman was on her way to America to look at universities. Her future husband who, had been in her country for his work, was travelling to America to write up and present his doctoral thesis. The thirteenth met her future husband when she was doing a placement as part of her college sandwich course in the business owned by her future father-in-law.

For at least four women and their spouses, it was the ability to speak a common language other than their own which helped them establish the relationship in the first place.

Initial Attraction: The Exotic Other?
Several factors were mentioned by the women as attracting them to their future spouse initially, and many of these factors indicate both what women seek in partnerships generally, as well as what is appealing about foreign men in particular. Seven women said they were drawn to their future husband because he was 'different'. Although this difference was variously defined, it alluded to personal qualities in the future spouse which either compared favourably with those of known others, or complemented some aspect of the subject's own personality in which she felt lacking. For one, he had a 'nice' nature, not like her previous boyfriend who had been jealous; for another it was because 'he wasn't overly excitable and hysterical like everyone in my family'. Another subject, who was herself rather quiet, said he was 'very boisterous, larger than life, unorthodox'. The above examples seem to have more to do with individual personality than cultural characteristics, but one subject commented on the man's manners being different from those of the English whom she described as 'cold', suggesting that she may have been attracted to a culturally different approach in the way in which men related to women. Several found their own countrymen rather 'boring': this feeling was perhaps sometimes stimulated by a dream of the 'exotic other' (see

Kohn, this volume), or, less romantically, based on positive early experiences of living abroad and relating to foreigners. Only one woman said she was attracted to her foreign husband primarily because he was a foreigner. However, an American of Canadian origin did remark that a great attraction for her was that her future French husband, like her, mixed with foreigners rather than his own countrymen in the international hostel where they both lived when students.

Our small sample consequently suggests qualified support for the complementarity principle in long-term relationships (Kerckhoff and Davis 1962). According to this view, people choose relationships in which their basic needs can be mutually gratified, often resulting in a pairing of apparent opposites. In one case there was an explicit comparison between the woman's father and her husband which demonstrates complementarity in the socio-economic sphere. She explained 'It was important for me to marry somebody who was not in my father's occupation because my parents were very poor. But somebody who had a steady job, and in this case a profession he was going to . . . I wouldn't feel poor all the time and that was important to me.'

On the other hand, similarity between spouses was also observed: seven of the women emphasized that they had a lot in common with their spouses. This generally referred to common interests. Not surprisingly, positive personal qualities generally associated with interpersonal attraction were found to be important here too. Six women mentioned admiration of their husband's intellect or intelligence. One subject remarked of her Jordanian husband: 'He knew more than I did . . . He broadened my vision . . . Maybe I was being an opportunist [because his higher studies meant she could learn from him].' Another liked the fact that her husband had 'a lot of intellectual interests . . . was open to new experiences . . . knew a tremendous amount . . . knew a lot about poetry and although he was a scientist he had a kind of feel for the humanities . . .' A third greatly admired her husband's intellect, his ability to write and 'his knowledge about so many things'.

Five women mentioned the warmth, sense of humour and/or liveliness of their future husband. Four mentioned good looks, and two sexual attraction (see also Kohn, this volume). One mentioned a 'mystical' sense of already knowing her husband when they first met, although as this was not explored further it is not clear what was meant.

The general picture emerging from the interviews was that these women were attracted by the same personal qualities as those who do not marry out. This suggests that personality and situational factors relating to the women themselves may yield clues relevant to their marital choice.

The Decision to Marry: Taking the Plunge
The decision to marry was not, for the most part, made in haste: the average time the couples knew each other before marrying was more than three years, just under

if we exclude the one exceptional case of ten years. This meant that those women whose partners remained in their country had time to get to know them better. However, in at least three cases, the time from the first meeting until the marriage was largely spent apart. The Russian subject, who met her future British husband when he had come as a tourist for five days, laughingly remarked that she had in fact known him 'only thirty-something hours altogether'. They continued their relationship by letter and six months later he flew back to Moscow to propose to her, and she had no hesitation in accepting.

Most women reported that they felt sure that their then boyfriend was 'the right man' for them to marry. Romantic attachment between the would-be partners was overtly or implicitly given as the main reason for marriage in most cases. The emotional ties were augmented by situational factors which affected the timing of the marriage. For one subject it was a case of an eligible man at the right time: she was finding the constraints of life in her home country increasingly irksome: 'Social control was closing in . . . You felt trapped in a pattern set for you . . . this made me determined to marry [him] . . . He was exotic, foreign, exciting and working in — [another country].'

For several women we gained the impression that their age was a factor in the decision. This was particularly so for one subject aged thirty-seven: after knowing her future husband for nine months, six months of which he was abroad when they could communicate only by phone, she was as anxious as he to get married because they both wanted children. Here awareness of the biological clock probably acted as an impetus, whereas external pressure may have played a greater role in the cases of two women now in their fifties who both commented that all their friends seemed to have married before them, in their early twenties; they were both in their late twenties when they married. One reported a growing sense of urgency conveyed by her family as she approached her mid-twenties. Two Middle Eastern women who married at twenty-seven and twenty-eight, which was well past the normal age of marriage for their particular cultures, similarly indicated that cultural expectations played some part in their decision to marry when they did.

In several cases it appeared that chance factors precipitated the actual timing of the marriage, although not the decision to marry. These included the death of the mother of one woman, followed by the collapse of her father. This unfortunate event may have been the spur to make the relationship permanent. In two instances the threat of impending separation because the men had to return to their countries for work led to the decision to marry at that time. The most idiosyncratic trigger to marriage in our sample was a house. One couple who worked together and spent six years of their leisure in each other's company, saw a house they both liked and wanted to buy and decided at that point to get married.

Overall, it seemed that many of the women in our sample were ready for the long-term commitment of marriage. They had completed their higher education, they had travelled, and were ready to settle down; there was perhaps 'a predisposition to wed' (cf. Surra 1990: 856), and an acknowledgment that it was time they did so.

Attitude of the Parents: Antagonism or Acceptance?

Eight women reported that their parent(s) disapproved of their daughters' choice of husband to some degree, though according to the women this was not *necessarily* because the men were foreigners.[4] In three cases of interracial marriage, the women denied that race was an issue for their families. Two women, however, reported that there was overt rejection of their chosen partner on *perceived* racial grounds. In one of these the woman was actually disowned when her parents learned of her relationship with her future, fair-skinned, Muslim husband, whose undesirability according to the mother – and the father usually followed what his wife thought – was total: he was not the right nationality, not Roman Catholic and 'worst of all he was Black'.

In the case of two Jewish couples the women stated that their parents had mixed reactions to the match as they were anxious in case their daughters would move to their husbands' countries. Both these women mentioned that their parents disliked their future son-in-law's nationality, indicating a hierarchical evaluation of groups of foreigners similar to that discussed by Breger in this volume. In one case this dislike was based on beliefs held by the subject's left-wing parents about a history of imperialist politics and anti-Semitism in the future husband's country; in the other, the parents (Jews of Sephardic origin living in Western Europe) appeared to hold a negative stereotype of the people in the Middle Eastern country from which the husband came.

Of the remaining parents who disapproved of their daughters' choice, two had never thought in terms of them marrying foreigners, and disliked the idea but also had other reasons for their disapproval. The first, a father, considered his future son-in-law's occupation (writer) as being of too low status. The second, a mother, was also ambitious for her highly educated daughter to improve her social standing through marriage. A British subject said that her future husband's being foreign was the least of her mother's worries: 'She was against anyone who wanted to marry her children.'

At least six women mentioned in the course of their interview that one of their parents was dead before they married. In three cases they believed that this may have affected the degree of opposition they might otherwise have met. Two Middle Eastern women had lost their fathers; their mothers allowed them greater freedom than they would have experienced if their fathers had been alive. A British subject said that if her mother had still been alive, she doubted if she would have had sufficient strength to oppose her and to go through with the marriage to her African husband.

Overall, we found disparate attitudes reported by the subjects in our small sample. It is likely that this variation is similar to that found among parents whose daughters do not 'marry out'.

Preparing for the Marriage

Romano (1988: 142) advises that couples intending to marry cross-culturally should find out as much as possible about the background, family and culture of the future spouse before getting married, ideally visiting his/her country and even paying an extended visit to the prospective spouse's family home. Most of our women did not attempt to do this, although prior to meeting their husbands six had visited their husband's country; two in the course of their work and four as tourists. Only two women interviewed knew their husband's family before marriage, and only one had travelled overseas, entirely of her own volition, to meet some members of her boyfriend's family.[5]

Whether or not they had visited their husband's country or met his family, for many of the women it was clear that the country of origin and the family of their future spouse were of less concern to them than more personal factors. 'You are marrying me, not my family', one subject was told, and this seems to have been the general attitude of the women themselves (but see Sissons Joshi and Krishna, this volume).

The same venturesome qualities were displayed over where they would live after marriage: nine were either happy to go wherever their husband wanted or were eager to leave their home country. Others hoped to stay in their own country but accepted that they might have to go elsewhere for their husbands' work. Only one subject mentioned feeling apprehensive before marriage about possibly living in her husband's country: she married her Iranian husband some three years after the Islamic revolution, six years after they first met.

Life Experiences (N=19)

In this section we look at the childhood, adolescent and young adulthood experiences reported by the women in our sample which we believe relevant to international mixed marriage. We concentrate on two areas: significant, positive experiences with people from different cultures; and the feelings reported by the women of being marginal within the community (society or family) in which they were raised. We believe that these two factors acted in tandem: the 'push' away from their own culture and the 'pull' towards people from other cultures. In other words, foreignness was seen by most of our sample as a positive quality in other people, but a negative one in themselves when experienced as marginality.

Internationalism: Previous Experience with Foreigners

Sixteen women reported significant interaction with foreigners before meeting their husband. Ten had lived abroad for at least a year and in most cases far longer, either because of their parents' work, their own work or studies. None of these women, however, married men from the countries where they had lived. This suggests that the attraction was not necessarily towards that with which they were familiar, but may have been part of the general allure of the exotic.

Predictably those with foreign antecedents had contact with relatives or family friends from other countries as they were growing up. They were accustomed to close family ties with those from other countries.

Two who had not travelled had met many foreigners through their work. These women reported mixing only with people from other countries and feeling more at ease with them. The remainder whose contact with foreigners abroad included extended school exchange visits and/or visits abroad as tourists also considered these experiences influential in developing their attitudes towards other cultures and countries.

Previous experience was not an important feature in every case, however. Three women had very limited contact with people from other countries. They had never travelled abroad and one of them commented that her husband was the first foreigner she had ever met.

Nearly half of the women interviewed reported that they had had several foreign boyfriends. Although the sample was very small, this may be a further indication of the attractiveness of 'foreignness'. In addition to common interests and other similarities of major importance, it would appear that these women sought relationships with men who were culturally different from themselves. Why this might be so, their personality characteristics and feelings about themselves will be addressed next.

Feelings of Marginality

Of the nineteen women interviewed sixteen reported feelings and experiences of marginality – of being different from others, or of not belonging, or of social isolation – for a significant period in their childhood, adolescence or early adulthood.[6] Most told of their distress associated with the experience of marginality but three women reported that although they felt they did not belong, they were not unhappy about this.

More detailed information is given on this topic because it seemed to us a highly relevant variable; most of the women raised this issue without probing from the interviewer and several related poignant anecdotes to illustrate this theme in their lives.

We have divided the material reported on the topic of marginality into three groups based on the following: feelings of being outsiders linked to structural marginality (ethnicity, culture, social class, and so forth); feelings of being an outsider within the personal domain (family, friends); and consciously choosing 'Otherness' (rejecting their own culture/society). These categories are not mutually exclusive; several women's stories illustrate more than one category but we concentrate on the predominant theme(s) which emerged in each interview.

(1) Structural marginality leading to feelings of exclusion.   For nine women their feelings of social and/or personal marginality were linked to their structural marginality, or what Imamura (1990) terms 'objective marginality'.

Four of our subjects were Jewish by birth and linked their feelings of marginality to that. Given the archetypical status of the Jew as outsider, this is not surprising. Two of the women reported deep feelings of isolation and unhappiness with their situation. One was brought up in a town in England where they were the only Jews and she was exposed to anti-Semitism. In addition, she felt excluded from the dominant culture as she was forbidden by her non-practising father to take part in the Christian religious activities in school. She 'missed out' on both Christmas and Jewish festivals. This woman married a man who had been brought up in a practising Christian family and reported that she always compensated for the lack of any festivities in her childhood by *really* celebrating Christmas with her children.

Another woman emphasized her Jewish ties whilst at the same time describing how she felt separated from the mainstream culture. This was exacerbated by other social features: her parents were immigrants who were not well integrated into the society in which they lived and they were poor. This woman's sense of isolation may also have derived in part from her status within the family: she was the eldest with two much younger siblings.

In contrast, the other two Jewish women did not seem perturbed by their outsider status, although both recognized it as significant in their lives. One was brought up in an area where she had felt different because she was a Jew in Christian schools, because she came from a liberal Jewish family in a community where most Jews were Orthodox, and because she had parents who voted Labour in a predominantly Conservative neighbourhood. In young adulthood she enjoyed being different and doing different things. The second, who moved to Western Europe from North Africa at age nine, commented that although culturally she felt French, she didn't really belong to any country. She was also different in her family and the Jewish community because she mixed mainly with non-Jewish foreigners. Interestingly, although both these women reported that they were not unhappy at being 'outsiders', they both formally converted to other religions. In one case the woman adopted her husband's religion and in the other both husband and wife converted to Islam, the dominant religion of the country in which they live.

In two cases feelings of marginality were associated with social class. Both women described how their mothers' ambitions for social recognition isolated their daughters from their peers and led them to reject their mothers' values. The immigrant mother of one had 'learned to talk, walk and dress' as a lady's maid when she first came to America. She tried to control her daughter completely: as a child growing up in Brooklyn she was prevented from playing with anyone from the neighbourhood because her mother did not consider the local working-class children to be suitable play-mates; she had to go to Mass daily; she described her mother making her into 'a dressed-up princess'. Later, when she won a scholarship to a private Catholic school in a middle-class area, she was again isolated from her school-friends because her family had no car to fetch her if she visited them.

For another subject, who had a foreign-born mother, her intellectually oriented family was different from those of her peer group at school. Her snobbish, polyglot mother disapproved of her mixing with people from 'the wrong background' in the country area where they lived. She commented: 'I could *really* feel when my mother disapproved of any of my friends . . . she let me know and I found it very hurtful.' As the eldest child in the family she felt the brunt of her mother's fussiness fell on her: '. . . till the day my mother died I was always nagging her about how my sister had an easier life than I.'

The feelings of marginality of a further three women were associated with experience of living in another culture in childhood or adolescence. The first, an Austrian woman, felt that she was drawn to foreigners because of her early experiences. She had spent several happy years as a teenager in an international community in Kuwait because of her father's work. It was when she returned to Austria that she felt different: '. . . the only time I really felt like an outsider was in Austria, my last year at school, when there were so few Austrians that I could associate with, that I could relate to.' Because of her earlier experiences of travelling, living abroad and mixing with people from a range of cultural backgrounds, she found little in common with others of her age who had always lived in one place; the latter seemed to her to be dull and narrow. All but one of her boyfriends were foreigners.

A similar picture was unexpectedly presented by a Russian subject who had spent several happy years in Cameroon with her family when she was a child. During her adolescence, she was sent back to the then Soviet Union for her education and lived with her grandmother whilst her parents remained abroad. It was then that she discovered how much her interests and experiences had diverged from her peers: she was not interested in dating, makeup and the other common concerns of teenagers both in the west and in the former eastern bloc countries. She was lonely for companionship and missed her family, especially her mother. The years in Cameroon had prepared her for marriage to a foreigner in another way also: when she and her British husband first met, the only language they had in common was French, which she had learned as a child while there.

The third woman in this sub-category showed several features previously observed. Her parents were immigrants and for a short time in childhood she lived abroad. Her academic family stood out from the others in the largely upper-class conservative community in which they lived: they were not members of the church, their children did not go to independent schools, and their political allegiances were different from those of their neighbours. They socialized mainly with their own compatriots and other foreigners. She was one of the few subjects who was not unhappy at her marginal status.

(2) Familial/personal marginality.   The stories of four women illustrate the feelings of marginality or isolation induced by the situation within their families. The clearest example of this is a Spanish woman raised in Spain and married to an Englishman. She reported feeling isolated from her own family. She was the firstborn in a family of four, and from the age of seven was raised separately, except for holidays, by a grandmother and half-blind godmother. 'You were never one of us', her siblings told her later. Her physical appearance, with red hair and freckles also singled her out from her sisters whom she described as more beautiful. As a young adult she had felt stifled by bourgeois Spanish society, and challenged her dictatorial father over her education and choice of husband. Rebellion against women's traditional role is a theme related by several women, especially those from the Middle East. It may be relevant that this woman was labelled by her own family as an outsider; she married very early (the youngest in our sample), and she married the first foreigner she had ever met.

The next subject, an American with Canadian parents, spent her early years moving from place to place in North America because of her father's work. This had not worried her when she was at primary school in Canada, but when the family moved to the United States, she felt lonely and rejected by her peers whose friendships were already formed. In adolescence, she refused to participate in the American dating scene which left her further isolated. The early death of her father, to whom she had been very attached, also left her feeling alone within her family because she felt her mother favoured her brother.

Familial conflict leading to feelings of marginality are also seen in the instance of a British woman with British parents whose aggressively working-class father came from the north of England and her socially ambitious middle-class mother was a southerner. The mother, according to her daughter, 'thought of herself as the bearer of culture in a pagan land', while her father was very much part of his own working-class locality. This subject experienced feelings of both social and personal marginality which were directly linked to this regional/class division of her parents. Later, in London, where she went to work to escape the class warfare waged at home, she felt an outsider because of her northern roots. In London she mixed almost entirely with people from other countries.

The last subject described an extremely happy, secure childhood and adolescence, where she had loved being with '200 brothers' in the boys' school where her father was deputy head and housemaster of the boarding section. She experienced feelings of exclusion and isolation in young adulthood after leaving school, for when she returned to her parental home the boys her parents were looking after 'weren't my brothers anymore . . . It was horrible . . . I went home to an empty house. Because of course those children did not know me. I was just that woman upstairs. That was weird.' Several years later, after living in a bedsit and feeling isolated, she moved into a large African household (in the same English city) where she felt at ease: 'I was just one of a crowd . . . And I didn't get noticed and I liked that.' Later in life she married an African.

(3) Escape from cultural gender roles. The following three women – all Middle Easterners – seemed to be rebelling against the conventions of their own countries, and sometimes their own families. These instances reveal the way the women used marriage to a foreigner to avoid the gender role expectations within their native countries. The first one married outside her religion and culture area. The other two married fellow Muslims from different countries in the Middle East.

For the first one her feelings of being different within her own society and family represent a case best-described as self-induced social/personal marginality: she *wanted* to be different. Jealous of her attractive elder sister whom she felt she could not resemble, she chose to succeed in academic work. Finding her own society restrictive, and distrustful of her own countrymen, she felt liberated in Paris where she went for post-graduate studies. 'France was the making of me', she remarked. There she made a point of mixing with the French rather than her own compatriots as her countrymen/women did.

Similarly, the next subject seemed to *want* to be different: she dressed differently, and refused to go out socializing like most girls did in her country. She said she had felt different within the family and freer from parental restrictions, perhaps because she was the youngest and her parents had 'satisfied their image of a son and daughter' in her older brother and sister. She commented that she did what she wanted, not caring what others thought, and suffered the consequences. She ignored criticism of her relationship with a foreign student in the university where she was a lecturer, and pointed out to the authorities that the male lecturers were not subject to the same criticism.

The third subject said she had always felt she was different from others; while others had many friends, 'I had my own world.' Unlike her schoolmates, she was not interested in boys. 'Because I was bright, I was different and a different future was expected for me', she commented. While others were interested in clothes she was considered 'odd' because she read whatever she could lay her hands on. This love of reading was shared and encouraged by her mother. She added her brother was also 'odd' in Turkish terms because he painted, an unusual hobby for a Turkish man.

Benefits of Cross-national Marriage

It can be suggested that a foreigner may be a more attractive proposition as a marriage partner both for those whose marginality has been a painful experience and for those in whom it did not cause distress. For the former it holds out the prospect of being able to distance themselves from elements in their own culture or family which they do not like; for the latter it affords the opportunity to express their marginality even further. As one subject remarked about herself in young adulthood, she seemed to be testing her liberal parents' outlook to the limit: 'I chose more and more outlandish boyfriends in one way or another . . . I knew my relationship [with the African she later married] would be a problem with my family and I made it into more of a problem . . . by telling them I had met this wonderful man . . . then I listed all the things they wouldn't like [his being Muslim, previously married and having children] . . . I think I was a rebel in the same way as my mother.'

For those women whose parents were very status conscious, a future son-in-law could not be assessed in the same way as a national from the woman's own country. This proved to be an advantage to several women who reported that their parents, particularly their mothers, considered 'no-one good enough' (see also Yamani, this volume).

In several instances women reported that they were attracted to their future husbands because they, too, seemed to be 'outsiders'. Although the structure of their alienation was often substantially different, these women felt that the shared feelings of marginality helped maintain the bond between them. For example, a British Jewish woman stated that her American husband, like her, was not part of the British class system, to which she felt she did not belong, and which she disliked intensely. For another British woman who grew up in the north of England and felt a stranger in London, her husband, like herself, was 'a floater', feeling that he did not really belong to his land of birth, Egypt, because of his Greek-Lebanese origins.

Personality Characteristics

In addition to the interviews, seventeen of the women filled out a paper and pencil personality questionnaire: the 16PF. An eighteenth, whose results are included here, took the personality test but was not willing to be interviewed. This personality measure was chosen as it has been extensively researched and has been demonstrated to yield reliable and meaningful scores. One of the most commonly used personality tests, it is designed to measure fundamental character traits which have been derived from factor analytic studies of personality. Both British and American norms are provided (see Anastasi and Urbina (1997) for a fuller description and evaluation). The results of the test discussed here are based on those subjects who are British or North American, or who have lived in England for several years.

We include a preliminary discussion of the results although we recognize that these should be treated with caution. Our sample was small and non-random. The women were tested many years after their marriages; the personality profiles we obtained were recent ones and not necessarily representative of those at the time of marriage. As such, these findings can only be treated as applicable to this particular sample at present. Taking these caveats on board, the test results indicated that the women in our sample are more imaginative and unconventional (Factor M), as well as more emotionally stable (Factor C) than the norm (significance levels p<.01). They were also more adventurous and uninhibited (Factor H), more sensitive to others (Factor I), and more experimenting, liberal and freethinking (Factor Q1) than the norm (significance level p<.05 for all three factors).

These findings support the impression given in the interviews. Certainly, by choosing a marital partner from another culture, the women are demonstrating many of these qualities 'in action', especially Factors M (unconventionality), H (adventurousness) and Q1 (experimenting). As has already been described, several of the women had shown independence of mind in rejecting their parents' view of whom to marry. They were experimenting and adventurous in their willingness to accept a marital partner whose background and culture they did not know. The majority now live in either their husband's country or a third country, several having moved many times, and enjoyed the experience. The lack of religious beliefs within our sample is also consistent with the high free-thinking, liberal and experimenting scores. Naturally, we do not suggest a causal relationship between these personality traits and the choice of marriage partner, but the personality characteristics consistent in our sample are those which 'fit' with an exogamous choice.

Concluding Remarks

Despite the limitations mentioned above, our study reveals certain salient variables which merit further research. These women resemble each other in certain definable ways. More than half had foreign antecedents; most had no religious convictions; many had experienced positive exposure to foreigners and foreign cultures, and had travelled or lived abroad. All but three of them had had life experiences which had left them in situations where they felt they did not belong to the social environment in which they found themselves (in childhood, adolescence, or early adulthood). The women had certain personality traits in common which supported the information given in the interviews: they were generally more adventurous, freethinking, unconventional and emotionally stable than the average. The match between personality traits and experiences (and attitudes) indicates 'a good fit', although the long time-lag between administering the personality measure and the date of marriage is acknowledged.

Cottrell (1973) suggested in her study of international marriages in India that they may be 'an extension and continuation of an already established international lifestyle'. Certainly some of our subjects had a well-established pattern of mixing with foreigners before marriage and the figures she gives for exposure to foreigners/ other cultures prior to marriage are similar to ours. However, our multi-cultural pilot study, unlike her much larger one (N=113) based on couples where one partner was Indian, indicates that other factors, particularly feelings of marginality, may play a major role. In several cases it was the experience of marginality itself which appeared to 'push' some women to mix with foreigners; in other cases it was the international lifestyle which led to feelings of alienation and isolation when the women returned to their home countries from abroad. Cottrell mentions that in only 15 per cent of her sample did rebellion, rejection or disillusion with country of origin appear to be an incentive to marry someone from another culture. She reported that only 4 per cent had felt rootless before marriage. Our data suggest a higher incidence of these factors which were linked to the feelings of marginality (structural, social or personal) expressed by sixteen out of the nineteen women we interviewed.

In her 1990 survey of research into international marriage, however, Cottrell states that 'People who marry out are, to some degree, psychologically, culturally, or socially marginal; at least they are not "dead centre". This should not be assumed to mean maladjusted' (Cottrell, 1990: 163). This certainly holds true for the women we interviewed. Since her survey contained no further information about these different forms of marginality, it is hoped that the present chapter will serve to highlight some of the variables involved for future research.

As a postscript we would like to note that despite the fact that it is estimated that nowadays over 55 per cent of marriages in the USA will end in divorce (Atwood 1993: 79), the women in our sample are in marriages that have stood the test of time, ranging from five to forty years, an average of twenty years.

Notes

1. For the purposes of this study it is understood that the international marriages were also cross-cultural, i.e. the women's husbands were born and brought up in different countries from their own. The term 'foreign' throughout the text will designate various nationalities according to the nationality of the subject in question.
2. The research took place in three countries in Europe during 1992–3. This was an opportunistic sample of predominantly middle-class, middle-aged, white women. Further details such as the nationalities of each couple and the number of women/men for each nationality have been deliberately omitted to protect the anonymity of the subjects. Since the main variable investigated is the similarity (or not) of women who marry internationally whatever country they may come from, we do not feel these omissions detract from the study, although we recognize that for the reader they would have been of interest.
3. One subject completed the biographical data sheet and the personality measure but was not willing to be interviewed.
4. Imamura (1986: 38) reported 76 per cent (N=21) parental disapproval for marriage of foreign women from many countries to Nigerian men.
5. Imamura (1986: 38) found that 47.6 per cent of her sample had been similarly unconcerned about possible difference in values before they married.
6. There is considerable research literature on the question of marginality extending back to the 1920s which we are unable to include in this chapter. See Park (1928), Stonequist (1937), Dickie-Clark (1966), Johnston (1976), Spitzer (1989) amongst others.

References

Adams, B.N. (1979), 'Mate Selection in the US: A Theoretical Summarization', in W.R. Burr, R. Hill, F.I. Nye and I.L. Reiss (eds), *Contemporary Theories about the Family: Research Based Theories*, Vol. 1, New York and London: The Free Press.

Anastasi, A. and Urbina, S. (1997), *Psychological Testing*, Upper Saddle River, New Jersey: Prentice Hall.

Atwood, J. (1993), 'The Mating Game: What We Know and What We Don't Know', *Journal of Couples Therapy*, 4, 1/2, pp.61–87.

Blau, P. (1977), *Inequality and Heterogeneity*, New York: Free Press. (Reprinted 1988)

Buss, D.M. (1994), 'The Strategies of Human Mating', *American Scientist*, 82, May–June, pp.238–47.

Cottrell, A.B. (1973), 'Cross-National Marriage as an Extension of an International Life Style: A Study of Indian-Western Couples', *Journal of Marriage and the Family*, 35, (4), pp.739–41.

——, (1990), 'Cross-National Marriages: a Review of the Literature', *Journal of Comparative Family Studies*, XXI, no.2, pp.151–69.

Dickie-Clark, H.F. (1966), *The Marginal Situation*, London: Routledge & Kegan Paul.

Imamura, A.E. (1986), 'Ordinary Couples? Mate Selection in International Marriage in Nigeria', *Journal of Comparative Family Studies*, XVII. no.1, pp.33–42.

——, (1990), 'Strangers in a Strange Land', *Journal of Comparative Family Studies*, XXI, no.2, pp.171–91.

Johnston, R. (1976), 'The Concept of the "Marginal Man": a Refinement of the Term', *Australia and New Zealand Journal of Sociology*, 12, 2, pp.145–7.

Kerckhoff, A.C. and Davis, K.E. (1962), 'Value Consensus and Need Complementarity in Mate Selection', *American Sociological Review*, 27, pp.295–303.

Kuo, E.C.Y. and Hassan, R. (1976), 'Some Social Concomitants of Interethnic Marriage in Singapore', *Journal of Marriage and the Family*, 38, 3, p.558.

Lee Sung, B. (1990), 'Chinese American Intermarriage', *Journal of Comparative Family Studies*, XXI, 3, pp.337–52.

Lykken, D.T. and Tellegen, A. (1993), 'Is Human Mating Adventitious or the Result of Lawful Choice?', *Journal of Personality and Social Psychology*, 65, 1, pp.56–68.

Park, R. (1928), 'Human Migration and the Marginal Man', *American Journal of Sociology*, 33, 6, May, pp.881–93.

Resnik, R.B. (1933), 'Some Sociological Aspects of Intermarriage of Jews and non-Jews', *Social Forces*, 12, pp.94–102.

Romano, D. (1988), *Intercultural Marriage: Promises and Pitfalls*, Yarmouth, Maine: Intercultural Press.

Rubin, Z. (1970), Measurement of Romantic Love, *Journal of Personality and Social Psychology*, 27, pp.295–303.

——, (1973) *Liking and Loving: An Invitation to Social Psychology*, New York: Holt, Rinehart and Winston.

Spickard, P.R. (1989), *Mixed Blood: Intermarriage and Ethnic Identity in Twentieth Century America*, Madison, Wisconsin: University of Wisconsin Press.

Spitzer, L. (1989), *Lives in Between: Assimilation and Marginality in Austria, Brazil, West Africa 1780–1945*, Cambridge: Cambridge University Press.

Stonequist, E.V. (1937), *The Marginal Man*, New York: Scribner.

Surra, C.A. (1990), 'Research and Theory on Mate Selection and Premarital Relationships in the 1980s', *Journal of Marriage and the Family*, 52, pp.844–65.

Whyte, M.K. (1990), *Dating, Mating and Marriage*, New York: Aldine de Gruyter.

4

The Seduction of the Exotic: Notes on Mixed Marriage in East Nepal[1]

Tamara Kohn

> Some enchanted evening
> You will see a stranger
> Across a crowded room
>
> And somehow you know
> You know even then
> That somehow you'll see her again.
>
> So fly to her side
> And make her your own
> Or all your lifetime you'll dream all alone.

Many readers may know these lyrics from the musical *South Pacific*. If not, they are probably familiar with the sentiments expressed in them. There is something particularly alluring, romantic, and challenging about a courtship with 'strangers' across cultural boundaries, however those boundaries might be defined. As an American student in the early 1980s, I met my future husband Andrew, who is English, as a fellow post-graduate student. Shortly after we had met, I went out with a girlfriend and told her about my first impressions of him – his 'sexy accent', 'mystery', 'kindness', 'reserve', his 'difference' in everything from his choice of dress, food and music to his style of writing. He had just thrown a big Guy Fawkes party and served Pimms, followed later on by Horlicks. He always said 'please' and 'thank you'. He was just so . . . 'English'. It is significant to know that he was the first English friend I ever had, so all the differences in taste and behaviour that I noticed were put into this hitherto-only-read-about category, 'the young Englishman'. This goes to show that the Other is always to some extent a creation by the Self.

The Anti-strategy of Attraction and Love

There is a good reason to begin this chapter about mixed marriage in Nepal with reference to what preceded my own 'mixed marriage'. Anthropological analyses are often full of double standards. Whatever inspires our own choices and behaviours is usually not good enough for tribal, 'non-western', 'primitive' others. My friend did not insist that my attraction to Andrew's difference was motivated by the need, either monetary or social, to form a union between our respective families. A notion of romantic 'love', and an aesthetic of 'Otherness' was all that was needed to justify such attractions.

Neo-functional descriptions of courtship and marriage continue to dominate the anthropological literature (see Rivière, who already raised this objection in 1971), and these allow no place for a simple attraction to the exotic Other. In fact, Jankowiak and Fischer (1992: 149) noted that the anthropological study of romantic love generally (either within one's group, or without) is 'virtually non-existent, due to the widespread belief that romantic love is unique to Euro-American culture'. Endelman (1989) offers an exception to this. From a psychoanalytic perspective he attempts to understand the extent of love's universality by comparing and contrasting case-studies extracted from ethnographies of 'tribal' societies around the world. Despite his worthy focus on love, his data is primarily drawn from works which were clearly not interested in the emotional, romantic experience of individuals. He offers a few exceptions in Polynesian, American Indian and other love poems but still concludes from the majority of his examples that 'something like our Western conception of love, though not entirely absent, seems to be *rare* in such tribal or transitional societies . . . And even rarer is "romantic love" as reality, or as expectation or ideal' (ibid.: 83–4). Such a conclusion is only as strong as the data upon which it is based. Our ideas about romantic love are constructed from our own history and come out of a particular definitional orientation which is Euro-American in character and scope. When you put this together with a popular and academic stereotype that imagines the 'tribal' Other to have neither the capacity, nor time and resources to indulge in romantic idealizations of others either preceding or during marriage, then you end up with a curious paucity of romantic description outside of European and American societies.

This bias is neatly encapsulated in the following quote by Rougemont:

In the East, and also in the Greece of Plato, human love has usually been regarded as mere pleasure and physical enjoyment. Not only has passion – in the tragic and painful sense of the word – seldom been met with there but also and especially it has been despised in the eyes of current morals and treated as a sickness or frenzy. 'Some think it is a madness,' Plutarch says. In the West, on the contrary, it was marriage which in the twelfth century became an object of contempt, and passion that was glorified precisely because it is preposterous, inflicts suffering upon its victims, and wreaks havoc alike in the world and in the self (1940: 71–2).

Here, then, we see how associations of morality and order/disorder are differentially imposed on love and marriage in the 'West' and 'East', as part of the stereotyped dichotomy between 'us' and 'the foreign Other'. At home one can do things that make no sense, and indeed a great aesthetic appears to lie in disorder. Those people far away that 'Westerners' imagine and some anthropologists study are seen as creatures steeped in order and morality.

The absence of 'love' in anthropological description is partly due to a clear tendency for ethnographers to problematize social institutions like marriage – especially intermarriage (cf. Yalman 1962) – to search for rules and meaningful patterns in social unions to the exclusion of all else. Bourdieu has allowed the individual to exercise choice – to be masters of the game of marriage and to act strategically (1990: 59–65). The game metaphor he uses is interesting, but the whole emphasis on strategy as the impetus for marriage does not leave room for the aesthetic spark, the romantic and wholly reckless anti-strategy of love, especially across culturally constructed 'boundaries'.

Interethnic Marriage in East Nepal

Yet, amongst the tribal people of East Nepal, love marriage is the norm, even if it hovers under a pretence of 'arranged marriage' which has been encouraged in the relatively recently Hinduized nation. Indeed, courtship across ethnic and linguistic boundaries is common, and the attraction and mystique of the Other motivates many potential unions. Before I can describe what I know of this attraction (second-hand, of course[2]), I must briefly introduce the location and the social environment of the people with whom I worked.

Tamaphok is a village in southern Sankhuwasabha district in the Koshi Hills of East Nepal, where my husband and I spent twenty-one months researching between 1989 and 1990. The homes in this 'village' are widely dispersed over a steep north-facing slope ranging from 3,000 to 7,000 feet. From the 'centre' of Tamaphok, where the school and a cluster of tea shops are situated, it is approximately a four-hour walk up several thousand feet to Basantapur, the nearest roadhead town. It is a nine-hour walk north-west to the Newar ridge town of Chainpur.

Tamaphok is considered by most residents to be the heartland of an ethnic group called 'Yakha', belonging to a larger cultural-linguistic group called the Kiranti, a people of Tibeto-Burmese origin. The Yakha see themselves as linguistically and culturally distinct from their neighbours, but would say that their closest Kiranti kin are the Limbu, followed by the Rais. The total number of Yakha in the region are estimated to be between five and ten thousand. In Tamaphok, there are over 180 Yakha households, interspersed by the homes of Gurung and Tamang (other Tibeto-Burman peoples) as well as Damai, Kami, Brahmins and Chhetris (caste Hindus whose ancestors migrated to the area during the last 250 years[3]). When we first went in search of the Yakha (who, despite brief mention in a number of texts, e.g. Hodgson 1858: 447; Bista 1987: 32, 38, had never before been the focus of ethnographic research), we discovered them in a village called Madi Mulkharka which is situated across the Maya Khola valley from Tamaphok. In Madi, however, most members of the large Yakha community spoke only Nepali, but no Yakha. We were directed to Tamaphok in order to find people for whom the language was very much alive. Quite a few marital unions have been made between Yakha of these two communities.

As others have noted, Kiranti women seem to have a great deal of control over their courtship and choice of marriage partners (Jones and Jones 1976: 72–3; McDougal 1979: 101; Bista 1987: 39). Interethnic and interlinguistic marriages take place in both directions. As well as in-migration of non-Yakha-speaking Yakha women from Madi and other communities, Limbu and Rai women from elsewhere also marry into Yakha-speaking families in Tamaphok. Conversely, Yakha women often marry non-Yakha or non-Yakha-speaking men, who can live up to several days' walk away from Tamaphok. These sorts of marriages between different Kiranti people are often preferred. The notions of 'boundary', 'ethnic group' and 'Other' we have developed in anthropology encourage us to describe the *peripheralization* felt by incomers from other linguistic groups and to ignore the sometimes *celebratory* aspects of interethnic marriage.

Also, some researchers have downplayed the sense of difference in these intra-Kiranti unions (for example, Jones and Jones 1976: 65). From an etic perspective, the various Kiranti peoples are linguistically and culturally related, and yet their languages are mutually unintelligible and the Yakha appear to be keenly aware of many significant differences in a number of cultural arenas. The emic sense of difference felt by women experiencing these unions should override any externally created conceptual terminology which often lumps together 'related' Others and reserves all comment on difference to extremes and exceptions (such as marriage between high-castes and untouchables). A third of all the Yakha households we interviewed in Tamaphok included at least one interethnic union, and there is no evidence to suggest that this pattern is purely a recent phenomenon (Kohn 1992).

The majority of these exogamous marriages are between Yakha and Limbu, followed by unions with Rai. The Yakha say that they used to regard the Rai as lowly in caste terms, and therefore in the past they would have avoided Yakha/Rai intermarriage. However, marriage with a Rai is now perfectly acceptable. This illustrates how rules and notions of hierarchy, where they exist, are negotiable and open to change amongst many of the ethnic groups of the Himalaya (ibid., cf.

Horowitz 1975). We could, perhaps, call this a situation of 'controlled abnormality' (a term usually reserved for ritual behaviour at, for instance, Mardi Gras festivities) because, while marriages across the ethnic divide of Rai and Limbu are acceptable, Yakha intermarriage with untouchables or high-caste Hindus remains, in general, unthinkable. Marriages with Gurung and Magar are likewise rare since the Gurung and Magar have tended to see themselves until now as 'higher' than the Yakha, Limbu and Rai in caste terms.

The Limbu and the Yakha are different from one another, and they are also different from the Rai. And yet they all sit under one umbrella in many respects, as the following examples illustrate. The stories that Chamba, a powerful Yakha shaman, told us from religious lore (the *muntum*) were given in a mixture of Yakha, Limbu, Rai and Nepali words. Charlotte Hardman has described Lohorung Rai psycho-physical substances which control Lohorung behaviour and their mental and physical states – *niwa, saya*, and *lawa* (1981). The Yakha also share these concepts, with only a few variations in detail. With the pro-democracy campaign in April 1990, communist activists, who were mostly literate Brahmin and Chhetri travelling politicians, spoke out publicly for the first time on what they thought to be key social issues. At a rally held in the school, they encouraged love marriages over 'repressive' arranged marriages, and the Yakha, Limbu and Rai women around me laughed, and commented together about how they have always had a tradition of love marriages. Several grumbled about how the party ought to gear its speeches better for local audiences. One Yakha woman turned to me and whispered, 'Listen to that – we never wash our mother-in-law's feet!' Perhaps the political turmoil in the country reinforced the common identity of these Kiranti wives. They joined together against a very different and less informed Other on this occasion but would not have, perhaps, on another.

All of this throws light upon common themes which would appear to run through many of the contributions in this volume: how might 'cross-cultural marriage' be

Caste Hierarchy:	Brahmin
	Chhetri
	* Gurung
	* Magar
	* Kiranti – Limbu, Yakha, Rai
	Lower caste groups
	Untouchables

* Tibeto-Burman peoples who are classified in the caste system as the Drinking Castes and who frequently intermarry.

Figure 4.1

defined? Where does the edge of one culture end and another begin? If one takes 'culture' to be 'the things one needs to know in order to meet the standards of others' (Goodenough 1981: 50) – a shared body of knowledge, belief and custom, for example – then one has to ask, not only 'how many of these "things" need to be shared?', but from whose perspective is the boundary of culture to be judged? Differences to which an outside observer may be attuned may not be significant to the subjects themselves. We see a convincing example of this in Jackie Waldren's chapter (this volume) when she shows us how reluctant her daughters were to see their marriages to Mallorquins as 'mixed' or cross-cultural. This discrepancy in viewpoint between the observer and the subject is turned on its head in my example from East Nepal. Obviously the relative invisibility of Yakha/Limbu or Yakha/ Rai intermarriage from the outside means that one cannot direct one's gaze at how strangers react to such mixed unions (as one might in a study of Anglo-Caribbean and Anglo-African couples in Brixton, cf. Benson 1981). The Yakha and Limbu couple, walking in an anonymous crowd in Basantapur bazaar, will not attract any raised eyebrows, intrigued glances or prejudiced remarks. And yet the sense of Otherness and difference is there within them in the context of courtship.

One can know this by hearing young women talk about the young men they would like to dance with at the bazaar, and about the features which distinguish other tribal groups from the Yakha. Most of these comments were made as the women and girls made their way from Tamaphok to the bazaar in Basantapur where they would expect to meet friends and potential partners for the 'rice dance' (*dhan nac* – Nepali/*chabak lakma* – Yakha). They would occasionally stop at a resting place on the steep ascent and comb each others' long black hair and tease each other about the young men to whom they were attracted.

Desire . . .

Attraction is a first step on the ladder of intermarriage and involves interest in and desire for the Other across a crowded room (in the case of this chapter's opening lyric) or up a mountainside (in the case of Tamaphok). What makes the Other desirable? What do we know of that Other before meeting him or her? Desire is about longing for what one does not have – a 'voraciousness' for an absent thing or person (Kristeva 1987: 159–61). It is in the insecurity, the unsure imagination of the unknown, that the intensity of desire is born.

. . . For Gold

In one conversation about attractions felt for the Limbu, an informant named Dil Maya said, 'Limbu husbands give much more gold to their wives than Yakha men.' Phuku Maya replied, 'Yes, the Limbu do everything bigger – they have much larger wedding processions – sixty *lokondi* compared to twenty *lokondi* for Yakha weddings – the *lokondi* wear much more gold.'[4]

These statements suggest that there are some motivations for Yakha women courting Limbu men which can be measured in gold. The interest women have in gold is, on the one hand, a material one, for gold jewellery often represents a rural family's entire life savings. On the other hand, it is also an interest in the romance intrinsic to the act of giving gold and bestowing beauty on new wives. The gold stands for more than wealth (measurable in grain, rice, labour power, and so on) – it is the last possible resource to be dispensed with in times of hardship because of the power it wields over the hearts and desires of others.

When a woman or girl shows another her gold, it is not passed from hand to hand, but it is displayed on the skin – the neck, the hand, the wrist, the forehead. Every time gold jewellery was exhibited to me, it was on the owner's body or my own. Gold holds much more than monetary wealth – its meaning is evident in the way it is handled, the way it affects the body and senses.

Gold may help to define the field of possibility – helps one to gaze with interest, perhaps, at available Limbu men – but it certainly does not do this without the aid of aestheticism, the tickle of excitement which comes from registering difference and 'foreign-ness' in speech, physique, attitude, humour. A look beyond the monetary skin to the aesthetic heart makes us recognize glimmerings of our own understandings of desire. As Baudrillard writes, desire 'is sustained only by want. When desire is entirely on the side of demand, when it is operationalized without restrictions, it loses its imaginary and, therefore, its reality . . .' (1979: 5).

. . . For Words

Many young Yakha women in Tamaphok commented on the beauty of the Limbu language. 'The Limbu language is beautiful. I have learned some words', said one before reeling off a comparative list of Yakha words and their equivalents in Limbu. Another commented, 'I like the sound of the Limbu language, don't you?' At the time, I remember trying to get more of a sense of this aesthetic from the girl, and I said that while I can recognize the difference between spoken Yakha and Limbu, it is hard to say *how* they sound different. She could only agree! Perhaps it is not just the English language which is bereft of good descriptive words for timbre and the aesthetics of accent.

Part of the beauty of another's language is in the things it can get away with which your own cannot. It allows you freedoms of expression and ultimately feelings which you may believe your own language (and perhaps culture) con-strains. Thus, one young woman, with a giggle and flash of eyes, told me that the 'Limbu get angry quicker – they are more frank and more bawdy. The Yakha think bawdy words are not good and only a few families use them – not so for the

Limbu.' Another piped in, 'some words in Yakha can be quite rude in Limbu. For example, "to pour water" in Yakha is *mangcuwa likma* (*pani sarnu* – Nepali), whereas in Limbu it means something very different!' (giggle, giggle) (*likma* means 'to enter into an opening' in Limbu (van Driem 1987: 458), a word with obvious sexual connotations). Here, quotes celebrating the timbre and beauty of 'the other' language are heard alongside comments which suggest that the other language is dangerous and racy – full of innuendo and heightened temperament. The giggles which accompanied the telling made me feel that whatever public Yakha opinion said about bawdy speech, these women desired to be let loose to experience it firsthand.

. . . For Home

One reflection which did not at first seem to fit with the Yakha female admiration of Limbu men was the following: 'Of course, if you pick a Limbu, it's best to marry one who lives far away because you have an excuse to go back to your natal home for longer periods of time.' Here the reality of life after marriage trickles through the headiness of courtship which precedes it. No matter how much gold, romance and attractiveness lures them away, and no matter how much they care for their husbands-to-be, women must remember that they are marrying into whole families of strangers who may not all be so desirable (as much the case when marrying within the Yakha as when marrying out). Desire for the exotic Other is complemented by desire to be in one's own natal home when the possibilities to do so are limited. Ironically, marrying into a village further from home ensures the most freedom of return. The further you go, the longer you can stay when you go back to your natal home.

If 'desire' for the Other – his gold, his language, his accent, and so forth – is expressed on the path to the bazaar, the seduction takes place upon arrival at the market-place where hill people of different castes and tribes gather to buy and sell food and other merchandise, and where much mingling and merrymaking takes place.

Seduction

If we begin with Baudrillard's suggestion that 'seduction supposes a ritual order, sex and desire a natural order' (1979: 21), then we can see that for the Yakha the ritual of seduction *par excellence* is the rice dance which takes place periodically in the bazaar, and at some other social gatherings such as weddings.

To dance the 'rice dance', anywhere from two to ten couples of young men and women from a variety of Kiranti groups hold hands in a circle and sway back and forth singing a repetitive song about 'love' in a forced vibrato. One short verse is sung syllable by syllable, stretching it out for many minutes. Yakha may choose to dance with other Yakha as long as they are not within the same clan group (*thar* — Nepali/*chon* — Yakha), but they may as often choose partners from other ethnic groups. Despite the excitement and enthusiasm for the activity and the various positive attributes of prospective dance partners expressed on their way to the bazaar, the women adopt an air of pain and sufferance as they stand in the circle. Then the swaying and singing commences and carries on deep into the night.

I collected rice dance verses on tape and in notes at many different venues during my fieldwork period; at weddings with clusters of girls at my elbows competing to come up with more examples, in house porches with men and women of different generations, in our 'sister's' room as she and several girlfriends practised singing some for dances to come. However, I never collected them at the place they are meant to be performed – the rice dance. There was certainly an air of seriousness which prohibited interference of tapeplayers and notepads at the actual dances. They were private performances despite their location outside (a 'public' domain). It would have been like recording lovers' whispers and utterances in a corner of a crowded party. Consequently, I can only report on a few verses in a local repertoire which may or may not have been used in performance. I was particularly keen to collect verses in the Yakha language, and a few examples of these verses follow. In them one might look for the poetic sentiments expressed.

> *chokchoki lomi lanung sori*
> *abaiba yungchi kanung sori*
> (Stars come out, with the moon, sit with me)

> *Tukurukgo ki'ma ribinungsari*
> *Chemgalu'ma beisbare*
> (Comb hair, red ribbon sari, sing song with me)

> *Machi go chama dunabe*
> *Tamaga leksa aningga ten kunabe*
> (Eat spicy rice from leafplate, You have come to our uncivilized village)

> *Cama ga cama taharbe*
> *Ningda go wa'iaga hola saharbe*
> (Mixed up food on leafplate, you perhaps live in the city)

While a non-Yakha speaker (including myself) could not expect to understand all the symbols, emotions and innuendo hidden in these snippets of verse, it is fairly clear that the words from the first two stanzas are romantic 'courting' material. The third involves ideas about self-denigration or the suffering (Nepali

– *dukkha*) of living in a village, as opposed to the supposed sophistication of a town, a theme which often arose in our discussions with Yakha (see Russell 1992). And the final verse seems to allude to the confusion of city life. The last two, regardless of their reference to the negative attributes of village and city, are about relations between people who come from different places and meet to dance together and this is the important detail relevant for this discussion.

Despite my own interest in collecting verses in the Yakha language, the girls I spoke to assured me that Yakha was not the preferred language in which to sing the verses. One said, 'Young people mostly sing rice dance verses in Nepali. Our grandparents sang them only in Limbu – therefore they all knew more Limbu language than we do today.' Another told me, 'The Limbu teach their children the rice dance and parents and children can dance together. We Yakha learn only from our friends and never dance with our parents.' What these statements suggest is that what is done today is a reflection of learning patterns and changing traditions.

But it must also be about how the verses are created and who they are created for. Of course it makes sense to sing together in a mutually understood language! A significant feature of rice dance verses is the freedom with which they are composed. Old ones are passed down between generations and new ones are happily created on the spot. Their brevity allows for any audience to pick up the words for the dance. As the lingua franca of the nation, Nepali is the language with the most potential for interethnic courtship today. If the courtship is between Yakha and Limbu, then it appears that Limbu (spoken by the larger and more dominant population) is more likely to be understood by Yakha than the Yakha language would be by Limbu. One woman told me that, 'Yakha language is not used often in the rice dance – it sounds too harsh.' On several occasions I was told an origin myth which explained why Yakha verses are fewer than Limbu ones (see Kohn 1992: 28–9). Whether it is because of the perceived harshness of the language or stories of the past or because of the need to be understood by others who do not speak the language, Yakha remains the least popular language for rice dance songs. I was particularly interested to be told that the verses I was given in Nepali were 'Nepali language but Yakha thought' (Kohn 1994: 16). But in the end, it matters more that certain feelings and thoughts are expressed and less that they are encased in any particular language. In other words, the true language of seduction is to be found at the level of thought and sentiment rather than vocabulary and grammar. As Baudrillard (1979: 8) writes, '. . . seduction represents mastery over the symbolic universe, while power represents only mastery of the real universe'.

From the examples of the rice dance verses given so far in this chapter, and comments from women about their attractions and preferences, let us take it as read that the Yakha are aware of cultural, linguistic and temperamental differences between themselves and the Limbu, and an appeal for a somewhat exotic Other is recognizable in many of their words. Their words also tell of their material or practical interests – certain interethnic alliances provide more gold, bigger weddings, or more opportunity to visit the natal home. The spontaneity and mystery of attractions to Others mingles with the practicalities and functions attendant on these attractions.

I would suggest that anthropologists tend to find such a mixture problematic, especially those interested in marriage within Hindu societies. Descriptions and analyses of love and infatuation do feature in the generally non-anthropological and non-marriage-focused literature on Hindu societies, but sentiments of love have not been seen or discussed in relation to the institution and process of marriage. It may feature in anthropological descriptions of family interaction (such as Trawick's 'The Ideology of Love in a Tamil Family', 1990: 37–63), but not in most descriptions of the marriage process. Macfarlane's comment that in most societies, 'marriage and individual sentiment are not connected, and marriages have been arranged' (1987: 142) epitomizes this bias and inaccurate polarization of experience. Fruzzetti's study of Bengali marriage suggests that love (*prem*) is something which is seen to grow out of marriage but has no part in the creation of it:

> Prem is . . . the exclusive basis of love-marriage; and townspeople regard such a union as cheap and immoral, destined to fail because of its very foundation: the illusory and impermanent nature of *prem*. Hindu marriages take place regardless of the couple expressing like or dislike, love or hatred, of each other . . . Bengalis stress that *prem* is a part of the husband-wife tie, but that love has to develop through time, growing in and through the *swami stri* (husband-wife) relationship. Bengali marriages are not devoid of love, but *prem* is not the main reason for the union (1982: 12).

That love marriage exists in Bengal or anywhere else in the Hindu world, however, regardless of its official standing in systems of arranged marriage, calls for a closer understanding of the experiential interaction of love and marriage. And yet, if studies of attraction, romance, seduction and love are to be contextualized within studies of marriage, an interesting dilemma is bound to arise. Which came first, the money/family/alliance or the attraction/romance/seduction? An archaic but ever-present focus on function and structure imposes a hierarchy of motivation for marriage. An escape from such a perspective considers marriage more holistically, more realistically.

Depolarizing Attraction and Alliance: The Yakha Experience of Marriage

The courtship of the exotic Other by the Yakha often ends in marriage. Even marriages which have technically been 'arranged' by parents according to Hindu tradition have often been urged or suggested by children who first met and danced together at the bazaar. Many unions are described as 'love marriages', and a smaller number are the result of 'marriage by capture' or 'marriage by theft'. These marriages take place within and between ethnic groups.

Alongside the aesthetic attraction there are other motivations for interethnic marriage. Marriage is proscribed within one's clan and, ideally, up to seven generations back with members of other clans. For the numerically small Yakha, this limits the number of appropriate marriage partners possible within the group and makes marriage outside more desirable (cf. Caplan re intercaste marriage in Belaspur, 1975: 139).

For the young bride, the initial settling-in period almost always seems to be lonely and difficult, no matter how helpful or friendly the groom's family are (cf. Bennett 1983: 180–6 on the experiences of high-caste Hindu brides in their married homes). Generally, members of the new family attempt to ease the incomer into the household by including her in their conversation and offering her instruction. When the bride is not from a Yakha-speaking ethnic group, then the family will begin by speaking to her as well as to others in her presence in Nepali, the lingua franca of Nepal. To some extent this is done purely out of the necessity to communicate sufficiently so that meals can be served, wood gathered, fields worked, and so on. As the bride spends longer and longer in the household and if she demonstrates her ability to learn Yakha, the rest of the family will speak more and more Yakha to her until virtually all family speech around the kitchen fire travels to her in Yakha and is replied to in Nepali or, after a number of years, in Yakha. People in Tamaphok consider that eight to ten years are required for incomers to master their language. However, an incomer who is unable to learn to speak Yakha with any fluency is not summarily dismissed as a lost cause, but through very complex linguistic contortions in both Yakha and Nepali, she is pulled into conversations and involved in all household interaction (Kohn 1992).

There is some evidence to suggest that while incorporation into a new home is always a gradual process, in some respects it happens more quickly for other women marrying into Yakha society than for Yakha women marrying out into other groups. Women who marry Yakha men will take their husbands' clan names during the initial marriage ceremony, whereas women marrying into Limbu households will keep their maiden clan names until final bridewealth payments are made. This may take ten to fifteen years, according to Limbu custom (Jones and Jones 1976: 64). The Yakha make the final bridewealth payments (known as *bhataha* – Nepali) relatively quickly, generally before the bride has had any children.

After these final payments have been made, the bride's natal family no longer holds responsibility for performing her death rituals. The responsibility is passed on to her husband's family according to Yakha tradition. Of all the main life-cycle rituals amongst the different hill tribes of East Nepal, funeral rituals demonstrate the greatest variation. The point at which an incoming bride is treated in death as an insider is of particular significance in a discussion about interethnic marriage.

When we talk of mixed marriage in a patrilocal society, it is tempting to observe only the incoming bride's adoption of local ways. She, however, does not arrive without bringing a bit of her Otherness with her. Certainly one of the most significant of her potential imports is a spirit (*cyang* – Yakha) which comes from her natal home. One of our neighbours had married a Rai woman whose grandmother had brought 'Atani', a Rai spirit, to live in his house. Many Yakha homes housed the 'Lahare' *cyang*, a spirit often brought by Limbu women into their new homes, and one which is famous for its expensive maintenance. Sacrificial offerings to the 'Lahare' *cyang* involve killing a buffalo, a sheep and sixteen chickens every three to six years. I have been told by several unmarried Yakha men that they would most likely try to find out what spirits a prospective wife had in her family. Some may be particularly costly and this could affect their choice of marriage partner (Kohn 1992).

Changes in the patterns of interethnic marriage are clearly apparent over time – both over the long term (as is illustrated by the current acceptance of Rai intermarriage, and the use of Nepali to ease the incomer's entry), as well as over the life of an interethnic union. Over the years, the bride is incorporated into her husband's world, while she simultaneously retains her separate identity with her natal home, her language and her somewhat portable spirit world. In our conversations with ageing non-Yakha women who had given birth to Yakha children in Tamaphok, the language of romantic intrigue was no longer there. I suppose these women were caught up in the here-and-now of daily work and survival – their hunts for exotic Others were long since over.

I have thus far not conducted research with children of 'mixed marriages' in the community, but it would be interesting to know how they identify themselves and others. Children in a Yakha-speaking community are bilingual, speaking both Yakha and Nepali, but it appears that those children with Yakha mothers pick up the language more quickly and fluently than those whose mothers are from another linguistic group and who must rely on their fathers, other kin and friends to learn the language. There is no apparent stigma attached to the child of mixed parentage; Yakha-ness is made out of all unions. This is a fine illustration of Strathern's notion that 'birth stands for sameness and marriage for difference' (1982: 93).

In this chapter, I have sketched how interethnic marriage is commonly sought by the marriageable Yakha of East Nepal. I have argued for the inclusion of aesthetic attractions in explaining such unions. I should stress again that courtship in East Nepal is not just an ethnic free-for-all. There are caste boundaries around the different tribal groups mentioned beyond which very few venture. But there are also significant cultural distinctions within these acceptable boundaries which are locally, if not externally, writ large. I think we would all agree that the allure of the Other may be seen to stretch across all cultures – from the 'stranger' in 'some enchanted evening', to my own flirtations with 'Englishness', to the Yakha schoolgirl on her way to the bazaar.

Notes

1. I would like to thank Luisa Elvira Belaunde, Joanna Pfaff-Czarnecka, Andrew Russell, and members of the Centre for Cross-Cultural Research on Women, for helpful comments on earlier drafts of this work. Some passages in this chapter derive from an earlier publication of mine on marriage (Kohn 1992).
2. I have discussed elsewhere the problem of working with second-hand experience (Kohn 1994: 25).
3. Damai (traditionally tailors) and Kami (traditionally blacksmiths) are both 'untouchables' in the caste system. Chhetris and Brahmins are ranked highest in the caste hierarchy. While Tibeto-Burman peoples have been somewhat 'Hinduized' by the Nepalese State, and they have been situated in the caste hierarchy (between these high and low castes), they are not identified as members of other caste groups.
4. *Lokondi* (Nepali) are the female friends and relatives who accompany the bride to the wedding ceremony in the groom's village.

References

Baudrillard, J. (1990, 1979), *Seduction*, London: Macmillan.
Bennett, L. (1983), *Dangerous Wives and Sacred Sisters: Social and Symbolic Roles of High-Caste Women in Nepal*, New York: Columbia University Press.
Benson, S. (1981), *Ambiguous Ethnicity: Interracial Families in London*, Cambridge: Cambridge University Press.
Bista, D.B. (1987, 1967), *People of Nepal*, Kathmandu: Ratna Pustak Bhandar.
Bourdieu, P. (1990, 1987), *In Other Words*, Oxford: Polity Press.
Caplan, L. (1975), *Administration and Politics in a Nepalese Town: The Study of a District Capital and its Environs*, London etc.: Oxford University Press.
Driem, G. van (1987), *A Grammar of Limbu*, Berlin etc.: Mouton de Gruyter.
Endelman, R. (1989), *Love and Sex in Twelve Cultures*, New York: Psyche Press.
Fruzzetti, L.M. (1982), *The Gift of a Virgin*, Delhi etc.: Oxford University Press.

Goodenough, W.H. (1981), *Culture, Language, and Society* (2nd ed.), Menlo Park, California: Benjamin/Cummings Publishing Co.

Hardman, C. (1981), 'The Psychology of Conformity and Self-expression Among the Lohorung Rai of East Nepal', in P. Heelas and A. Lock (eds), *Indigenous Psychologies*, London: Academic Press.

Hodgson, B.H. (1858), 'On the Kiránti Tribe of the Central Himalaya', *Journal of the Asiatic Society of Bengal*, 27, no.5, pp.396–407.

Horowitz, D.L. (1975), 'Ethnic Identity', in N. Glazer and D.P. Moynihan (eds), *Ethnicity: Theory and Experience*, Cambridge, Mass. and London: Harvard University Press.

Jankowiak, W.R. and Fischer, E.F. (1992), 'The Cross-Cultural Perspective on Romantic Love', *Ethnology*, 31, no.2, pp.149–55.

Jones, R.L. and Jones, S.K. (1976), *The Himalayan Woman: A Study of Limbu Women in Marriage and Divorce*, Prospect Heights, Illinois: Waveland Press.

Kohn, T. (1992), 'Guns and Garlands: Cultural and Linguistic Migration through Marriage', *Himalayan Research Bulletin*, 12, nos.1–2, pp.27–33.

——, (1994), 'Incomers and Fieldworkers: A Comparative Study of Social Experience', in K. Hastrup and P. Hervik (eds), *Social Experience and Anthropological Knowledge*, London: Routledge.

Kristeva, J. (1987), *Tales of Love*, New York: Columbia University Press.

McDougal, C. (1979), *The Kulunge Rai*, Kathmandu: Ratna Pustak Bhandar.

Macfarlane, A. (1987), *The Culture of Capitalism*, Oxford: Basil Blackwell.

Rivière, P.G. (1971), 'Marriage: A Reassessment', in R. Needham (ed.), *Rethinking Kinship and Marriage*, London: Tavistock.

Rougemont, D. de (1956, 1940), *Love in the Western World*, New York etc.: Harper and Row Publishers.

Russell, A.J. (1992), 'The Hills are Alive with the Sense of Movement: Migration and Identity amongst the Yakha of East Nepal', *Himalayan Research Bulletin*, 12, nos.1–2, pp.35–43.

Strathern, M. (1982), 'The Place of Kinship: Kin, Class and Village Status in Elmdon, Essex', in A.P. Cohen (ed.), *Belonging: Identity and Social Organisation in British Rural Cultures*, Manchester: Manchester University Press.

Trawick, M. (1990), 'The Ideology of Love in a Tamil Family', in O.M. Lynch (ed.), *Divine Passions: the Social Construction of Emotion in India*, Delhi, etc.: Oxford University Press.

Yalman, N. (1962), 'Sinhalese-Tamil Intermarriage on the East Coast of Ceylon', *Sociologus*, 12, pp.36–54.

5

Crossing Racialized Boundaries: Intermarriage between 'Africans' and 'Indians' in Contemporary Guyana[1]

Yoshiko Shibata

Introduction

Intermarriage is not a new phenomenon, either in Guyana or in the Caribbean as a whole. 'Intermarriage' here includes co-habitation, locally known as common-law relationships or 'live home'/'shack-up', and fairly steady 'visiting' relationships. Caribbean societies are known for their dynamic ethnic heterogeneity and the consequent production of diverse, mixed people, the amalgamation of cultures and the formation of unique Creole cultures. However, if we look at those societies carefully, it becomes clear that each case is different.

The topic of interracial relationships in Guyana has been the focus of heated discussions over the years, but little academic study. Intermarriage seems to represent the most problematic area of interracial relationships. It links all kinds of issues, and stereotypes rather than actual experiences influence most people's opinions. In Guyana, intermarriage – especially between 'Africans' and 'Indians' – has remained very controversial and is generally avoided (Shibata 1993).

Guyana is a multiracial, multi-ethnic country, often called 'the land of six peoples' (Swan 1957). The latter fall into the following broad status hierarchy, not always, however, reflected in individual wealth: Europeans or Whites (mainly of Dutch and British origin), Portuguese (commonly used as a separate ethnic classification in Guyanese literature), Africans,[2] East Indians, Chinese and Amerindians.[3] The census also includes 'Mixed races' as a residual category covering people who are not normally counted within the 'six peoples'. The categories, though seemingly racially so distinctive, are in fact politico-cultural constructions. They tend to link with economic, political and religious interests. Actual physical differences have been blurred by acculturation and interracial sexual relationships which have produced 'mixed' children, but nevertheless people try to identify themselves with one of the categories. It is believed that membership of one category is essential, but trying to be a member of more than one at a time is difficult.[4] Many people, because of their mixed physical or cultural backgrounds, need to make a conscious choice about the category to which they wish to belong. Ambiguity may easily cause uneasiness and conflict. Interracial marriage invariably leads to identity problems for the families concerned and undermines the social divisions upon which political and economic life have been built.

Guyana is notorious for its history of racial conflicts, often very violent, between the two major groups, 'Africans' and 'Indians' (cf. Glasgow 1970). Naturally these have inhibited the most intimate relationships between them, such as intermarriage. Here 'Africans' means Afro-Guyanese or Blacks, descendants of slaves imported since 1621, and (following the abolition of slavery in 1834) indentured labourers from other nearby West Indian societies and Africa. 'Indians' are descendants of labourers from the Indian sub-continent and are often called 'East Indians' in the Caribbean and sometimes Indo-Guyanese in Guyana to avoid confusion between these and indigenous 'Amerindian' peoples. I will use 'Indians' here to mean East Indians rather than indigenous Amerindians. The Indians were transported between 1838 and 1917 under indentureship schemes, and for some time afterwards small numbers continued to come into Guyana (Daly 1974).

During my fieldwork in Guyana in 1991 (September) and in 1992 (August–October), I conducted interviews with both successfully and unsuccessfully intermarried men and women. I interviewed forty-eight people in depth, thirty of whom were women, and talked informally about interracial marriage and related issues to many other people. Most of the interviewees lived within Greater Georgetown, but the rest came from a wide range of different geographical, socio-economic, and cultural sectors. In this chapter I shall use my field data to elucidate the kind of difficulties that arise in intermarriage between Africans and Indians. I will emphasize especially women's points of view, as intermarried women, rather than men, have been the most common targets of criticism, harassment and abuse. Firstly, I give a brief explanation of conflicts between Africans and Indians. Secondly, I try to deal with contemporary norms of marriage in Guyana along with common ethnic/racial stereotype images. Thirdly, I provide a case-study typical of the intermarried women I interviewed. Finally, I try to summarize some of the common problems this case-study indicates.

Brief Background of Interracial Conflicts

The 1980 census (Table 5.1) shows that out of a population of just under 760,000, Africans and Indians together compose roughly 82 per cent.[5] Guyana is unique amongst Caribbean societies[6] in the dominance of these two 'rival' groups and the

Table 5.1. Population by Ethnic Categories. 1980. Per cent.

Indian	African	Mixed	Amerindian	Portuguese	Chinese	Others*
51.38	30.49	11.04	5.20	0.004	0.003	1.20

* Others comprise Europeans other than Portuguese, as well as citizens from countries in the Near East such as Syria and Lebanon.

sharp sense of conflict along racial lines between them, since the rest of the small population has not been able to function as a kind of buffer.

Relationships between Africans and Indians still largely stem from the historical interplay between plantation economies, colonialism, and political interests. Guyana was developed as a sugar plantation colony based primarily on slavery. Following abolition, to maintain the plantation economy, the large labour force was replenished under an indenture system that recruited workers from Africa (mostly Sierra Leone), other West Indian societies, the United States, Portuguese Madeira, the Azores, Cape Verde, Malta, China, and British India. Indians were the most important both in terms of number and labour cost. By and large, ex-slaves left the plantations at the earliest opportunity, especially for work in the towns and cities. New indentured labourers would work for lower wages than the ex-slaves, under living conditions similar to those that had prevailed under slavery.

Regardless of caste or importance, Indians came to occupy the lowest social strata as estate labourers. Ex-slaves began to feel superior to indentured 'coolies' not only in terms of status but also in relationship to other cultural factors. For example, they found the 'coolies'' language odd, and incompatible with their own, and they considered their religion to be 'pagan'. The majority of ex-slaves had already become acculturated with each other and in fact formed an Afro-Creole culture, which to them was closer to White European culture, the source of the dominant ruling power. Hence, they thought they were superior to the new coloured immigrants. On the other hand, Indians saw Africans as mere ex-slaves, who had lost their cultural authenticity and were inferior to Indians because of their 'uncivilized' way of living. Whilst the ruling White class suppressed African customs, Indian practices (as long as they did not hinder the allocation of work on the estates) were left alone. Prejudice and ignorance between Africans and Indians were cleverly maintained through the British policy of 'divide and rule', so as not to give them a chance to become united and possibly rise up together in insurrection or other resistance against the plantation and colonial system (see also Smith 1962; Moore 1987).

The social hierarchy based on race and colour was carefully maintained during colonialism so that the more closely a person's features and skin colour approached those of White Europeans, the higher they could rise in the social scale – most notably of course in marriage (particularly for women) and employment. This social hierarchy based on physical characteristics was fairly rigid and upward mobility was still limited. In the case of intermarriage, children tended to share the category of whichever of their parents was darker and of lower status. Thus no formal mixed or clearly 'Creole' cultural identity developed among such people. (The rise of nationalist movements has made it easier for them to feel neither African nor Indian but Guyanese, but in practice it is still very difficult to separate any aspect of daily life from its racialized components.) Among the coloured categories, intermarriage with a partner higher in socio-economic position and whiter (i.e. hypergamy in terms of status and phenotype) remains highly appreciated or sometimes the goal of desperate aspirations.

On the other hand, although marriage between Africans and Indians might be expected because they shared similar interests as exploited labourers (indeed this happened within the restricted world of some plantations, where the supply of partners was strictly limited), as communities they have continued to struggle against each other as economic rivals and recently, more importantly, for political empowerment and cultural recognition.

Contemporary politics have thus become indelibly linked with racial and ethnic identities and conflicts (cf. Despres 1967, 1975; Williams 1991). Major political parties have recruited their supporters primarily according to 'race', so much so that political allegiance can be manipulated very easily through racial discourse. The vast majority of People's Progressive Party (PPP) supporters are Indians. The opposition is the African-dominated People's National Congress (PNC). Though they have been bitter rivals, the parties shared the same origin, the PPP, which mobilized people for independence. The party split in 1955, during the process of de-colonization, mainly because of ideological differences between the late Cheddi Jagan,[7] an unrepentant Communist committed to a Marxist-Leninist approach, and the late Linden Forbes Burnham, ex-President and a notorious despot, staunch Africanist and 'nationalist'. Their disagreements were accompanied by a rapid heightening of racial tensions. Two years following the split, Burnham formed the PNC. The conflict between these two sections has continued to grow visibly worse since then.

On top of internal conflicts, fear of communism prompted Britain and the USA in particular to interfere with the local democratic process. It is widely believed that the most vicious of the racial riots between Africans and Indians from 1962 to 1964 were set ablaze because of outside political conspiracies. This is the period people remember as making indelible the resentment, antagonism and hatred between Africans and Indians, and prompted a habit of emigration which has almost halved the population.

The PNC managed to keep power through fraud, bribery, violence, and clever manipulation of the security forces and civil service strata, besides other means of subjugating the Indian majority and reducing their access to political power. They did not forget to ally with some wealthy Indians to display their 'fair' approach to ethnic problems. However, in the general elections in October 1992, the PPP, with the Civic Movement, riding a wave of support for democracy and human rights, finally swept to power in the first 'free and fair' elections for twenty-five years. The PPP/Civic campaigned on a broad anti-PNC front and promised that the Prime Minister would be from the African community.

Such political polarization along racial lines has inevitably increased racial prejudice in people's minds. In fact, many Indians sometimes felt intensely intimidated under the previous PNC government. Such an atmosphere was scarcely conducive to intermarriage.

Contemporary Marriage Norms

While the young and educated sections of society in particular have been attracted by British/American cultural norms and lifestyles (see also Gopal 1992), basic ideas about marriage are still derived from long-retained ideas of ethnic and religious endogamy. Crossing such boundaries has been taboo, especially those between Africans and Indians. Indians in particular may become terribly bitter. When asked, most Guyanese, even Indians, nowadays smile and say something like 'people mix freely and marry anybody in Guyana because we are already mixed'. However, these same people may confess their inner feelings in lower voices with remarks such as 'we had better stick to our own race and must be proud of our blood. Those mixed are low', and so forth. Indian parents are likely to disapprove strongly and interfere if a child chooses an African partner. They may even throw a child out of their house, totally severing home and family ties, if (s)he (especially a daughter) shows any inclination towards this type of intermarriage. If still undeterred, young couples may elope. About 70 per cent of my interracially married interviewees (particularly women) told me how they suffered because of intermarriage.

Little has changed to soften the underlying mutual suspicion and hatred between Indians and Africans which have prevented intimate social mixing, not to mention intermarriage. People, especially in Greater Georgetown and big towns, may emphasize the recent 'harmonious' atmosphere and may stress how the number of interracial couples and families has visibly increased. But a brief increase in intermarriage is not the same as a decrease in prejudice and in fact such an increase can add extra force to local prejudice and antagonism. It can be perceived as highlighting new weaknesses in the racial barricade, perhaps due to recent educational and job opportunities, that need to be shored up.

Despite the pretension to lack of prejudice and a willingness to marry anyone regardless of race, both Africans and Indians still think racial endogamy is best. The reasons are many but can be summarized by saying that physical differences have become the marker of differences of supposedly incompatible social and cultural systems, including significant religious affiliations, which have formed two totally separate life and value systems (see also Assensoh and Alex-Assensoh, this volume).

The roots of African culture in Guyana stem from the different ethnic cultures of West and Central Africa (see also Smith 1953, 1956). But acculturation began from the moment of boarding the slave ships, resulting in considerable cultural creolization, for example, the creation of fictive kinship networks (Jayawardena 1962). Indian indentured labourers were mostly from North India (Uttar Pradesh and its surrounding areas), coming through Calcutta, and from the Tamil South, coming through Madras. Acculturation likewise began on the ships. Between 1865 and 1917 their religions were estimated as follows: Hindu 83.6 per cent, Muslim 16.3 per cent, Christian 0.1 per cent.[8] Jayawardena's study (1966) shows that over 80 per cent belonged to the lower castes among the Hindus.[9] The majority spoke creolized Bhojpuri (a dialect of Hindi), but soon needed to learn the masters' language, i.e. English, a creolized version of which would become a lingua franca of plantation society. It is common for both Africans and Indians to find that however much they would have liked to transplant their original cultural packages intact, with no functional changes, they were not able to do this. Therefore, what they call 'tradition' in Guyana refers to a creolized amalgam, full of reinterpretation and re-working of homeland cultures. Moreover, although the process of creolization was largely separate for the African and Indian communities, there was nevertheless some merging together based on mutual observation and interaction. Both communities, however, have tried to emphasize their own distinctiveness, and the incongruity of the other culture. Such a process abounds in stereotypes, not least of which are sexual.

Current Ethnic Stereotypes between Africans and Indians

The general images of Indian women have been fairly favourable to them and relate mostly to their subordinate domestic roles: keeping to the house, more likely to remain a virgin until marriage, beautiful, docile, modest, frugal, diligent, always thinking of future development. They are said to be humble, making men feel protective, treating husband and what they consider 'tradition' with due respect. They are supposed to be faithful, devoted, family-oriented, good homemakers and housekeepers, who are willing to 'sacrifice' themselves for husband or family.

Some negative images, however, derive from these same positive images (for example, too dependent, or too docile), but they are not counted negatively in terms of mate selection as most Guyanese men have preferred to play a *macho* role. There are more spiteful images, such as Indian women pretending to be virgins, but being whores in reality. In fact, many men, both African and Indian, laugh at the popular 'nice' images of Indian women as 'decent', and 'chaste' and say: 'only dem parents know nut'ing about dem darters! Even school gals dem put deir close in de bags and change 'n go fe men and get money.'[10] Popular male opinion is that nowadays more than 80 per cent of prostitutes are Indians, whereas about twenty years ago there were hardly any, though this comment is hard to substantiate.[11]

Indian men have also been credited with some of the positive images mentioned above. For example, emphasis is placed on being handsome, diligent, frugal, thinking in the long term, vibrant, knowing the art of sacrifice for the family, respectful of relatives and cultural traditions. Male dominance and relative affluence (especially in savings, holding jewellery and land) are almost always cited. These images again can easily be related with negative images such as stingy, untrustworthy, lying, jealous, vengeful, bossy, short-tempered, brutal, pessimistic, racist, womanizer, sexist, and so forth.

Such negative images have naturally been created largely by non-Indians. However, almost all my Indian female interviewees who had had African partners shared very negative views, particularly towards the kind of bitter prejudice and narrow racism sometimes openly expressed towards Africans. They confessed 'straight' or 'pure' Indians to be the most racist in Guyana. Indian women do not easily forget witnessing their mothers' miseries at the hands of their Indian husbands. Such memories can be a strong motive to avoid Indian males and choose as her own close friends or partner a man who is not Indian. The most available among non-Indian males within the vicinity are African or mixed, especially *douglas*, who are the offspring of Indians and others.

Images of African women by other ethnic groups have tended to be negative, constructing them as morally and sexually dangerous, outside of and threatening to the moral ideals of Indian female roles. African women are criticized for being not only ugly, but bawdy, promiscuous, too low, too easy, always thinking of men, sex or clothes. Their non-subservience to men is represented as being too independent, too bossy, and 'warrish' (meaning aggressive). They are accused of having no self-control, being noisy, intolerant, merciless and unscrupulous, abusive to the point of violence, callous, and on the whole uncivilized. They are said to be thriftless and never to plan for the future. Of course some of these images can make them attractive to enterprising Indian men for sexual pleasure, commonly called 'sporting',[12] but not for marriage. Indian men in general have felt inhibited from long-term attachments through fear of being dominated and losing face. At the same time, these same stereotypes offer Indian women pride in themselves and respect for their own culture, whilst creating a suspicious and cautious attitude towards other groups, especially Africans. Theirs is a conservative attitude towards life, without much exposure to wider society. It is easy for them to develop a sense of superiority and disdain towards African women, coupled with an intense jealousy towards them for their supposed sexual abilities, their independence and control over men. It is interesting to note a frequent comment that if an Indian woman goes out with an African man, she will disgrace 'the whole Indian nation', whereas if an Indian man chooses an African woman, it is not just a personal matter but also a matter of 'civilizing Africans in general'.

Most of the stereotypes of African men are very negative and derogatory, too. In addition to those applied to women, there are more, which emphasize untrust-worthiness and general lack of (culturally rooted) principles to the point of criminality. They are said to live according to mere taste and the feeling of the moment, often in squalor, moving on when it suits them, with little or no due regard for religion and 'proper' behaviour. They are said to be not only inappropriately carefree, but idle braggers who are womanizers, sexist and brutal. Their behaviour is not only socially reprehensible, but criminally threatening via their supposed alcoholism, thieving and drug dealing. In short, they are represented as a cause of social problems, opposite in behaviour to 'good' Indian men.

However, many Indian women who know African men well in the neigh-bourhood, at school or at work, may see such images as quite misleading. Such women tend to agree that they are treated much better by African men than by Indians. It is Indian men, rather than African men, they might criticize as 'alcoholic', 'idlers', 'violent', 'gamblers', 'too much womanizing', 'sexist', 'racist', and so forth. Examples of typical positive images for contemporary African men as well as women include: 'stronger and more potent in sex' (as Indians tend to 'get excited and roused too soon', so that 'women will get far more and lasting pleasure by African men'), 'freer in mind', 'standing on their own feet', 'more sympathetic' and 'brooking no nonsense'.

African women may be afraid of Indian men as being 'not cultivated', 'always wanting and doing his own ways', 'getting very vexed too easily', 'cursing often' and 'taking up tools to kill soon', as well as sexually less potent. Those Indian men who have had African women as girlfriends, classmates or close colleagues at work appreciate qualities such as their beauty, their sense of values, independent will, and skills of dealing tactfully with difficult situations. Their praise is certainly sincere.

These predominant racial stereotypes have probably remained almost unchanged since the introduction of indentured labourers and have contributed powerfully to the avoidance of interracial marital partnerships (see also Breger, this volume).

However, there are forces for change. Images and attitudes towards marriage and sexual relationships have been influenced by modernization and rapid permeation by contemporary Euro-American cultures. Changes in religion, education and employment have made it easier for people to base their opinions on closer observations and more direct personal contact than has been generally possible in the past. The effect has been to increase further the opportunities for members of either group to meet in a wider variety of ways, and loosen somewhat the shackles of tradition in the selection of partners. However, such a challenge has also provoked a backlash, so that it is too soon to speak of a real breakdown of traditional prejudice, especially since political rivalries continue to follow and maintain racial contours.

Crossing Boundaries, Creating Conflicts: Pearl's Case

To illustrate some of the problems related to intermarriage, and the consequent challenges a wife must rise to, I introduce one story from my interviews in 1992. All the personal names used are pseudonyms.

Mrs Pearl Singh, aged thirty-seven, calls herself Black more than *dougla*. In 1974 she married an Indian, Krishna, who is one year older, and she first lived with him and their children in a fairly mixed (racially and socio-economically) community in the suburbs of Georgetown. They had recently moved to a more middle-class area of East Coast Demerara near Georgetown. She has worked as a salesperson at an insurance company, as a managerial secretary in a hotel and so on. She has a loving, positive, outgoing personality. She is firm in her attitude to life, clearly proud in herself without being pushy.

Her paternal grandfather, a rich Indian manager in a rural sugar estate, fell in love with an African school headmistress in the same community. But in those days, such a marriage was totally unacceptable and impossible. The secret of their relationship could no longer be maintained when the headmistress became pregnant. She gave birth to a boy and was confined to the birth room for nine days, according to African custom. On the very day she was allowed to go outside, she drowned herself in one of the backdams. The baby boy was taken to his maternal grandparents, but instead of raising him, they decided to abandon him. He was found by an African maid from the house. This maid, probably in her thirties, had unfortunately lost all her three children, the last one very recently. She decided to take him as she was still able to breastfeed. This boy is Pearl's father. The boy's father later married an Indian. There was talk of taking the boy to his father, but the father never wanted to see him, for reasons unknown. Later on he contacted the boy occasionally, but none of the boy's close blood relatives were much involved in his upbringing.

This *dougla* boy married Pearl's mother, Laxmi, whose grandparents are from Madras and remained Hindu. Laxmi was a widow already when she met him. Her first husband was a Chinese, Mr Chin. However, before Mr Chin met her, he had already married someone else and could not get a divorce easily. After some time, Laxmi and Mr Chin married officially in an Anglican church. After four years of marriage he died of typhoid, leaving four children of 'different' features. Pearl was Laxmi's fifth child, her first in the second marriage. So Pearl has African and Indian 'blood' plus some Chinese cultural influence in her. She normally identifies herself as Black or African as she is the darkest in the family though she is fully aware of her 'mixed blood' and occasionally emphasizes it. As shown above, from the grandparents' generation, interracial sexual relationships occurred, and from her parents' generation (both paternal and maternal) the family was already interracially mixed. Pearl was brought up with her Chinese–Indian half-siblings and surrounded by interracially mixed aunts and uncles, and remembers all siblings were treated equally by the parents. She had not experienced nor witnessed any racial prejudice among her own relatives up to her own marriage.

When she was seventeen, she started to work and met a 'pure' Indian youth, Krishna Singh, at a Jehovah's Witness Kingdom Hall. She did not have any substantial interference from her parents when she started to go to the Kingdom Hall, since her father is not a staunch Hindu, and her mother was associated with the Anglican church (although Pearl did not tell me whether Laxmi chose to convert from Hindu to Anglican or just agreed to use the church as an acceptable way to legalize her marriage, whilst retaining her Hindu affiliation). Krishna was already a 'witness' though his parents were Hindu. With his help, she was baptized the following year.

They wanted to be married, but both families opposed this. From Laxmi's attitudes especially, Pearl sensed racial problems were involved, though her *dougla* father seemed rather neutral. To Krishna's parents, a son marrying a Black girl was totally out of question. His parents consulted local *pundits* and even *obeahmen* (African traditional magical counsellors or healers) to prevent the relationship going any further. They also tried other Hindu approaches, but all in vain. They even arranged for him to marry a Hindu girl, but he simply refused to see her.

Their courtship was purely platonic as they were committed Christians. She, however, remembers how they used to be jeered at whenever they walked out together. They could go to a cinema only under the supervision of one of her aunts and dared not even hold hands inside. When she took him to her house just to chat on the veranda, Laxmi always came to check and tell them, 'Time is up!' After he had gone, she would loudly warn her that neighbours could hear them and she should be ashamed of herself.

They married at the Registry without parental consent, but with considerable help from church members, including financial support. They had only a small reception. At first they needed to go back to their parents to sleep after work until they finally found a small place to live together. Though they started from scratch with only the very basic daily utensils, they were happy in their new married life.

Pearl's mother-in-law, Parvati, was especially unkind to her from the beginning but avoided intimidating her in public. She kept criticizing her behind her back. Pearl tried her best to retain her cheerfulness despite unkindness from her in-laws.

When she had their first baby, an Indian-looking girl with straight hair and fair skin, Parvati was so excited that she wanted to keep the baby with her. Pearl refused. Parvati continued to show 'a nice face' to her but never stopped speaking ill of her. Parvati started to offer them food and used to put 'something' into her plate which she couldn't identify. However, Krishna somehow always switched his plate with hers, much to the surprise and disappointment of Parvati. Strangely the stuff put into the plate did not work on him.

One day, whilst Pearl was hospitalized, she was again offered some food, which tasted strange. Suddenly she became extremely hot and tried to reach a window, but blacked out in the corridor. Later Krishna's brother disclosed that Parvati had put something into her food. Parvati used to do other things which really annoyed Pearl. She heard similar stories from other African women who married Indians and were given poison, or were made to suffer in other ways.

Another horrifying story concerns the mysterious death of Pearl's last son who was the darkest of all her children. Krishna's sister used to look after him carefully and told the story to Krishna after the son's death. This boy died at the age of one year and nine months and suffered persistent diarrhoea for over a year without any convincing medical explanation. He used to be given drinks regularly by Krishna's family, and it seemed likely that this was the cause. Krishna's sister told him that Parvati used to say the boy had to die. Pearl suspected this might relate to Kali Mai Puja, which is a local sacrificial cult of Madrassi origin. In Kali Mai, for some purposes, clients are requested to offer a living sacrifice. Pearl was not sure whether the son became the sacrifice or not, but noticing Parvati's absence at his funeral and other signs, she suspected Parvati of killing the child. Krishna himself sadly began to be suspicious of his own mother. But with no convincing evidence, they could not accuse her openly nor show even the slightest suspicion over this matter.

Pearl still has some problems with her in-laws but fortunately no longer serious ones since her son's death. Despite all sorts of interference just because of her 'blackness', particularly from in-laws, Pearl can laugh as she tells these stories. She tries to hold firmly to her principles of life – in her case, Christian faith, and she told me it would have been impossible to make an interracial marriage work without a shared faith. She strongly believes in the importance of sharing religious commitment for survival and success in both public and private domains, to solve inconsistencies and conflicts, and to give people courage and power to continue to bear or fight against recurring unpleasantness and persecution.

Although she emphasized how shared Christian commitment had helped their marriage to be successful so far, and that she had never felt marital difficulties, she admitted she had sensed cultural differences with Krishna. She decided to adapt herself to his satisfaction rather than confronting him or his cultural values. Such cultural differences were not serious to her, but seemed so to him.

For example, while they were walking on the street, if she happened to meet her male friends, she naturally responded to them cheerfully and would stop to chat, sometimes even holding hands with them. To her this just reflected her personality as well as the common expression of friendship among her Black and mixed peer groups. However she began to notice how he would become silent for a while. Rather against his will, he disclosed eventually that such openness had upset him, emphasizing he was not jealous but that such behaviour was not 'right' or proper for a wife. She quickly remembered the importance of the vows that an Indian wife would make and the lecturing of the *pundit* during the *kaniyadan* at a Hindu wedding ritual, which for Hindus is very important. What Smith and Jayawardena observed in 1958 has not changed radically. A Hindu wife is still expected to obey her husband faithfully and serve his family, though it is no longer regarded as a duty to get his permission before going out or to be accompanied by his family members when in public (Smith and Jayawardena 1958).[13] Pearl became more conscious of how, unlike Krishna, she had not been brought up in Indian ways, despite having an Indian mother and *dougla* father who seemed culturally more Indian. For Krishna, the ideal image of gender roles for marriage partners has been Hindu (in this case, the more standardized 'orthodox' type of Sanatan Dharma Hinduism, not the more 'reformed' or 'modernized' type of Arya Samaj) or Indian (i.e. as opposed to any other ethnic/racial group in Guyana), rather than Christian. Accordingly, he expected Pearl to show docility, obedience and faithfulness to him rather than being so outgoing and sociable, particularly to other males. She therefore decided to stop greeting her male friends as she used to and began to feel her husband's quiet satisfaction again.

She thinks that interracial marriages, especially between Africans and Indians, should be encouraged as racially mixed people tend to have less prejudice against racial stereotyping and make an effort to see people as individuals. She would not disagree with their children's choice of interracial partners. In her opinion interracial marriages could work in the case of (Christian) religious endogamy though she was not sure about Hindu or Muslim cases. She emphasized the importance of common moral values: these helped to overcome racial and cultural differences, and to reach compromises more easily.

Problems Experienced

Pearl's story features problems and aspects of marriage which seem to be common to other interracially married couples. First of all, many couples based their relationships on their own free will, love and respect, which often upset their parents. The majority of Indian parents still try to arrange, if not force, the marriage of their children, particularly daughters. Even in the case of Brahmins, who have shown most concern over their own caste and *varna* and their general prestige in society, caste endogamy has decreased dramatically due to the difficulty of finding suitable candidates because of the creolization process stemming from indenture-ship. Most orthodox and conservative Hindus, however, still try to stick to *varna* endogamy (as well as village exogamy), with the minimum norm of at least religious and racial endogamy. For this purpose, arranged marriages have been preferred, though often children's opinions have been consulted (see also Smith 1959a; Rauf 1974).

Encountering other religious groups and, above all, other ethnic groups has acted to consolidate the sense of Indian-ness in Guyana. The sharp contours of Indian ethnic identity have been constructed largely by interaction with other ethnic groups, especially Africans. The expression of this identity has changed according to the dynamics of such interaction. Religious and sectarian endogamy has been strongly recommended in order to maintain their ethnicity. On the other hand, being surrounded by other racial and ethnic groups and having contact with them through both secular and festive occasions has increased interracial/ethnic interactions, which might well develop into more intimate relationships. For a long time, if Indians desired to go up the social ladder, to escape the stigma of very low status and plantation or agricultural work, they needed to go through procedures which they detested. These included government school education, conversion to Christianity, and then obtaining certain kinds of occupation, particularly in the public sector (e.g. civil servant or school teacher), or professions such as lawyer, doctor or chemist. The effect has been to widen the opportunity for relatively progressive, flexible, practical young people to break away from hitherto accepted mores. Nevertheless, whilst interreligious and intersectarian marriages based on free will and love have become tolerable if the couples are both Indians, interracial unions remain the subject of considerable scorn.

In Pearl's case, the couple share the same strong faith, and this has bonded them together despite all the difficulties which normally accompany intermarriage. Among interracially married couples, the degree of success, stability and the sense of happiness seems higher in cases of religious or sectarian endogamy. Among the interracially married who share the same faith, there are many cases where they met their spouses in the same church or at religious functions. But those who have crossed religious or sectarian boundaries tend to share either the same racial background or have 'mixed blood' themselves.

In Pearl's own family, there were already 'mixed blood' members, which is why she thinks she did not have really strong opposition from her parents. When surrounded by 'mixed blood' family members, especially when these are in the same household or close relatives, people tend to have fewer inhibitions about interracial marriage, particularly if they did not have any early experience of racial prejudice.

'Pure' Indian parents express more concern about their children's marriage than any other racial or ethnic groups. If an Indian chooses an African, it is said the couple and their descendants will sink down the social hierarchy. Popular ways to hinder and interfere in a couple's relationship (even after marriage) include food poisoning or other kinds of physical harm, snubbing, abusing, or chasing them away. Even sexual harassment, physical violence, kidnapping or death threats may be experienced. In-law relationships are often harsh, especially at the beginning. They may become the prime cause of marital conflict as harm can be done very subtly and yet very effectively. However, all my interviewees survived such hardship largely because they managed either to cultivate or strengthen strong and liberated personalities, and to maintain their independence, confidence and pride, both in themselves and in their marriages.

Many interracially married women have experiences of working outside the home either as professionals, specialists of some sort or clerks. Exposure to a wider social world increases the opportunity of meeting different kinds of people in various situations, and would certainly widen their range of potential partners. Earning their own income has given them economic independence and stronger control over their own life-course outside parental influences. Relative economic independence has brought a sense of personal freedom, pride and confidence, which certainly helps them to solve problems. Many interracially married couples seem to be sensitive to individual and cultural gaps. However, those who are happily married are more eager to appreciate the differences and accept them. They seem to emphasize the importance of openness rather than remaining silent and hiding their feelings.

It is against married women rather than men that most criticisms are targeted (see Breger, this volume). It is commonly agreed that women can be more harshly bullied than men particularly when they cross normative boundaries. Quite a few interviewees spoke of the hostility – even violence – of neighbours and/or in-laws. It seems to take longer for African wives with Indian husbands to overcome or at least reconcile in-law conflicts than for Indian wives, who tend to be treated much better by African or mixed in-laws. In each case wives need to cultivate tactful ways to avoid problems. In addition, they tend to get more support and cooperation from their partners to solve problems than in the case of racial endogamy. Facing many difficulties can strengthen such women's minds and any faith they have. After enduring racial humiliation for some time, they may eventually get less interference and gain a better reputation.

Choice of residence can also be problematic. Many inter-married couples live in rather urban and fairly mixed communities, which are expected to be more tolerant of racial mixing. It seems the degree of segregation, racial prejudice and tension is higher in predominantly Indian communities than in African ones. If the racial obstructions become unbearable not only for the couple themselves but for their *dougla* children,[14] they could leave the community and try to settle down in a more mixed community.

They all admitted their change of values and attitudes towards racial relationships and life in general. Some show bitter criticism and resentment about Indians' narrow-mindedness, ignorance and scorn towards Africans and their culture. Indian women's experiences of expulsion from Indian families and/or communities after choosing African partners may pull them away from Indian cultural traditions and values, however reluctantly, and draw them closer into African communities. The longer they stay and develop friendly relationships with predominantly African communities, the more likely they are to become accepted and appreciated by Africans. In due course, they have begun to appreciate African ways of life and values, or become very practical and worldly-wise about cultural matters.

People have recently started to emphasize the increase in intermarriage and 'mixed' children. Many corners of villages, towns and cities have become more mixed racially and some might even be described as 'integrated'. However, those who have intermarried still tend to be topics of conversation and derogatory remarks. Interracial marriage between Africans and Indians is still highly controversial and despised, though other forms of intermarriage have become more tolerated, albeit never without some difficulties.

What seems significant here is that although interracially married people who have survived so many problems and difficulties try to underline the importance of racially bias-free attitudes, the very fact they needed to do so tells how deeply people are still preoccupied with racial prejudices. These are also closely related to gender issues. One positive sign is that many women and men who intermarried racially are no longer much concerned about race, nor afraid of being considered 'outcaste' any more, so that they can feel free from racial stereotyping and even biased gender images. In addition, many of them are conscious of playing a role as bridges between the races and trying to mitigate conflicts and groundless prejudice and stereotypes.

Notes

1. This paper is based on fieldwork in Guyana for about ten days in September and October, 1991, and ten weeks from August to October, 1992. The project was supported financially by the Ministry of Education of Japan under the leadership of Dr T. Maeyama. I have given talks and presented papers based on this research for a monthly seminar of the Association of Black Studies held at Osaka Gakuin University in 1993 and in different seminars at the University of Oxford and at the annual conference of the Society for Caribbean Studies in Oxford in 1994 (Shibata n.d.1, n.d.2, n.d.3).
2. In contemporary Guyana, people use 'Africans', 'People of African descent', 'Blacks', 'Negroes', and less frequently 'Afro-Creole' and 'Creoles' interchangeably. 'Negro(es)' does not necessarily seem to carry a derogatory connotation, judging from the frequency and the variety of people using it regardless of 'racial' backgrounds. Only those who are exposed to such ideologies as 'Black consciousness' and 'African cultural heritage' may avoid 'Negro(es)'. 'Africans' themselves have used 'Negroes' referring to themselves. However, Naipaul noted some resentment toward the usage of 'Negro' in 1962 among Africans (Naipaul 1963: 99).
3. Although such a rough sketch is generally accepted, we must remember that within each category there exist economic differences and ranking, particularly among Africans and Indians. Many of the older Chinese, who are distinguished from new immigrants, have become largely creolized. Africans, Indians and Chinese are no longer categorized hierarchically in this order.
4. Most people tend to identify with one of these six categories even though their blood is mixed. Only those clearly unidentifiable or 'really clearly mixed' may say they are 'Mixed Races', for example, those first generation of mixed parentage and those whose physical features show obviously mixed traits of several races. However, the same person may identify differently according to context.
5. The Mixed category is mainly chosen by those with African 'blood' (called 'coloured', and particularly before the early 1960s, 'mulatto' (offspring of Africans and Whites)). Including these, Indians and those with African 'blood' together compose over 92 per cent of the total population.
6. Trinidad and Surinam have similar Indian/African polarities but cleavages are not drawn as sharply as in Guyana.
7. Jagan died in 1997 and his wife Janet Jagan was elected president of Guyana in January 1998.
8. Smith (1959b). In 1960, Hindu 70.3 per cent, Muslim 16.3 per cent, Christian 1.1 per cent.
9. He mentioned that 2.1 per cent of the population was officially registered Brahmin and 9.1 per cent was Kshatria. However, these figures might be lower because the new and confused situation of indentured life made it possible for many Indians to claim rather higher names of caste and varna than their original ones, cf. Bassier 1993: 61. See also Nath 1970; Jayawardena 1963.
10. Regardless of race, it is said girls who accept even a drink from a man are expected, in return, to provide a sexual service for him.

11. Sometimes teenage girls, especially among the lower class, are said to be 'encouraged' or 'ordered' to stay out on the street till very late by their parent(s) just in case they may bring extra cash by prostitution. Even middle-class women were said to have been eager for the chance of meeting white sailors when a big ship came into port and tried to invite them to their homes for 'special entertainment'. Many prostitutes seem to be from broken families and/or marital relationships, and those whose pre-marital and extra-marital relationships ostracized them as 'shameless', 'sex-starved', and so forth.

12. Even a young *pundit* told me with a meaningful smile that his *mother* expected him to have this kind of 'sporting' before he formally married somebody *suitable*.

13. Even in the contemporary Hindu weddings I observed during my fieldwork, these instructions by a *pundit* were still very much an important part of the ritual.

14. Shibata (n.d.3) deals with mixed-identity problems of *douglas*.

References

Bassier, D. (1993), 'Indian Lower Caste Cult Worship in Guyana: Their Faith in 1988', in T. Maeyama (ed.), *Ethnicity and National Integration of Asian-Latinamericans: A Study on Inter-Ethnic Cohesion and Conflict* (Preliminary Report in Japanese), Shizuoka: Cultural Anthropology Course, Department of Sociology, Shizuoka University.

Daly, V.T. (1974), *The Making of Guyana*, London and Basingstoke: Macmillan Education Ltd.

Despres, L.A. (1967), *Cultural Pluralism and Nationalist Politics in British Guiana*, Chicago: Rand McNally.

——, (1975), 'Ethnicity and Resource Competition in Guyanese Society', in L.A. Despres (ed.), *Ethnicity and Resource Competition in Plural Societies*, The Hague: Mouton.

Glasgow, R.A. (1970), *Guyana: Race and Politics among Africans and East Indians*, The Hague: Martinus Nijhoff.

Gopal, M.M. (1992), *Politics, Race, and Youth in Guyana*, San Francisco: Mellen Research University Press.

Jayawardena, C. (1962), 'Family Organisation in Plantations in British Guiana', *International Journal of Comparative Sociology*, 3, 1, pp.43–64.

——, (1963) *Conflict and Solidarity in a Guianese Plantation*, London: University of London/Athlone.

——, (1966) 'Hinduism in British Guiana', *Comparative Studies in Society and History*, 8, pp.211–40.

Moore, B.L. (1987), *Race, Power and Social Segmentation in Colonial Society: Guyana After Slavery, 1838–1891*, Philadelphia, etc.: Gordon and Breach Science Publishers.

Naipaul, V.S. (1963), *The Middle Passage*, London: Andre Deutsch.

Nath, D. (1970, c.1950), *A History of Indians in Guyana*, London: published by the author, Second revised edition.

Rauf, M.A. (1974), *Indian Village in Guiana: A Study of Cultural Change and Ethnic Identity*, Leiden: Brill.

Shibata, Y. (1993), 'Intermarriage between Indians and Blacks Which Should Be Preferably Avoided: A Sketch on Guyanese Cases', in T. Maeyama (ed.), *Ethnicity and National Integration of Asian-Latinamericans: A Study on Inter-Ethnic Cohesion and Conflict* (Preliminary Report in Japanese), Shizuoka: Cultural Anthropology Course, Department of Sociology, Shizuoka University.

——, n.d.1, 'Crossing Boundaries, Creating New Categories: Intermarriage in Guyana', Paper presented to the seminar at the Centre for Cross-Cultural Research on Women, Queen Elizabeth House, Oxford, June 1993.

——, n.d.2, 'Controversial Intermarriage between 'Africans' and 'Indians' in Guyana', Paper presented to the Ethnic Relations Seminar, St Antony's College, Oxford, June 1993.

——, n.d.3, 'Neither Black Nor Indian: Dougla-ization, Creolization and Guyanization', Paper presented to the Annual Conference of the Society for Caribbean Studies, St Stephen's House, Oxford, July 1993.

Smith, R.T. (1953), 'Family Organization in a Coastal Negro Community in British Guiana: A Preliminary Report', *Social and Economic Studies*, 1, 1, Mona, Jamaica: Institute of Social and Economic Research (ISER), University of the West Indies (UWI).

——, (1956), *The Negro Family in British Guiana: Family Structure and Social Status in the Villages*, London: Routledge & Kegan Paul; Mona: ISER, UWI.

——, (1959a), 'Marriage and the Family amongst East Indians in British Guiana', *Social and Economic Studies*, 8, 4, pp.321–76.

——, (1959b), 'Some Social Characterictics of Indian Immigrants to British Guiana', *Population Studies*, 8, 1, pp.34–9.

——, (1962), *British Guiana*, London: Oxford University Press.

——, and Jayawardena, C. (1958), 'Hindu Marriage Customs in British Guiana', *Social and Economic Studies*, 7, 2, pp.178–94.

Swan, M. (1957), *British Guiana, the Land of Six Peoples*, London: Her Majesty's Stationery Office.

Williams, B.F. (1991), *Stains on My Name, War in My Veins: Guyana and the Politics of Cultural Struggle*, Durham and London: Duke University Press.

6

The Politics of Cross-Cultural Marriage: An Examination of a Ghanaian/African-American Case

Yvette Alex-Assensoh and A.B. Assensoh

Introduction

In the United States, there is a surprising dearth of scholarly research about marriages between African-Americans and their kith and kin from the African continent. There is even a paucity of popular material on this subject. This is because most research on US mixed-race marriages largely neglects marital relations between sojourning Africans and African-Americans (Larsson 1965: 1–201; Johnson and Warren 1994: 17–24). Instead, most researched publications have traditionally focused on marriages between Jews and Gentiles, or on Whites intermarrying with Blacks, Asians, Native Americans or Hispanics (Johnson and Warren 1994: 25–80).

This scarcity of overall research material on African/African-American couples may also be attributable to the politics and discourses of race in America, which often mute issues of culture in favour of issues of colour (Wilson 1987: 109–24; Hill and Jones 1993). However, marriages between Africans and African-Americans are not new: there is overwhelming evidence that young, marriageable Africans – both male and female – started coming to the United States as early as the mid-1800s in search of the proverbial golden fleece, including quality higher education (Williams 1980: 232–3; Vaz 1986: 12). The largest initial wave of these marriages occurred during the 1960s in the crucible of the African Liberation and the American Civil Rights movements. This was in spite of such marriages being seen as extremely challenging due to differences in the cultural and social backgrounds of such couples. Therefore, as underscored by many experts on marriage, it is most correct to see all marriages – including those between continental Africans and Africans in the diaspora or African-Americans – as a series of adjustments and, also, as 'the joining of two lives at the most personal level' (Norment 1982: 100).

Certainly, scholars know very little about the macro- and micro-political forces that affect these particular cross-cultural marital relations. Therefore, the exploratory research here intends to fill this obvious yawning gap by examining both the macro- and micro-effects of politics on marriages between Africans and African-Americans in the United States. Specifically, the study will address the influence of the politics of race, the politics of international relations and the politics of cultural differences on marital relations between Africans and African-Americans, with specific references to African-American and Ghanaian marital relationships.

The Macro-Politics of Race

Pervasive in the literature on cross-cultural marriages is the concept of the Other or 'outsider' in referring to marriage partners from different cultural backgrounds. While Africans who emigrate to America are in some respects culturally different from African-Americans (who may become potential marital partners), in the context of the dominance of the politics of race in America, their similar skin colour helps override awareness of their cultural 'Otherness' in American society. This politics of race not only plays a decisive, muting role in marital relationships between Africans and African-Americans, but it also means that many such marriages are perceived by others, especially the authorities, primarily as marriages of convenience, to obtain entry into America, and are therefore suspect, as discussed by Chua-Eoan in a report entitled, 'Tightening the Knot: A new law gets tougher on fraudulent marriages' (1986: 35). For example, in the mid-1980s the conservative Reagan administration swiftly tightened rules and amended American immigration laws regarding such marriages by creating the new so-called conditional basis of lawful permanent residence status, whereby any foreigner marrying an American citizen now has to wait two further consecutive years to prove that their marital union is 'genuine' before being able to obtain her or his residential papers through such a marriage (see also Breger, this volume). The new stringent immigration laws have been enshrined in a federal document entitled *Code of Federal Regulations* (US Government 1995: 299–303).

Obviously, from the years of slavery to the era of reconstruction and, indeed, during the two phases of the Civil Rights movement, African-Americans, who were once known as either Negroes or Black Americans, have made great strides in their personal lives. For example, during the post-Civil Rights era, many achieved middle-class status as well as being elected or appointed to important political offices in increasing numbers. Nevertheless, regrettably, African-Americans still hold 'outsider' or Other status in American society (Farley and Allen 1987: 20–5; Hacker 1992: 67–199). In the 1930s the legendary W.E.B.

DuBois first published his book, *The Souls of Black Folk*; in it, he *inter alia* lamented the Otherness of African-Americans – then called Negroes – and also forcefully underscored the unfortunate crucible of race or the colourline in defining all relations in American society (DuBois 1961: 16). As recently as 1996, Sam Fullwood was forced to re-affirm these conditions in his own work, *Waking from the Dream*. In this book, he decried the myth of Black assimilation into American racial and economic mainstreams, confirming that African-Americans still remain largely invisible in their country of birth (DuBois 1961: 16–17; Fullwood 1996).

Consequently, the problem of Otherness, as it relates to adjustments and acceptance by the larger American society, is constrained by the fetish and dividing line of colour for all Africans who emigrate to America. This unfortunate plight affects all Blacks in America without regard to ethnic background or nationality. As a result, the negative influences that the issues of Otherness might pose for some cross-cultural marriages are not as problematic for African/African-American couples because they already share an 'outsider' position. In fact, this shared plight of Otherness, of being excluded, is often considered to be the basic unifying force, attracting and subsequently binding Africans and their African-American partners together. Furthermore, as a psychological tie as well as a shared political position, it serves to facilitate social networks which may lead to romantic involvement and marriage. Chua-Eoan (1986: 35) amply demonstrated that Blacks from the West Indies also suffer similar Otherness situations in their marriages to African-Americans.

Indeed, racial discrimination against Blacks in America during the 1960s and 1970s prompted Blacks to establish ideological connections with the similar plight of Africans in colonized Africa, in their search for positive collective identity, thus de-emphasizing cultural differences whilst emphasizing political similarities. The American Civil Rights movement, begun in the mid-1800s, and Africa's active decolonization processes in Ghana (the former Gold Coast), Nigeria, Kenya and elsewhere helped blur obvious cultural diversity as they united Blacks in the diaspora and those on the mother continent (Africa) under the banner of the Pan-Africanist Movement and Black Consciousness, led by such indefatigable Black leaders as DuBois (USA), George Padmore, C.L.R. James (Caribbean), Kwame Nkrumah (Ghana), Jomo Kenyatta (Kenya), Julius K. Nyerere (Tanzania) and others (Assensoh 1989, 1998; Van Deburg 1992). Indeed, many African/African-American marriages at that time occurred in an effort to unite these groups in the name and spirit of Pan-Africanism, although as Norment noted, 'an American Black woman might know little of the cultural and personal ramifications of polygamy, the custom of having more than one wife [sic, spouse] at a time' (1982: 100).

Research on racial inequities in criminal sentencing, as well as the disproportionate percentage of black men sent to penal and correctional institutions in the United States, also have import for discussions about cross-cultural marriages between African men and African-American women (Wilson 1987: 63–92). This research shows that disproportionately more black men are sentenced than white, thus altering the sex ratio, and reducing the pool of potential endogamous marriage partners for black women. As the number of marriageable African-American men continues to plummet, coupled with the sharp rise in educated and successfully employed middle-class black women, well-educated and successful African men will undoubtedly continue to become a highly sought-after alternative. This will occur in spite of Norment's claim that the African-American woman may not be cognizant of cultural and personal ramifications of some of the cultural-cum-customary practices of African brothers from the continent, including the Islamic practice of a man of the faith being able to marry up to four wives, or the practice of polygyny found in many African cultures (Norment 1982: 100).

The Macro-Politics of International Relations

Cross-cultural marriages between Africans and African-Americans are also affected in several respects by prevailing international policies and relations between the United States and various African countries, as well as the internal politics of the respective African countries. First, in any given year, US immigration policies strictly regulate the total number of African nationals allowed to enter the United States for educational, occupational, political refugee and other reasons. The 1924 Immigration Act, for example, rigorously limited the number of non-white immigrants, a travesty that was not officially corrected until 1965. Although the recent more liberal immigration policy – including the so-called visa lottery – has facilitated an increase in visas issued to citizens of African nations, present-day problems in Africa such as alleged drug trafficking and the Ebola virus epidemic in Zaire, combined with increased xenophobic anxieties about what is perceived as the negative effect of immigration on the US economy, have further limited the number of African nationals permitted to enter the United States.

To make matters worse, in October 1986, the US Congress passed a very restrictive alien-marriage law to help the US Immigration and Naturalization Service (INS) 'guard against those who wed simply to become citizens' (Chua-Eoan 1986: 35). The new 1986 alien marriage rule, signed into law by the conservative Reagan administration, puts the onus of proof on both partners in the marriage, the American citizen and the foreign spouse. Thus, both partners are obliged to go to the local immigration office (or District Immigration Office) to file a joint application for 'permanent residence status', whereas in the past, only the American citizen was required to apply personally for her or his foreign spouse. Then, after the application is jointly filed and the appropriate fees paid by both, the new foreign spouse is given only a 'conditional lawful permanent residence status' that can be revoked within two years if found to have been obtained by fraudulent or illegal means. In addition, the couple now has to wait a further two consecutive years before filing a new application jointly to seek a change of status from conditional to permanent residence status. The rationale is that if the marriage is contracted fraudulently to help the foreign spouse regularize her or his immigration status, then it is unlikely that the couple would still be together after this period of time, and so could not jointly file this second application, thus supposedly closing this immigration loophole (see US Government 1995: 299–303).

In addition, the political climate in the respective African countries can also determine the number of nationals who may immigrate to America in search of education, employment, better opportunities and subsequently perhaps marriage partners. Economic austerity, ethnic strife, civil war and a lack of technological advancement at home have often been known to spur mass immigration of African nationals to America in search of broader and more profitable horizons. Indeed, many African/African-American couples met on college campuses as they pursued a common quest for higher educational credentials (Norment 1982: 100). Therefore, the politics of international relations is very important as it controls both the supply and availability of African mates for African-Americans in the United States, and also the demand for such mates.

While the foregoing macro-political forces have largely facilitated African/African-American mixed marriages, the micro-politics of culture can have a disconcerting influence on these unions.

The Micro-politics of Culture

There is an axiom that politics is the art of compromise; if so, then the politics of mixed or cross-cultural marriages augur well for a healthy dose of compromises. In addition to the idiosyncrasies that married couples typically either have to resolve or endure, individuals in cross-cultural marriages have to contend with cultural-cum-ethnic differences, different perceptions of the definition of marriage, and a range of stereotypes. All of the foregoing issues have the potential to wreak havoc on marital relations between Africans and African-Americans, as in any mixed marriage, especially if both parties are not willing to engage in serious compromise.

Many areas of a couple's life call for major compromises. For Ghanaian couples in general, Dr Christine Oppong has underscored that the earning, management and allocation of material resources are crucial issues with which all husbands and wives have to deal. They form part of the decision-making process in marriages involving Ghanaian men or women, and this process is of importance both to the couple concerned and to their dependants. Oppong also notes that practices and expectations may vary considerably (Oppong 1981: 85). From our own three-year marital experiences, where the husband is Ghanaian, the wife African-American, the term 'dependants', in a Ghanaian context and as used by Oppong, refers both to the nuclear family and to members of the large extended family. This extended family is both patrilateral and matrilateral, and also often incorporates children from previous marital unions, children from family inheritance (whereby the husband 'inherits' the property and families of deceased relatives), mothers, fathers, brothers, sisters and a host of other relatives. In this way, marriage is something much larger than the union of two people.

However, when a Ghanaian national chooses to marry an African-American, the foregoing scenario would take on an added dimension as the couple would nevertheless still be expected to act in unison as a couple on all decision-making matters, to show their compatibility and that their marriage was working at all levels. For example, in the case of a typical Ghanaian marriage, where both partners are from Ghana and belong to the Akan[1] ethnic group, Oppong explained that their major sources of livelihood are individually earned and individually controlled incomes, and they live in a form of segregated marriage mode (Oppong 1981: 85). In a Ghanaian/African-American marriage, however, especially in the USA, everything is done through a concerted effort, and an earned income, for example, belongs to the couple equally as a joint union. At this juncture, the couple is following an American notion of marital union, but not the Ghanaian prescription, whereby Ghanaian family members feel they have a *bona fide* say in the couple's life, ranging from their financial well-being to the number of children they should have.

Certainly, culture plays a crucial role in colouring perceptions of American society, which, in turn, has an important influence on marital relations between Africans and African-Americans. Cultural and social distinctions have been further blurred by a flurry of works published on the doctrine of Afrocentricity, defined by Molefi Kete Asante of Temple University, USA, as 'the most complete philosophical totalization of the African being-at-the-center of his or her existence' (Asante 1987: 125). Asante, indeed, sees Afrocentricity as an African or African-American way of living, behaving culturally, socially or otherwise, seeing everything through the 'bi-focal' perspective of Pan-Africanism or total Blackness. However, very often the commonalities of culture are emphasized, without adequately underscoring the important cultural differences that also exist (see Asante 1987). These differences include (1) the clash between a self-oriented culture and a communal culture; (2) the clash between definitions of marriage based on extended family ties and one based on the union of two individuals; and (3) the clash between conflicting images and stereotypes Africans and African-Americans may have of each other.

There have, indeed, been instances where American or European observers of Ghanaian/African-American unions have felt that certain African cultural or customary practices could lead to the destruction, undermining, or malfunctioning of the new cross-cultural family unit (Landis and Landis 1977: 13). These include situations in which an African mother-in-law or father-in-law insists on the couple producing children until a male is born; or when relatives insist in letters from Africa that their son or daughter should continue to worship and pour libations in honour of their earthly gods or ancestors back home. There are many more that we as a couple have not (yet) personally experienced, although we know of several other couples who have suffered through this insistence. In addition, the partners in a couple would have known each other for a while and, as a result, would have built up trust between them. Yet individuals observing from the outside may cast insinuations, and also harbour the suspicion that since polygamous relationships have existed in Africa from time immemorial, it inevitably means that in the end the Ghanaian husband would necessarily also seek other wives, so destroying the Ghanaian/African-American relationship. This is not always the case; many of these marital unions have endured all the pressures as well as the stereotypes of American society, and nevertheless survived (Vaz 1986: 5).

Stereotyping, Acceptability and Personal Happiness

In an earlier study similar to Oppong's study of middle-class Ghanaian marriages, Assensoh (1986) emphasized how in Ghanaian marriages at that time the wife often played subservient roles. This situation has become incorporated into the stereotypes some American and European observers suspect are reenacted in today's marriages between Ghanaians and their African-American partners. For example, he noted *inter alia* how Ghanaian wives, several years ago, could not open their own bank accounts, nor could they obtain their own individual passports or drivers' licences without the approval of their husbands (Assensoh 1986: 55–8). Oppong, however, recounts the changing trend in gendered power relations of the Ghanaian wife back home, including the complaint of a Ghanaian husband – a lawyer by profession – to the effect that today, 'women in Ghana like their independence too much! They will not have joint bank accounts with their husbands' (Oppong 1981: 95). In essence, the study accentuates the fact that Ghanaians have come of age when it comes to marital relationships, and that neither the male nor the female would like to take a partner – let alone one from America or Europe – for granted.

Furthermore, policy analysts have argued that the manner in which an issue or problem is defined determines, to a large measure, the manner in which it will be resolved (Ripley 1985: 93–130). Similarly, the manner in which a marriage is defined or perceived determines what is acceptable as its roles, relationships and boundaries. Indeed, research has shown that differences have often existed in the definition of marriage as perceived by many Africans and African-Americans. In many West African cultures, for example, where extended kinship systems exist, a marriage is seen as the joining of two extended families; therefore, the extended family remains an important integral part of the marital relationship. In contrast, the African-American's perception of a marriage is that it is the union of two individuals. As a result, in the wedding vows of many Protestant marriages individuals are called on to 'forsake all others and cling to his/her spouse', as stipulated biblically. Thus, while the extended family is perceived as an integral part of the marital union in the West African – or specifically in the Ghanaian – notion of marriage, the extended family is generally viewed as external to the core relationship of a couple in the African-American concept of marriage, across classes. Certainly, unlike the case of an indigenous Ghanaian marital relationship, extended family ties do not become the norm in the Ghanaian/African-American conjugal relationship, especially when the couple resides in the United States (Oppong 1981: 21,98).

These different expectations of and attitudes towards including or excluding kinfolk, and the nature of obligations and duties due to them, can very easily set the stage for various conflicting situations, especially as they relate to marital decision-making, finances and child-rearing. Therefore, the would-be Ghanaian/ African-American couple need to iron out such differences before they embark on their marriage. Indeed, many couples have done so to the extent that, similar to our own Ghanaian/African-American marital situation, extended family members can be assisted whenever they need help, especially if it can be afforded. However, this is not done as a formal established obligation, but is more flexible, contrary to the situation Oppong described in her work on middle-class African marriage as 'a recognition of obligations to assist parents, to help brothers and sisters, to educate sisters' children' (Oppong 1981: 85). On the contrary, marriages in the United States are often viewed as partnerships, wherein the wives and husbands make joint decisions about the marriage and the nuclear family.

There is a widespread stereotype in Europe and America that marital decision-making practices in West African countries – of which Ghana forms an integral part – are comparable to fiefdoms, whereby each man or husband is seen as a semi-tyrant, who can unilaterally rule his household without either contributions from or the concurrence of his wife. However, our research on African/African-American marriages has shown that, for various reasons, not all African men expect such wifely subordination, and in such families there is little conflict over spousal roles. For example, due to religious backgrounds, superior educational training, and cultural influences from Europe and America, many men from African countries have come to eschew the so-called traditional view of male and female roles. As a result, some of these men are very capable cooks, fathers and housekeepers. Contrary to expectations, however, what has been shown is that many African women married to African-American men have come to re-accept patriarchal notions of male superiority and specific roles for women at home in their marriages. Therefore, many African-American men have said publicly that they would always prefer an African woman to their own African-American women, who believe in the equality of sexes. Indeed, Norment confirmed this point in his own study: 'African women are described by their [African-] American husbands as more supportive and less domineering than the typical [African-] American woman' (Norment 1982: 103).

Collectively held group stereotypes and ethnocentrism can also have detrimental effects on the marital relations between Africans and African-Americans. On the one hand, there is a wide range of both negative and positive stereotypes held by African-Americans about Africans, from 'uncivilized people who live in jungle huts or even in trees', to 'marvelous schemers', who are 'elitist', 'opportunistic', 'super-intelligent' and 'disdainful' people (Gibson 1984: 160; see also Kohn and Shibata, this volume). There is some evidence to support the 'schemer' stereotype, since there have been occasions when a male African has lied and exaggerated to 'entrap' an African-American woman into a relationship: for example, sometimes the son of an African peasant would claim to hail from a royal family, and a gullible African-American woman would fall for such a lie or exaggeration (Moikobou 1981: 173).

On the other hand, Africans also have negative stereotypes of African-Americans: these range from 'lazy', 'immoral' or 'materialistic', to 'self-centered' or 'criminally inclined' (Gibson 1984: 160). Some Africans – not necessarily Ghanaians, of course – maintain that they are superior to African-Americans because of the latter's enslaved past. Williams quoted an African student emphasizing this many years ago on an American campus, 'We are free men and not freedmen' (Williams 1980: 234). Such unfortunate assertions and contentions do very little to cultivate, promote, or nurture mixed marriages between Africans and their African-American kith and kin in America. In the end, Africans and their African-American spouses are, therefore, expected to overcome these stereotypes as well as diverse intrusions if a successful marital union is to continue to exist.

Furthermore, many White Americans believe that African-Americans should learn from and model their behaviour on the success of their counterparts from Africa, who supposedly work harder than African-Americans as a group (Gibson 1984: 160). Consequently, 'White America' has used this rather amorphous, homogenized positive view of 'Africans' as a so-called 'model minority', in order both to criticize African-Americans as well as to urge them to achieve similar standards of academic excellence, small-business successes, and independence from government handouts as well as programs (Gibson 1984: 160). This model, of course, places the blame for a wide variety of social problems on the shoulders of African-Americans, and absolves other groups, and governments, from any responsibility to take action themselves.

At the same time, Africans and African-Americans may also harbour idealized stereotypes and, sometimes, unrealistic expectations of the foreign Other, which predispose them to become involved in cross-cultural unions, but which are based on an unrealizable romanticized image of their partner. For example, many African-American women regard African men as exotically appealing (see Kohn's chapter on the attraction of the exotic Other, this volume), while others have held the mythical belief that all African men who make it to America are rich and socially well established. Feeding into this romanticization of the foreign Other are life-history anecdotes that some African-American women have found African men to be more suitable mates, much more stable, astute and mature than their African-American male counterparts. On the other hand, African men have often claimed that they were drawn to African-American women because of their sexual liberation, their skill at romance, and their economic potential.

While stereotypes can hinder the development of very cordial relations between Africans and African-Americans in general, the personal expression of ethno-centrism within a spouse's family and circle of friends can also be detrimental to a particular marital relationship. In discussing with us their friendships with African women, many African-American women, now married to African men, were of the opinion that there have always been high levels of resentment and antipathy towards them from some African women. These negative feelings stem, to a large measure, from the fact that unmarried or divorced African women are distressed to realize that their so-called good and marriageable men are no longer available to them as potential spouses, and that, instead, these men have married out to foreign or African-American women. The insult to the injury is that the men even appear to be happy with their choice. Some African-American wives of African men have reported that African women can be very subtle in displaying their hatred for such unions, while others are distressingly blatant. These instances of ethnocentrism, utter contempt and public display of sheer hatred for African/African-American marital relationships by these African women not only interfere with the marriage, but also tend to undermine the broader aspects of the couple's social networks. Above all, they highlight issues of cultural-cum-ethnic differences, which are often otherwise muted by America's focus on colour and race. However, what is heartening for many African-American spouses is the fact that whenever they accompany their Ghanaian (or African) spouses on visits to Africa, parents and other relatives on the continent observe the rules of warm and encompassing hospitality typical of Ghana (and many other African cultures) that make them feel welcome. Under such circumstances, the ethnocentric, bitter and unfriendly attitudes very often shown by some America-based Ghanaian (or African) women – often divorced and desperately in search of husbands for themselves – no longer matter.

To a large extent, this exploratory research has reinforced the contention that cross-cultural marriages between Africans and African-Americans in the United States are viable entities that should not be studied either in isolation or in a vacuum. Rather, to appreciate the complexity of these *bona fide* unions, future analyses should use contextual, multi-faceted perspectives, with an emphasis on the personal and public effects of micro- and macro-political factors such as racial politics, international relations, and deeply seated cultural underpinnings in general.

Note

1. Akan is the dominant ethnic group in Ghana, made up of Ashantis, Fantis, Akims and Akwapims.

References

Asante, M.K. (1987), *The Afro-Centric Idea*, Philadelphia: Temple University Press.

Assensoh, A.B. (1986), *Essays on Contemporary International Topics*, Devon: Arthur Stockwell.

——, (1989), *Kwame Nkrumah of Africa*, Devon: Arthur Stockwell.

——, (1998), *African Political Leadership: Jomo Kenyatta, Julius K. Nyerere and Kwame Nkrumah*, Malabar, Florida: Krieger Publishing Company.

Chua-Eoan, H.G. (1986), 'Tightening the Knot', *Time Magazine*, 15 December, p.35.

DuBois, W.E.B. (1961), *The Souls of Black Folk*, New York: Fawcett.

Farley, R. and Allen, W.R. (1987), *The Color Line and the Quality of Life in America*, New York: Oxford University Press.

Fullwood, S. (1996), *Waking From the Dream*, New York: Random Books.

Gibson, J. (1984), 'Toward Understanding between Africans and African-Americans', *The Black Collegian*, November/December, p.160.

Hacker, A. (1992), *Two Nations: Black and White, Separate, Hostile, Unequal*, New York: Ballentine Books.

Hill, H. and Jones, J.E. Jr (1993), *Race in America: The Struggle for Equality*, Madison: University of Wisconsin Press.

Johnson, W.R. and Warren, D.M. (1994), *Inside the Mixed Marriage*, New York: University Press of America.

Landis, J.T. and Landis M.G. (1977), *Building a Successful Marriage*, 7th Edition, Englewood Cliffs, N.J.: Prentice-Hall.

Larsson, C. (ed.), (1965), *Marriage Across the Color Line*, Chicago: Johnson Publishing Company.

Moikobou, J. (1981), *Blood and Flesh: Black American and African Identification*, Westport: Greenwood Press.

Norment, L. (1982), 'What Kind of Spouses do Africans Make?', *Ebony*, February, pp. 100–5.

Oppong, C. (1981), *Middleclass African Marriage: A Family Study of Ghanaian Senior Civil Servants*. Boston: G. Allen and Unwin.

Ripley, R. (1985), *Policy Analysis in Political Science*, Chicago: Nelson-Hall.

US Government (1995), *Code of Federal Regulations*, no.8, 9 January.

Van Deburg, W.L. (1992), *New Day in Babylon*, Chicago: University of Chicago Press.

Vaz, K. (1986), 'Tired of Turkey: Try a New Game: The Pursuit of Intimacy between Africans and Afro-Americans', (unpublished manuscript), Indiana University: Bloomington.

Williams, W. (1980), 'Ethnic Relations of African Students in the United States with Black Americans, 1870–1900', *Journal of Negro History*, 65, pp.228–49.

Wilson, W. (1987), *The Truly Disadvantaged*, Chicago: University of Chicago Press.

7

Freedom of Choice or Pandora's Box? Legal Pluralism and the Regulation of Cross-Cultural Marriages in Uganda

Sanyu Semafumu

Introduction: Of Legal Regulation and Rational Decision-Making

Choice and Law in Marriage

One of the central tenets of orthodox liberal thought is that in arriving at important decisions people will look to, and be guided by, the law as laid down and/or recognized by the state. Indeed, the liberal ideal of the rule of law as a political and legal doctrine is premised on the assumption that social order facilitates greater enjoyment of individual choice and freedom. To this end, citizens have a common desire and interest in having laws to guide them, not just in situations of conflict, but in the day-to-day and long-term management of their lives (for example, Arblaster 1984: Chs 2–3).

At the same time, it is widely acknowledged that such law is not the only, or even necessarily, the main means of achieving social order. Yet, at the level of policy formulation and implementation, belief in the central role of law in social regulation and social change is pervasive. Campaigns for law reform on various issues suggest that this view of the power of law is shared by many ordinary people. One obvious inference to be drawn from such belief in the centrality of law is that, when taking key decisions, people will presumably consider the possible effect of any relevant legal provisions in weighing up the available options.

As regards their long-term personal happiness and well-being, the choice of marriage partner is probably the single most important decision most people ever make or have made for them. Moreover, marriage as an *institution* is generally viewed by state and social authorities as central to the overall well-being, stability, and continuity of human societies, adding to the importance attached to choosing the right spouse.[1]

There are many variations in the practices by which marriages are formed and regulated. For example, while Europe, the United States, and countries influenced by their legal traditions give legal validity only to monogamous marriages, many African countries recognize both monogamous and polygamous marriages. Where such plurality of marriage forms is found, the choice available is largely determined by the religious, racial and/or ethnic identity of the parties. These countries thus seem to offer greater freedom to choose how one marries, and, therefore, they also offer some choice in the marital obligations to which one wishes to be subject. If indeed people do make rational choices after considering the likely outcomes of each of the available options, then where choice exists for marriage forms, it is plausible that people would take into account the regulatory regime to which a particular marriage is subject.

This chapter presents the preliminary findings from a small pilot study exploring to what extent and how a multiplicity of legally available options may influence people's choices of marriage form and partner. The study was carried out in the East African country of Uganda. Participants were asked what factors informed their choice of partner, and whether their choice was influenced by the likely legal consequences of that particular type of union. Behind these questions there is a wider aim: to examine state regulation of personal relationships in a culturally and legally complex society in flux.

Global Variations in Marriage Practices

In most highly industrialized countries, the choice of marriage partner is seen as a largely private or personal affair, taken with little interference from the state apart from formalities about prohibited degrees of kinship and consanguinity, the ages, sex and marital status of the intended partners.[2] Beyond a certain age, there is no legal requirement for parental consent to the marriage, though the family's blessing on the union is usually valued.

In other cultures, these are matters not for the spouses alone, but for their families and wider social group. The implications of this for the choice of partner vary. The marriage may be arranged by the families with little or no involvement by the intended spouses, or they may be left to choose their own partner, subject to family approval. The category of marriage may also be limited by factors such as sex, age, and degree of kinship.[3]

The form of marriage also leads to important differences in the legal consequences of the relationship. Amongst these are whether the marriage is monogamous or polygamous; the extent to which the relationship created by the marriage is a private one for the spouses, or one that binds the immediate and/or extended family; the wife's rights to matrimonial and other property; and the ease with which a marriage can be entered into and dissolved.

Regulation of Marriage in Uganda

Cultural Diversity

Uganda's indigenous population consists of at least fifty-six distinct ethnic groups.[4] The degree of difference between their respective cultures varies.[5] For example, geographically distant pastoralist communities have similarities not shared by closer neighbours from an agricultural tradition. On the other hand, local linguistic groupings overlay the pastoralist/cultivator distinctions, with the result that there may be strong similarities in language alongside important cultural differences. There are also stereotypes suggesting temperamental differences between north and south, east and west, which could influence a particular group's perception of the suitability or otherwise of members of other groups as marriage partners.

Religious distinctions are important. They tend to be sharpest between Christians and Muslims, but exist between the Christian denominations as well, sometimes transcending ethnic identities and loyalties.[6] The customary indigenous religions continue to influence even some committed Christians and Muslims.

Plurality in the Law Regulating Marriage in Uganda

Prior to colonization, marriage between indigenous Africans was regulated by the customary law of each ethnic group.[7] The colonial administration set in place by the British towards the end of the last century created a regime under which a number of different types of marriages had legal validity. Limited recognition was given to the relationships formed under the customary practices (often polygynous) of the various ethnic groups.[8] Africans could continue to 'marry' under them, while those who wished could enter monogamous marriages regulated by statute. Interracial marriages had to be performed under statute, and there were also provisions recognizing 'Mohammedan' and Hindu marriages.

Post-independence regulations have retained the plurality of marriage forms that characterized the colonial period, but there have been changes in the law, as well as in the rationale for the plurality. Four forms of marriage are recognized under the current law, each with different significance regarding access to property and wealth, rights and obligations to the partner and the extended family, divorce proceedings, and numbers of spouses permitted:

1. statutory or civil marriage under the Marriage Act. Christian marriages are usually legalized under this Act by the signing of the marriage certificate as part of the ceremony;
2. Islamic marriages under the Marriage and Divorce of Mohammedans Act;
3. Hindu marriages under the Marriage of Hindus Act;
4. customary marriages under the Marriage of Africans Act and the Registration of Customary Marriages Decree 1973.

With fifty or so different ethnic groups in Uganda, each with its own distinctive rules on marriage, it may be argued that in reality the law recognizes not four, but fifty-three forms of marriage.[9] However, there are broad similarities that justify use of the term 'customary marriage' with reference to relationships formalized by the fulfilment of the rites and practices recognized by the relevant ethnic group(s) as necessary for the creation of a valid marriage. For example, all customary marriages are presumed to be potentially polygynous; the marriage is the outcome of agreement between families rather than the spouses alone;[10] and the transfer or exchange of some property is considered crucial to the formation of such marriages.[11] Customary marriages were relegated to second-class status under colonialism.[12] Post-independence laws have tried to rectify this. The 1973 Registration of Customary Marriages Decree affirms that customary marriages have the same legal status as marriages under other laws.[13]

The Law in the Books versus the Law in Action

The aim of the present regulatory regime is to allow the individual to choose the system of law under which s/he marries, and then to stick to that system until any marriage(s) contracted under that system is (are) lawfully dissolved. So if A marries B and C under customary law, A cannot then contract a valid civil marriage with D while the earlier marriages subsist, and any attempt to do so would amount to an offence under the law.

A cursory examination of marriage practice in Uganda suggests, however, that the separation between marriage systems is not always as rigidly observed as envisaged by legislators.[14] Many couples will go through at least some of the formalities of a customary marriage even if they are marrying under civil and/or religious law. This is not unlawful. However, going through the subsequent ceremony *with a different partner* would be. Where this happens, it is likely to involve a man purporting to marry a second or subsequent time. Such relationships are widely accepted in the community as valid marriages, even though they are both invalid in law and bigamous. Well-intentioned community leaders may unwittingly abet law-breaking by encouraging men in polygynous marriages to go through a Christian marriage with one of their wives without dissolving the other marriages. Law-enforcement personnel appear reluctant to follow up or prosecute the often blatant contraventions of the law. While in some cases this law-breaking is due to ignorance or misunderstanding of the law, in others it is deliberate.

The Decision to Marry: Cross-Cultural Marriages in a Context of Legal Pluralism

Methodology

This project constitutes the preliminary stage of a larger investigation. Five articulate and well-educated women were interviewed about their decision to embark on a relationship with a man from a different religious, ethnic and/or racial background. They were asked how these differences influenced their decision to formalize the relationship, and how they then chose the system under which to marry. The extent to which the latter decision has shaped their marriages, and shaped perceptions of their and their spouse's roles in the relationship were explored.

Belief in the rationality of decision-making presumes a subject equipped with a reasonable understanding of the factors relevant to the decision. A major consideration in choosing participants for the pilot study was that they understood the system of marriage regulation in Uganda, and the implications of their choices in this regard. They were questioned to determine how far they had understood the legal options available to them at the time they made the decision, rather than purely with the benefit of hindsight. The women interviewed were in relationships that they and their communities defined as mixed or cross-cultural. Those in such relationships have a wider than average choice of legal systems under which to regulate their marriages: these included civil, religious and various customary marriage regulations. Table 7.1 shows the range of options available to the five informants and their partners. (Pseudonyms are used.)

Informants were interviewed individually. The interviews were informal and loosely structured. On average, interviews lasted two and a half hours. Informants' husbands indicated their willingness to be interviewed in the next stage of the study, which will help further the investigation of gender differences in the use of the system.

All five informants were conscious of the cultural differences between themselves and their future partners from the start. In two cases, the difference appears to have been a factor in the decision to start the relationship. For Grace, it was an act of rebellion against what she had felt were stifling expectations of her by her 'eminently respectable' family. Edith was anxious to avoid a relationship with someone of her late husband's ethnic group. For the other three women, the difference was not a significant factor in the decision to start a relationship, and the decision to go further and marry their partners appears to have been despite, rather than in part due to, the differences.

Table 7.1.   Regulatory Pluralism in Cross-cultural Relationships. Choice of Marriage Systems Available to the Couples Surveyed.

Names, Ethnic Origin and Religious Affiliation of Couple	Types of Marriage Available to Couple under Ugandan Law
Anna: Ganda, Christian *married to*: **Abby**: Ganda, Muslim	Civil,* Christian, Islamic, and Ganda Customary.
Hanifa: Ganda, Christian (converted to Islam) *married to*: **Badru**: Ganda, Muslim	Civil,* Christian, Islamic*, and Ganda Customary.*
Edith: Samia, Christian *married to*: **Chris**: Ganda, Christian	Civil,* Christian,* Ganda Customary, Samia Customary.
Grace: Itesot, Christian *married to*: **Dennis**: Swedish, Christian	Civil,* Christian*, and Itesot Customary.
Irene: Kiga, Christian *married to*: **Fred**: Itesot, Christian	Civil,* Christian,* Itesot Customary, and Kiga Customary.

* indicates the legal system(s) under which the couple purport to be married.

Reactions to Choice of Spouse

Informants reported having to overcome some degree of family opposition. They all felt that their status at the time helped them in this, for as professionals or college students, there did appear to be some expectation that they would be more independent than their less educated counterparts.

It emerged that the degree of resistance to the marriages by the families was in part determined by their assessment of the woman's eligibility. Hanifa, who converted from Catholicism to marry Badru, an older Muslim man, in an Islamic ceremony, said that because she was several years out of university, and a high-flying career woman, she was perceived by her family as becoming increasingly more intimidating to men, and therefore as less marriageable. While they strongly disapproved of her choice of husband, they were also quite pragmatic about preferring her to be married to him than to no one. Edith, whose first husband had been wholly satisfactory to her family, was widowed early, and so regarded as unlikely to find another equally suitable man. Having done her duty by them with her first marriage, they accepted her marrying to suit herself the second time around.

Grace, very tall, slim, and of dark complexion was regarded as relatively unattractive by her own ethnic group, where plumpness and fairer complexions are preferred. Her decision to marry out therefore raised less dissent than would have otherwise been the case.[15]

Anna and Irene were rated as at least reasonably marriageable by their families. A 'suitable boy' was already lined up for Irene, leaving her family even less amenable to her choice of an outsider. Family acceptance was obtained through negotiation, accomplished by winning over a respected elder relative or family friend, and using this support to break down the resistance. Irene said that ultimately an important tactic had been to make clear to her parents that they had no real means of preventing the marriage, and stood to alienate her by rejecting her chosen partner. This strategy, coupled with parents getting to know the fiancé, generally achieved the desired result. In the case of Hanifa, however, the parents refused to attend the wedding and made it clear that those relatives who did were there in their own capacity, not as representatives.

Meeting Strangers: Opportunities and Attitudes

Space limitations here mean that I cannot discuss all the case-studies, so to illustrate the types of issues that are taken into account I have chosen one from each end of the range of marriage choices, with one informant choosing one type of marriage law, whereas the other chose three. Detailed extracts from these two interviews are given later in this section, but it seems appropriate to start with an overview of the findings about which it is possible to generalize.

All five informants met their future husbands while living away from close family control and supervision. This created opportunities for the development of relationships that would have been unlikely to get off the ground in other circumstances. Equally important was the women's perception of themselves as more cosmopolitan in outlook and preferred lifestyle than the older generation and their less highly educated friends and relations.[16] The women's views on how the form of marriage and the identity of their spouses might affect the rules by which the relationships would run were discussed. There was a consensus that if you married in Church or had a civil ceremony, the marriage was intended to be monogamous and 'modern', and you could demand this of your husband. The women saw the various areas of difference from their partners both as a challenge to be overcome, and as an important reason for the continued success of their marriages, in that people expected them to fail, which made the couple even more determined to prove them wrong.

In the case of the two women who married Muslim men, the possibility of being subject to Islamic law required careful consideration. In Uganda, Christians and Muslims tend, for historical reasons, to see their differences as negative.[17] To marry across this particular religious barrier is seen as marrying out, even where the couple belongs to the same ethnic group as in the two cases below, or both are only nominally religious, as in one of the cases.

Informants' Perceptions of their Relationships

Case-study 1: Anna and Abby.   Anna was raised in a church-going but otherwise not particularly committed Protestant home. She married Abby, a lapsed Muslim. She was totally unwilling even to go through the motions of an Islamic marriage. Fortunately, Abby did not want one either, and as they were living abroad at the time of the marriage, they were not as subject to family pressure as they would have been at home. As it was, they had a civil ceremony and returned to Uganda over two years later with a *fait accompli*.

Anna's reasons for rejecting an Islamic marriage included the following: the fact that the woman did not have any role in the marriage ceremony, the acceptance of polygyny, the possibility of unilateral divorce by the husband (*talak*), and the expectations of her husband's family, had she been married in Islam, that she would be a proper Muslim wife. The advantage of a civil ceremony was that both partners knew they were contracting a monogamous marriage, and any departure from this would be in the full knowledge that it was illicit. It would make some difference to the regulation of the marriage, in that a civil ceremony symbolizes a modern marriage. By this, Anna said she meant a marriage in which traditions about how a wife should care for her home, children and husband are still important, but she is not 'ruled' as in customary or Islamic law, and she is not obliged to tolerate his family and their demands to the same extent as under custom, where she is considered to be 'their' wife. For example, a wife married under customary law might be expected to keep open house for an endless stream of relatives visiting from the village, while one married in modern style might be treated more warily, especially by those not belonging to the immediate family. After eight years of marriage, Anna was sure that the form of her marriage had given her greater freedom than she would have had had she married in either an Islamic or customary ceremony.

Unusually, she and Abby had not performed any of the practices necessary for the formation of a customary marriage.[18] She did not think this made any difference to the way their families perceived the marriage. Both of them fulfilled the expectations of the key members of their respective nuclear and extended families. For example, they each attended social functions as expected by the families, and relatives from each side turned up on those occasions when in-laws were expected to be present, such as funerals. The children had been duly presented to his family for naming, and had both clan and Islamic names. She felt her children were not viewed as different by her family or non-Muslim friends.

The form of marriage has important implications for the wife's rights to property.

In Anna's view, the form of her marriage made it clear that the matrimonial property was jointly owned. The matrimonial home was in joint names, and she held equal shares in their business. Abby had always made it clear to his relations that she had a share in all the property, and a say in how money was spent. She knew this displeased some of them, who clung to the traditional view of a man's property being that of his clan. If he died suddenly, some of them might not be above trying to grab what they could. In Anna's view, this would be tantamount to theft from herself and her children, and she would not let it happen to her. 'I would lock up everything that can be moved then show the family the documents in joint names. I'd call in the police if necessary.' If she ever left Abby and there was any dispute, she would go to court for the equal share she felt was her due.

One area in which the differences between them surfaced was funerals, where Islamic practices differ from both customary and Christian ones. Since, according to Kiganda customs, attendance at burials is a key obligation on the part of family on both sides, the differences did tend to get thrown into relief. The other was in some of the taboos about pork and alcohol, but this was a minor inconvenience. Anna was satisfied that she had chosen well. Moreover, she was sure that the initial reservations that her family had had about her marrying out had been overcome by the obvious success of the marriage, and their inability to find any real fault with Abby. In her assessment, the cultural differences, which she did not see as extensive, were a source of strength rather than of stress to their marriage.

Case-study 2: Hanifa and Badru. Like Anna, Hanifa too came of a Christian family and married a Muslim man, but there are important differences between the two women and their marriages. Hanifa's family were devout Catholics (the extended family including a nun and a priest in its ranks). Her husband Badru and his family were practising Muslims. Unlike Anna, Hanifa was considerably younger than her husband when they met. He already had two wives married under Islamic law, with five children between them. Matters were further complicated by the fact that both families came from the same small town, one with strong Islamic and Catholic communities. He is something of a pillar of the Muslim community. There was therefore no question of a civil marriage, as his marrying a Christian was bad enough for the family's standing without being compounded by not having an Islamic wedding. Hanifa had to convert to Islam, as well as marry under Islamic law. She took a Muslim name. It was not, she said, an easy decision, but in some ways having to make these concessions strengthened her bargaining position. Badru was fully aware of the strain that her involvement with him had placed on her relationships with her family. Her misgivings about marrying him, and in an Islamic ceremony, were similar to those of Anna's, and aggravated by the expectations of family and friends on both sides, who lived in the same town. Her price for agreeing to his terms was that he divorced his other wives and followed up the Islamic marriage with a civil ceremony. As to her role as his wife, this was not such a source of difficulty, for one of her major attractions for him was her modernity, including her image as a competent professional woman. He wished her to continue being these things, as well as a good Muslim wife.

Badru was unable to divorce his wives without making his family pariahs in their community. Instead, he undertook to provide for them but to cease relations with them. A quiet civil ceremony followed their big Islamic wedding. They had also honoured some of the key customary ceremonies, which would have been the case even if each had married someone of his or her own faith.[19]

At the time, Hanifa was fully aware that the civil ceremony on top of the existing Islamic marriage was unlawful and of no legal worth. However, her reasons for having the ceremony were to do with 'diluting' the expectations that she felt would have been promoted had she had only the Islamic and customary ceremonies. It also seemed to make her family feel better, and in her opinion, it reinforced Badru's view of her as being more than the ordinary Muslim wife. For Hanifa, the civil ceremony symbolized that her becoming a Muslim wife was not tantamount to her accepting the totality of what this might signify to other people, including her husband.

Thirteen years into the marriage, how did she think the differences and compromises over the form of their marriage had shaped the relationship? Like Anna, Hanifa felt the differences had strengthened rather than weakened their marriage. However, she emphasized that she had staked a great deal in the face of family who not only thought that the marriage would fail, but would have been glad if it did. Badru had similarly placed his credibility on the line, though she felt that being a man he had less to lose by failure. Both of them had tried hard to stick to their part of the bargain. Their biggest crisis had occurred three years into the marriage, when Badru had had a child with one of the wives he was supposed to have left in all but name. They had survived though, and she was confident there would not be a repetition.

In retrospect, Hanifa felt making the marriage work had been much harder and more complicated than she had anticipated. For instance, she was taken aback at realizing that she was expected to be a Muslim in more than name. On Fridays she had to go to the mosque and, given Badru's status in the community, she had had to become involved with Muslim women's groups. She was expected to encourage everyone to use her Muslim name. Her three children were being raised as practising Muslims.

On the other hand, she had continued to do well in her career, always with Badru's support. Most of her family now accepted and respected him. Her marriage had gradually broadened the collective mind of her family, as exposure to Islamic beliefs and culture had made them confront their ignorance and prejudices about Muslims. Nevertheless, there was still a degree to which she felt alienated from her husband and children in their 'Muslimness'. No matter how well she acted the role, she was not at heart a Muslim.

Hanifa felt that the existence of differences between them often worked in her favour. For example, Badru had changed all his business documents to include her as a shareholder in his businesses, a position which neither of his other wives enjoyed. To her, this affirmed their marriage as a partnership of equals, albeit with him as first amongst them. Others might construe it as him being under her thumb. He confounded them by publicizing it as evidence of the complete trust and confidence that he, as a good Muslim, had in his wife. Few of his colleagues of any faith could boast of similar shows of confidence or egalitarianism. To mock him for these qualities would reflect badly on their own marriages and/or attitudes to their wives.

Hanifa had also been able to negotiate other aspects of her rights to property by highlighting her potential vulnerability as an outsider if she were widowed. Given his other family commitments, she argued that it was best if she and her children were secured during his lifetime. Badru understood, perhaps even shared her fears, and they were now provided for in case of divorce or death, with little scope for legal challenges to the settlement.

Marriage Regulation and the 'Implicit Theory of Legal Pluralism'

What is going on in situations such as that of Hanifa and Badru, where people mix and match marriage systems as suits them, regardless of the actual provisions or intentions of the law?

The theory of legal pluralism may offer a way of analysing the operation of marriage laws as described here.[20] Legal pluralism may be said to exist in a social field where behaviour that accords with more than one legal order occurs (Griffiths 1986: 1–55). A distinction is drawn between pluralism 'in the weaker sense' on the one hand, and pluralism 'in the strong sense' on the other. The former refers to state-sanctioned (juridical) pluralism. The latter describes 'social science' pluralism, or how the concept is generally understood in the social sciences. This refers to any situation where a group follows regulations other than those laid down for them by the state, and is a feature of all complex societies (Griffiths 1986: 1–55).

In an important study, Sally Falk Moore concludes that all such societies are organized at various fields or levels, ranging, for example, from the family to the workplace. Each subgroup within the larger polity evolves concrete rules for its own regulation, which may be in harmony or at odds with those of the wider social order. Law can then be defined as the 'self-regulation of the semi-autonomous social field' (Griffiths 1986: 38). The social field is *semi*-autonomous because it is not a normative vacuum, waiting to be filled by the laws of the latter, but rather a self-regulating unit which:

> generates rules and customs and symbols internally . . . it is also vulnerable to rules and decisions and other forces emanating from the larger world by which it is surrounded. The semi-autonomous social field has rule-making capacities, and the means to induce or coerce compliance; but it is simultaneously set in a larger social matrix which can, and does, affect and invade it (Moore 1978: 55–6).

This theory of legal pluralism defines 'law' as the normative order by which any social group achieves internal regulation. Tensions between the demands made by the different social fields to which a person may belong might explain why legislation frequently fails in practice to achieve the effect expected and intended by governments. It may also explain what is going on in regulatory systems such as that governing marriage in Uganda, where the prevalence of pluralism in both senses results in complex juxtapositions of regulatory norms and expectations.

If we accept the situation as one of legal pluralism in both senses of the term, then couples in cross-cultural relationships can be seen as members of semi-autonomous social fields in which the accommodations and compromises regarding each other's differences are a part of the normative ordering of that particular field.[21] While some of the rules are consistent with the diktat of state law, others contravene it, and yet are accepted within the social group as imposing obligations on those who marry under them. Thus the bigamously married man is expected to accord his 'wife' such status as to make it obvious that she is not just a girlfriend or mistress. A Muslim man in Badru's position should treat his earlier wives with respect, but is expected to show Hanifa the special status that is implied in having purportedly married her under the civil law. That he committed an offence under state law by the latter act does not appear to change the expectation of his social group that he will fulfil the obligations that the act symbolizes for them.

It is interesting to note that this subversion of state law occurs within, and is informed by, the parameters of state law. So although the rules by which people choose to regulate their marriages may be at odds with the official rules, they are often recognizably hybrids of a variety of state-sanctioned provisions, rather than completely new or different. Whatever the similarities of form, the differences in legal effect are unambiguous. Marriage in accordance with state regulations confers the legal status of 'married' on the parties, which in turn gives rise to rights and obligations that the state can often be called upon to enforce between the spouses and/or against third parties. On the other hand, the sanctions for failure to comply with the expectations imposed by marriages that are not in accordance with official regulations are unofficial. Apart from the disapproval of one's social group, there is the possibility of involving friends, families and so forth as mediators in any serious breach of the agreed rules. The pressure that these groups can impose is informal, but nonetheless effective. Maintaining the support and respect of friends and family is important to the well-being of the individual, and pressure can be increased by making compliance a matter of the honour of the immediate group to which one belongs.[22]

Conclusions

The pilot study reported on here was small, and highly unrepresentative of Uganda's population. The following are therefore closing observations rather than con-clusions as such. First, the case-studies reported here suggest that cross-cultural marriages in a context of both juridical and social-science pluralism represent a continuum of degrees of compliance with the state's regulatory framework. They range from cases such as that of Anna, where the law is being applied more or less as intended, to Hanifa, where the couple are 'married' under three different systems of law, and are in fact subverting the state's regulatory regime. The other three marriages that were looked at in the study fall along different points between these two extremes.

It seems that the existence of various types of marriage presents considerable scope for manipulation of the regulatory scheme as a whole. In the case of cross-cultural relationships, the even greater range of choice can be manipulated to reflect the complexities of the relationship. The study findings suggest too that when they are in a position to do so, women are not any less willing to manipulate the system to suit their needs and interests than their male counterparts.

It also seems that people may be more concerned about marrying in ways that earn their relationships the recognition of the various social fields with which they most strongly identify, than about the legal status of the relationship. It may be that if forced to choose between recognition of the marriage by their respective cultural (including religious) groups, and legal recognition, the former would be more important to the majority of people, at least at the time they take the decision, though perhaps not necessarily in the long term.[23]

If the state wishes to shape or regulate society in a particular way through law, the situation described here suggests that something is missing from the formula by which the legislation was devised. Perhaps it is an inadequate understanding of the complexity of a multicultural, multifaceted society. The tendency of positivist legal method is to compartmentalize, to put people and relationships into neat, discrete categories. Personal relationships formed and conducted in an increasingly multicultural and changing social context are not so readily pigeon-holed. Furthermore, legislation does not emerge to fill a normative vacuum. New laws do not necessarily result in transformation of vested interests, so wresting people away from the old normative order (unless strictly enforced). This aspect of the process of shaping social mores does not appear to have been adequately looked into by those who advocate law reform as a means of achieving change.

In countries like Uganda, cross-cultural marriages will continue to occur with greater frequency as old barriers break down. Such relationships highlight the dynamism of culture, rather than its immutability. Examining them can offer insights into how the law's subjects may choose to interpret and apply the law to suit their own unique needs, irrespective of legislative and policy intentions. Such situations should continue to be a fertile ground of study for those who wish to obtain a clearer understanding of the processes of law and social change.

Notes

1. At present, global concern about the institution of marriage is focused on the correlation between marital instability and increased levels of social dysfunction, including under-achievement and delinquency amongst young people.
2. See, for example, the *Marriage Acts* for England and Wales, 1949–86. In addition to the requirements of these Acts, the nationality of the intended partner may present further scope for state involvement, for example where it is necessary to comply with immigration regulations in order for the couple to live together. Cf. also Breger's chapter in this volume.
3. An example is the age restrictions imposed by Uganda's *Customary Marriages Registration Decree*, 1973.
4. These are listed in Schedule 1 of the *Constitution of the Republic of Uganda*, 1995.
5. As used in this paper, the word 'culture' is given the wide sense used commonly by anthropologists, as referring to the entire set of beliefs, values, norms, practices and so forth of a people.
6. Two of the main political parties that emerged in the period leading up to the end of colonialism were in fact identified respectively with the Protestant and Catholic churches.
7. To speak of 'customary law' obscures the great complexity of cultural identities and practices that lie behind the term. In addition, questions have been raised about the extent to which the customary law pertaining since the colonial era was in fact customary, or indeed instead a creation of the various interests that coalesced to interpret and apply it as such. See, for example, Snyder (1981).
8. This was subject to the practice or custom in question not being 'repugnant' to the concepts of morality or natural justice determined by British law. For a discussion see Allot (1970: Ch.5).
9. The Kalema Report (1965) gives perhaps the most thorough overview of the customary practices of the various ethnic groups.

10. Some commentators have characterized these marriages as being agreements between the male members of the two families, see Tamale and Okumu-Wengi (1992). This can be misleading. Amongst the Baganda, for example, the bride's paternal aunt (*ssenga*) had a crucial role in determining the suitability of the intended groom. It may be important to distinguish between the role of female *members* as opposed to *non-members* of the clan in these arrangements. See also Musisi (1993).

11. The decision in the case of *Ayiiya v. Ayiiya*, reported as High Court Divorce Jurisdiction Case No. 8 of 1973 is to this effect. Contrary to the general belief that bridewealth flows from the groom's family to that of the bride, there are variations in the practice. Amongst the Bakiga of Southern Uganda for example, the bride's family give substantially to that of the groom. Amongst their Banyankole neighbours, there is a substantial flow of gifts between the families and to the couple.

12. See the case of *R v. Amkeyo* (1917) East African Court of Appeal, in which such marriages were characterized as a form of 'concubinage'.

13. Consequently, the decision in *Alai v. Uganda* (1967) EA makes an interesting contrast to that cited in the previous note. For a discussion, see Semafumu (1991).

14. These observations are based on the author's five-year experience of legal practice and involvement in popular legal education in Uganda. For a fuller discussion, see Semafumu (1991). Other information emerges from the interviews, discussed below.

15. All three women apparently shared their families' assessment of their chances on the marriage market. However, only the first said that this influenced her decision to marry her husband. Perceiving oneself as relatively unattractive to one's own cultural group would appear to predispose one to marrying out, see Khatib-Chahidi et al., this volume. It is worth recording that all those interviewed wanted to marry, regarding it as important for their personal happiness and for their standing within the family and wider social group.

16. Indeed, their views seemed to throw up fundamental questions about the extent to which a shared socio-economic group and educational background creates more of a common culture than does shared ethnicity or religion.

17. Islam arrived in Uganda earlier than Christianity. In the 1870s, the two faiths competed fiercely for royal converts, culminating in armed struggle in the 1880s. For a discussion and further references see Rowe (1988) 267–79 and especially 268–73.

18. Typically, these would include *okwanjula*, the formal introduction of the man to key members of the woman's family and clan. The brideprice, often just a token, would be set at this time, as would a date for completion of the series of pre-marriage exchanges. On this date, the man's representatives must fetch the bride, bringing with them certain customary items (*kasuzze katya*). Without this ceremony, she cannot leave her natal home, and customarily, if any single ceremony signifies that a marriage has been contracted, this is it.

19. See previous note.

20. For a comprehensive review of the evolution of the theory of legal pluralism, see Merry (1988: 869–96).

21. The social field here is comprised not necessarily of other couples in similar relationships, but of the particular couple and the circle of family and friends who are

party to, privy to, or witnesses to the arrangement arrived at by the couple, and whose censure would be aroused by breach of the agreement.

22. Important reservations exist about whether this kind of rule and sanction can properly be called law. Unfortunately, there is not the space to go into this discussion here, but see, for example, Tamanaha (1993: 192–217.)

23. The longer-term implications of opting for social rather than legal recognition for a relationship are especially important on the death of a partner, as enforceable rights to property often depend on whether there was a legal marriage.

References

Allot, A. (1970), *New Essays in African Law*, London: Butterworths.

Arblaster, A. (1984), *The Rise and Decline of Western Liberalism*, Oxford: Blackwell.

Griffiths, J. (1986), 'What is Legal Pluralism?', *Journal of Legal Pluralism*, 24(1), pp.1–55.

Kalema Report, Government of Uganda (1965), *Report of the Commission on Marriage, Divorce and the Status of Women*, Entebbe: Government Printers.

Merry, S.E. (1988), 'Legal Pluralism', *Law and Society Review*, 22(5), pp.869–96.

Moore, S.F. (1978), 'Law and Social Change: The Semi-Autonomous Social Field as an Appropriate Subject for Study', in S.F. Moore, *Law as Process: An Anthropological Approach*, London: Routledge & Kegan Paul.

Musisi, N. (1993), 'Women and State Formation in Buganda', in R. Collins (ed.), *Problems in African History*, Princeton and New York: Markus Wiener.

Rowe, J.A. (1988), 'Islam under Amin: a case of *déjà vu*?', in H. Hansen and M. Twaddle (eds), *Uganda Now: Between Decay and Development*, London and Nairobi: James Curry and Heinemann Kenya.

Semafumu, S. (1991), 'Between a Rock and a Hard Place? Women in the Pluralistic Legal Systems of Africa', conference paper at the Haldane Society 'Symposium on Africa, Democracy and the New World Order', London School of Economics, December.

Snyder, F. (1981), 'Colonialism and Legal Form: The Creation of "Customary Law" in Senegal', *Journal of Legal Pluralism*, 19, pp.49–90.

Tamale, S. and Okumu-Wengi, J. (1992), 'The Legal Status of Women in Uganda', in *Women and Law in East Africa*, Kampala: WLEA Publications.

Tamanaha, B. (1993), 'The Folly of the "Social Scientific" Concept of Legal Pluralism', *Journal of Law and Society*, 20, pp.192–217.

8

Love and the State: Women, Mixed Marriages and the Law in Germany

Rosemary Breger

The Course of True Love

Many anthropological and sociological models of marriage and the family in highly industrialized European and American societies implicitly assume that restrictions on spouse choice are primarily informal. Social scientists tend to look at socio-cultural or psychological factors influencing freedom of partner choice, but seldom at formal legal constraints and the public stereotypes and assumptions behind these.

In fact, the German state, like many other countries, imposes a wide range of formal constraints not only in defining what the state expects and tolerates in a marriage relationship, and thus in defining categories of acceptable marriage partners, but also in exercising a fairly tight control on its citizens' right under European law to marry non-nationals. Generally, the more atypical these outsiders are perceived to be, the more stringent the state control.

State interference with the right of its citizens to free choice of spouse encompasses delays and refusals to grant entry and temporary residence visas to the foreign spouse, delays and refusal to grant permission to marry, and restrictions on the foreign spouse's rights to reside and work in Germany. Furthermore, by fostering certain views about foreigners, the state contributes to and legitimizes by its very authority negative discourses about them. These discourses may find their way into how civil servants apply their powers of discretion when considering applications regarding marrying a foreigner; at the very least, they promote a general unease regarding Otherness.

The state thus clearly indicates that marriages with foreigners are undesirable, and defines foreigners through its actions as somehow inferior, and the right of free choice of spouse (Articles 12 and 14 of the European Human Rights Convention) is converted into a favour granted – unwillingly – by the state. There seem to be, arguably, three central related issues. One is controlling access to citizenship and the rights and duties it entails. Another concerns state ideology of marriage and the family, through which the reproduction of new citizens is controlled – or threatened – by outsider incorporation. Behind both of these is an uneasy national self-definition, complicated by the various nationalisms of Germany's past.

This paper takes a preliminary look at the personal implications of such laws, and at the assumptions and public discourses surrounding them. Given the difficulties mixed marriages face, perhaps one can contend that those which experience and survive the stress and tensions caused by formal factors and their by-products must be particularly strong!

The thoughts explored here are based on my own experiences, on those of about eighteen other mixed-marriage couples I knew well from fieldwork, academic and personal situations, on other experiences related in a cross-cultural women's group of which I was a member for about eighteen months, and on experiences related in a foreign students' club at my German university.

From Workers to Spouse: Foreigners in Germany

Historically, there have always been people from many different cultural origins living in the geographical area encompassed by modern Germany: given Germany's geographical position in central Europe, the complexities of European population movements and trading routes, this is hardly surprising. Furthermore, from the end of the nineteenth century until the mid 1970s, foreigners were actively recruited in large numbers by industry and state to work in Germany. For example, at the end of the nineteenth century, large numbers of Poles from Prussian-controlled Poland were recruited to work in the coal mining and smelting industries of the Ruhr, and then from 1955 onwards, Germany signed recruitment agreements with Italy (in 1955), then Spain and Greece (in 1960), Turkey (in 1961), Morocco (in 1963), Tunisia (in 1965) and finally Yugoslavia (in 1968). Recruitment stopped in 1973 in the face of the oil-based recession (Treibel 1990). At first, work permits and contracts were short term, but the cost of renewing the labour force every year caused industries to lobby government for longer and renewable contracts. This meant that many of these so-called *Gastarbeiter* (guest-workers) remained in Germany. Germany still, however, insists that it is not a country of immigration, and therefore sees no need to give its large population of foreigners any local, regional or national civil rights.

The vast majority of foreigners now living in Germany are thus recruited workers and their families, or the succeeding generations of such people. There is also a small number of people with refugee status, and an even smaller number of economic elite migrant groups: the managers and top employees of multinationals. By 1989, there were 4.8 million foreigners (7.5 per cent of the population), with Turks comprising nearly 32 per cent of all foreigners.

Marriages to non-Germans have increased slowly but steadily since the end of the Second World War. Mixed marriages comprised 7.7 per cent of all marriages registered in Germany in 1980, and 9 per cent in 1989 (Wolf-Almanasreh 1991 using government census data). There have been two obvious ways people come into contact with potential foreign spouses: firstly, children of migrant workers have been to German schools and made Germans friends, and secondly, since the 1960s, increased tourism especially within Europe has taken Germans to a wide range of countries, including those of their foreign-worker population. The following statistics refer only to marriages registered in Germany (source, Wolf-Almanasreh 1991).

An interesting feature is that German female exogamy (out-marriage) consistently exceeds male exogamy (as it does in France, the United Kingdom and the United States, cf. Barbara 1989; Spickard 1989; Crester 1990), with only 38 per cent of all exogamous marriages between 1969 and 1989 being between German men and foreign women (Wolf-Almanasreh 1991, p.23ff.). From his research on mixed marriages in France, Barbara (1989) maintains that the weaker a social group is, the more likely it will control the out-marriage of its women, who become what he calls 'forbidden persons'. However, as discussed in the Introduction here, this assumes that marriage preferences are all controlled – and subscribed to – by the ethnic group. It ignores that the majority culture, as well as other minority ethnic groups, may themselves construct social distances and choose not to marry persons from a particular group (e.g. Spickard's (1989) discussion of the role of stereotyping and physical appearance in maintaining social distances). It also does not account for the fact that Japanese and Chinese women in America, from the beginning of this century onwards, when they belonged to very low-status groups, consistently preferred to marry out, whereas their men preferred to send back to the home country for their brides (Spickard 1989; Lee and Yamanaka 1990; Lee Sung 1990).

In addition, German men and women tend to choose foreign spouses from different groups of countries, see Figure 8.1. Wolf-Almanasreh (1991) noted that choices of foreign partner have changed as home economic conditions have changed, and as borders have become more permeable, especially to the east (see the Introduction for a discussion of factors influencing choice).

German women have shown a long and marked first preference for husbands from the United States, amounting to between 12 per cent and 25 per cent of all foreign husbands. Italians, Austrians and Yugoslavs, and within the last fifteen years Turks, have all ranked next highest in choice of husbands. Altogether, men from central Europe account for about 60 per cent of their exogamous marriages. Men from Asia, particularly Iran, India and Pakistan, form up to 10 per cent of choices, from Africa up to 8 per cent, whereas only a tiny percentage are chosen from South and Middle America.

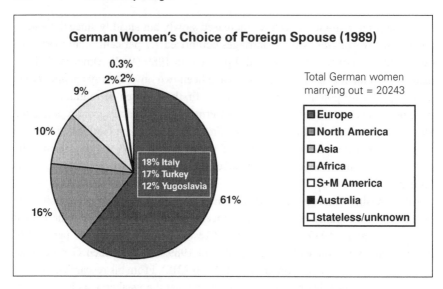

German Women's Choice of Foreign Spouse (1989)

0.3%
2% 2%
9%
10%
16%

18% Italy
17% Turkey
12% Yugoslavia

61%

Total German women
marrying out = 20243

■ Europe
▨ North America
▨ Asia
□ Africa
□ S+M America
■ Australia
□ stateless/unknown

German Men's Choice of Foreign Spouse (1989)

0.3%
5% 1%
4%
20%
4%

20% Poland
17% Yugoslavia
11% Austria

66%

Total German men
marrying out = 15669

Source: Wolf-Almanasreh 1991 pp.28–9, own calculations and graphics

Figure 8.1.   German Choice of Foreign Spouse (1989)

Very little systematic research on a sufficiently large scale has looked at these gendered patterns of choice, so that the reasons suggested below should be seen as working hypotheses, still to be tested. Perhaps one can conjecture that American men were favoured in the past as a means of escaping a war-ravaged home, and later, because the United States still exerts a glamorous fascination on many young

Germans, with a popular myth of freedom of living and self-expression. Perhaps many German women choose Italian and Turkish men because of the seduction of the exotic stereotypes (see Kohn's and Waldren's chapters, this volume): swarthy Mediterranean good looks, a flirtatious enjoyment of women's company (not often expressed by young German men in the same way), and an open *joie de vivre*. Although these are stereotypes, there is certainly a core of truth in the different types of and attitudes to flirtation and courtship rituals. It is more difficult to speculate about why nearly a tenth of foreign marriages are with men from different parts of Asia. Many came to study at German universities, and met their partners there. Some were met during travel, and some were foreign workers or their children, born and brought up in Germany.

German men marry out far less frequently than do German women. Women from Europe and Asia are their favoured choices of foreign spouse, see Figure 8.1. Two-thirds of their foreign brides in 1989 were from Europe, especially Poland, Yugoslavia, Austria and Italy. As the border to Poland opened, there was an enormous increase in percentage of brides from Poland, from less than 10 per cent in 1987 to over 20 per cent in 1989. The number of brides from Asia, particularly the main countries of sex tourism, has risen over the last ten years from being negligible to amounting to about one-fifth of all foreign brides. Proportionately, German men marry half as many Africans than do German women, and only one-quarter as many Americans.

As working hypotheses, one could suggest two main sets of reasons which could plausibly affect men's marriage choices. One is to do with constraints placed upon women. Choices of wives could be restricted by the wife-giving group; some cultures may guard marriage access to their daughters more strictly than to their sons especially when the group is politically a minority, as Barbara (1989) suggests. In addition, control over and discrimination against women often means that when a child is sent abroad (e.g. to Germany) either to work or to university, it is often the son and not the daughter who is sent, resulting in higher proportions of foreign male students and workers than female. The other set of reasons is to do with German men's own choices, which involve their definitions of gendered marriage roles, masculinity and femininity.

To determine why Polish women should prove to be such popular brides currently, we need to consider firstly whether their German husbands are themselves of Polish origin. In the Ruhr area especially, there is a large minority of descendants of Polish indentured labourers, who came to work in the Ruhr mines from Prussian-held Polish territories. Perhaps men from such families still have some connections with Poland and met future brides on visits there, or perhaps they felt a desire to develop a sense of their Polish heritage via marriage. This information is, unfortunately, now largely unavailable. Secondly, some work on current life in Poland indicates that Polish women accept the dual or even triple burden of work, sometimes with two jobs and housework, and do not expect male help, in other words, they are willing to impose immense burdens on themselves with strength and resourcefulness (Höllinger and Haller 1990). It remains conjecture, but perhaps some conservative German men may choose such strong partners, who accept a strictly gendered division of labour and authority at home, in preference to more feminist-aware German women.

The latter reason certainly plays a part in unreconstructed German men choosing women from the Philippines and Thailand as partners. There has long existed in German literature (dating back to the sixteenth century, cf. Breger 1990) and in the media an image of the exotic, sensual, subservient 'Asian' woman, whose chief aim, according to this stereotype, is to please and obey her husband. This is so prevalent that there is a widespread notion amongst certain sectors of German men that in fact Asian women make far better wives than German women, with their 'aggressive anti-male feminism'. This in turn has resulted in marriage bureaux being opened in several Asian countries, such as the Philippines, Taiwan and Thailand, and it is mostly through these that such brides have been found. These bureaux seek primarily foreign brides for German men and not foreign husbands for German women. Some of these institutions are barely a cover for prostitution rings extending to Europe, but some do actually broker wives for a fee to both parties. Conservative tabloids in particular emphasize the contrast between such 'feminine' and praiseworthy Asian women, compared with 'hard', 'selfish' and 'unloving' German women who have supposedly lost their femininity through feminism (Breger 1990). It is no coincidence that the majority of Asian wives come from the main sex tourism countries visited by German men: sadly, wife as obedient but active sex object, dependent on male attention and money sometimes sums up the (expected) power relationship fairly accurately, see below.

Nation-State and Imagined Community

Historically, the rise of nation-states has meant that within the debate about citizenship rights and duties, certain membership criteria have become important politically, legally and ideologically (and therefore highly charged), such as the notion of sharing a common culture or common values (Gouldbourne 1991). The notion of nationality, of forging a common political membership on the basis of an assumed common culture and language, that is, the somewhat coercive creation of an imagined community on a national level, has played a central role in the history of Germany at least since the beginning of the nineteenth century, and still does (Snyder 1978; Smith 1986; Turner 1990). The existence of foreigners and of cross-cultural marriages within the society both highlights the contested non-homogenous nature of national identity, as well as acting as a foil against which national identities can be developed, hardened and publicized (Hobsbawm and Ranger 1983; Gluck 1985; Mouer and Sugimoto 1986; MacDonald 1994; Essed 1995).

To understand the political role of nationalism in Germany, one must remember that before the Napoleonic conquest, there were 1,789 sovereign entities in the German geographical area, reduced to thirty-eight at the Congress of Vienna in 1815. The Germanic principalities were unified only in 1871. These various polities by no means shared the same values, nor even followed the same dominant cultural centres (there were French, Austrian and Prussian-based cultural centres). Regionalism prevailed; there was not even an accepted standard German language until Bismarck's *Kulturkampf* policies deliberately reduced these diversities via educational and administrative centralization reforms (Snyder 1978; Smith 1986). There was no sense of any unified German nation as such prior to this. Currently, Germany is undergoing yet another public debate regarding nation, identity and belonging consequent to reunification and the incorporation into the German nation-state not only of East Germany, but also of German migrant communities from various parts of the old Soviet Union. As Räthzel (1995) points out, national unification is never 'complete', it is an ongoing process.

The German romantics of the nineteenth century played a key role in deliberately creating a sense of overarching identity. Through their strong selective emphasis on old Germanic folk tales, they created pan-Germanic national heroes out of saga figures, and pan-Germanic virtues out of their characters. Romantics fiercely believed in an identifiable and unique German spirit, an inherent national character based on blood line: free to experience inner emotions, untainted by French rationalism, heroic, where brave deeds counted high. This spirit was to be found amongst the *Volk*, the rural life and rural traditions. In romanticism's idealized and moralistic dichotomy between pure nature and corrupt town, it was assumed that these 'rural traditions' were all the same. It was clear not only to philosophers such as Hegel and Fichte, but also to musicians (e.g. Wagner), writers (e.g. the Grimm brothers), and most importantly, politicians such as Bismarck, that the concept of a national character, assumed to be deeply embedded in ancient folk traditions and history, could help unify the diversity of the Germanies (Snyder 1978; Smith 1986). This was further supported by nineteenth-century evolutionary theories, which assumed a hierarchy of civilization and development of humankind, with white Europeans at the apex. The German, Christoph Meiner, produced a simple classification based on the beauty of white and the ugliness of black. His work influenced Gobineau, who developed the concept of a master Aryan race in *Essai sur l'inegalité des races humaines*, which became one of the underpinning works bolstering Nazi racism (Burke 1972).

The significance of the notion of national character, besides as a political rallying cry, is that it assumes there *is* such a thing as a majority culture, common to all regions and classes, without internal conflict, unchanging; a closed monolithic culture, whose edges are easily identifiable. Germany had never been such. Räthzel (1995: 165) maintains that a superordinate collective definition of Self, a unifying concept of 'German' that incorporates not only the regional differences within both West and East Germany, but also the political traditions and economic practices between the old 'West' and 'East' Germanies, is one way in which post-reunification Germany attempts to overcome 'horizontal differences and vertical antagonisms to form a shaky unity'. It furthermore assumes personality traits are inherent, therefore difficult if not impervious to change. 'National character' is supposedly characteristic of an entire group of people, irrespective of age, class and region. This concept has far-reaching significance when civil servants use their discretionary powers to 'judge' whether a foreigner can be granted certain rights for which the principle of 'ability to integrate and accept German culture' is central. So in this way, culture becomes politicized.

The concept of collective Self is necessarily linked to that of collective Other (Said 1978; Miller 1982; Kreiner 1984; Dower 1986) in what Gamson and Modigliani (1989) called 'sets of interpretive packages' within the broad discourse. Intrinsic to this is evaluation of both Self and Other within changing socio-economic contexts. Where Other's differences to Self are emphasized, instead of similarities, Other is constructed as alien, positively as a mirror of what Self has lost, or negatively as a threat. The most dangerous construction of Other is as the 'enemy within' the state, which constructs groups of resident foreigners stereotypically and racially as, at best, a social problem, at worst a national threat (see below; see also the media analyses by Link 1985; Thränhardt 1985; Merten 1986). Räthzel notes that even the most sympathetic media discourses on foreigners tend to present them in terms of social problems, thereby immediately invoking the state's powers to interfere – to aid or to restrict – and thus in the process also reaffirming the power of the state. It results in the implicit assumption, reinforced by law and collective self-definitions, that Other cannot be allowed to be manifestly different and expect to be accorded equal rights or status.

It also results in governments – and social scientists – espousing policies and theories envisaging the incorporation of outsiders, if this is to be done at all, only by way of 'integration'. When looked at in detail, this almost always means becoming like the majority, giving up public domain statements of cultural difference. Behind this there lurks the assumption therefore that there is indeed a 'national culture' and 'national character', however 'collaged' these may be out of personal prejudices and stereotypes, and Germany's history of nationalisms. In Germany, as in many other nation-states, integration forms a leading principle in naturalization law, which civil servants must apply when considering foreigners' claims in areas where they have discretionary powers, such as naturalization requests, marriage applications, or residence and work restrictions.

The Tyranny of the Observer: Foreigners as a Social Problem

German officials have the right to apply their discretion in deciding on the acceptability of a foreign spouse, and thus of the marriage, in accepting foreign documentation, imposing limitations on the length of the first residence permit, and on deciding which rights are retained or forfeit in cases of divorce or death.

German law is restrictive, but in many cases open to interpretation. Nevertheless, it is clear that foreigners are not generally regarded highly, and that access to all levels of civil and citizenship rights is strictly protected. Castles (1984: 77) quotes the guidelines for officials in how to apply the 1965 FRG Foreigners Law: 'Foreigners enjoy all basic rights, except the basic rights of freedom of assembly, freedom of association, freedom of movement and free choice of occupation, place of work and place of education and protection from extradition abroad' (cited in Cohen 1993: 122).

Earlier studies of German-media discourses about foreigners, such as those by Scheuch (1982), Götze (1985), Thränhardt (1985), Merten (1986) and Breger (1990) indicated the existence of a widely held hierarchy of acceptability, depending on the nationality and culture of the group of foreigners. At the top of the hierarchy are those groups of foreigners considered almost equals, who are often portrayed neutrally if not sometimes positively in the media. They tend to look similar to Germans, have a culture that seems similar, and their countries are powerful and wealthy trading partners. At the bottom are groups of foreigners who are considered completely alien, and who are often portrayed very negatively in the media. They tend to come from cultures considered very unfamiliar and different to German cultures, where physical differences are easily noted, and whose countries are neither important trading partners, nor very significant politically in current German politics, that is, their images parallel the power relationships between the countries (Foucault 1980).

These cultures are often portrayed in terms of the racist concept of 'national character', and their cultures as 'lesser' cultures, 'less developed', 'less wealthy', 'less democratic'. Merten (1986) showed how groups of foreigners were constructed in terms of 'social problems', in which stereotyped negative character traits were said to cause the 'foreigner problems' in Germany, and that the mere presence of foreigners was often depicted as being threatening to German culture, values and interests. Furthermore, typical of the hegemonic relationship between majority and minority, foreigners very seldom speak for themselves even in positive representations: mostly German authors write about them, or largely ignore any voice from them, in what Said aptly called 'the tyranny of the observer', and Ardener called 'muting' (Ardener 1978; Said 1978; Merten 1986; Breger 1990, 1992). Räthzel (1995) later noted that different German groups have differing ideas about which sets of foreigners could perhaps be incorporated into an expanded concept of 'nation' consequent to reunification. For example, liberals in former West Germany have agitated to include long-term Turkish residents within a broader concept of nation, whereas conservatives favour an end to any admission of foreigners, except the so-called ethnic Germans (German communities from abroad, especially from the former Soviet Union). What Räthzel is saying therefore is that the notion of German nation today, unlike under fascism, is open to (fierce) debate about diversity and inclusion or exclusion.

This discourse is also gendered. Foreign men are often portrayed as criminally dangerous, sexually threatening (e.g. Wobbe 1995), and as direct competition for 'honest' German men's work. The reality, however, is more that 'guest-workers' were hired for the lowest status, worst-paid jobs, competing for these more amongst themselves and young unskilled German workers (Heckmann 1981; Korte 1987). Foreign women tend to be portrayed as culturally beyond integration, keeping to themselves at home within the heart of their ethnic community. As mothers, they supposedly teach their children ethnic customs and mores, which are often presented as inimical to German culture. In this way, the home is portrayed as the centre of ethnic identity and practices (i.e. the gendering of the 'ethnic essence', cf. McDonald 1994). Their motherhood is demonized by criticizing ethnic fertility rates, while their children are represented as a source of social problems through their supposed potential to delinquency, which is perceived as an unwelcome drain, or scrounging, on state welfare meant for German citizens' needs. Foreign mothers and their families are thus being constructed as morally outside the 'norm', outside the 'imagined community' (cf. Introduction, in Lutz et al. 1995).

Wobbe (1995: 93), in her work on the gendered construction of community in Germany, notes that the latter is closely linked with the construction of sexual vulnerability in relation to the gendered power to violate ('our' women are threatened by 'their' men's aggressive and dangerous sexuality): '. . . as a powerful instrument of social closure . . . gender relations occupy one of the central dimensions in the construction of community/*Gemeinschaft*' (p.91). If public officials accept this sort of discourse uncritically, it must surely affect their decision-making.

Entering the Citadel: Entry Visas and Permission to Marry

There are several legal barriers foreigners must pass before being allowed to marry a German and remain and work in Germany, some of which are applicable to all foreigners seeking residence in the country, whether they marry a German or not. Briefly these are:

to prove that the marriage is 'proper' and not one of convenience, i.e. the rule of primary purpose;

to supply the authorities with certain documents, depending on reason for residence, but always including a police clearance statement from the home police without which they will not be granted permission to marry;

to undergo a medical examination by a state doctor, the exact obligatory extent of which varies from *Bundesland* to *Bundesland* and which includes an AIDS test in Bavaria;

if they want to work in their professional field, they should apply to the *Kultusministerium* or appropriate professional body to have their foreign qualifications recognized and be given an equivalent German status;

and if they work in areas protected by professional bodies and national law such as medicine and pharmacy, they are not allowed to practise unless a definite benefit to the state can be proven, and a need for such workers that Germans cannot provide can be shown.

Foreigners who seem as though they will require state support, either because of chronic ill-health or disability, or through lack of employment chances, are also refused permission to marry.

When a mixed-nationality couple decides to get married in Germany, they are immediately faced with problems caused by laws restricting entry and residence of the foreign partner. Because there is a range of conditions applicable to allowing foreign fiancé/es to enter and remain in Germany, the authorities have the power to use their own discretion in applying or modifying them, and in expediting or slowing down the process of application. Thus, the personal stereotypes and prejudices of individual civil servants can influence the ease with which a couple starts a life together.

Becoming engaged to a German citizen does not automatically give the foreign fiancé/e any right to reside in Germany; not even a tourist visa will be granted once marriage has been mentioned. Partners from countries requiring tourist visas need to apply for permits to enter Germany in order to marry, or, if already married abroad, in order to 'bring the family together'. This generally takes between six to twelve months to obtain (Wolf-Almanasreh 1991: 81). If the couple can prove that they are doing their utmost to get married as soon as possible, temporary permits are issued to the date of the marriage. However, it is up to the civil servant dealing with the case to decide what proof to accept or not. In my own case, applying from abroad for a visa to enter Germany to get married there was met by complete surprise and unpleasantness from the petty official at the desk. Luckily the official had to ask the senior officer on duty about the course of action he should take. The latter recognized my husband's name and came to deal with us personally, with a great deal of friendly advice and support, to the extent of providing me with a covering letter allowing me – against the normal course of action – to obtain German character references once I had entered Germany, and not before.

My husband had tutored his daughter at the university, and she had reported that it was thanks to him that she had passed her exams.

Official guidelines require that one of the primary considerations is to check whether those concerned – and especially non-EU citizens – are attempting to use marriage to a German citizen only as a means of gaining access to residence and work permits, thus invoking the 'primary purpose of marriage' rule. *Standesamt* (Registry) officials are required to ask whether the marriage is for 'proper' purposes; that is those of procreation and family building envisaged by Father State and Father Church in their ideologies of family and gender roles. Thereby, women are immediately associated through their domestic reproductive roles and therefore also through their bodies with the vulnerable ethnic centre; it is part of the social construction of family roles that ascribes parenting responsibilities primarily to women, ignoring any role fathers could play except as providers (Barker 1978; see also Evans 1993 on sexual citizenship).

This often leads to the most intimate and probing questions being asked. If a young couple says that they do not want any children, although they have no health reason for not having a family, permission to marry is always refused. 'Suspect' couples may also be checked up on after marriage, although this is actually now illegal. I myself was subject to two such visits, whereby the official said he wanted to see if I was 'settling in easily', but the wish to look over the apartment (to check that my husband and I were indeed living together), questions as to the whereabouts of my husband, and the suspicion regarding lack of family photographs made me realize that something else was at issue.

The German state also recognizes as legitimate marriages only love marriages: arranged marriages with foreign brides are deeply suspect and often result in entry-permit refusals (as happens in England). The great irony of this position is that non-arranged love marriages have become common in Europe only in the last century, and form an extremely small percentage of all marriages worldwide (see Kohn, this volume, on the flexibility of arranged marriages).

Permission to marry is given only when the couple has produced all the documents required by law; delays in waiting for documents to arrive, in getting them translated, and then getting them accepted by the authorities as valid equivalents can amount to over a year, during which time any previously granted visa may have expired, forcing the foreign partner to leave the country. This has happened so often that the IAF (*Interessen Gemeinschaft der mit Ausländer verheirateten Frauen*, rather awkwardly translated as Lobby Group of Women married to Foreigners), an association formed by German women married to foreign men, regards this as a deliberate strategy to hinder mixed marriages. What is perhaps not immediately obvious is the human side of delays: not just frustration, anger, enforced parting, but also that foreign fiancé/es have generally given up their jobs in their home countries in order to move to Germany, so may have no secure income to return to, and no way of knowing how long either home or German authorities may take with providing and approving papers. Added to this is the burden of a return fare, which may be very high. This is not a good emotional start to a marriage.

The IAF also reports that officials can be particularly tardy and unhelpful in cases of German women wanting to marry foreign men. It notes that officials may ask such women to show why they are not marrying Germans before stamping letters to embassies or passports for the foreign fiancé; they may also be warned in the most lurid terms about the lifestyle in the country of their fiancé, and several have been insulted.

> For example, G, a highly educated German women was helping her fiancé, who was an Indian from Uganda, to obtain all his papers. He had obtained higher degrees in England and Germany, but nevertheless the official dealing with the case insisted on calling him a barely educated 'primitive'. The official warned her that she would be expected to live in strictest purdah within an unaccepting and over-crowded household, and to bear child after child until she had had at least five or six sons. He said that she was wasting her blonde beauty, and demanded to see her parents to ascertain that they approved of the marriage, even though she was above the age of consent, because he did not want to be party to such a potential family disaster. She refused, and it was only after enduring a great deal more of this harrassment that the official finally continued with the case. (Many years later, they are still happily married, living in a sophisticated, cosmopolitan environment.)

Previously, women automatically lost their German citizenship on marrying a foreigner. This seems to indicate that in this situation German women are being constructed as 'signifiers of community' (Wobbe 1995), the gendered centre of ethnic identity ideologically and through their bodies, so that their wish to marry outsiders, especially those constructed negatively, is equated with betrayal. It is common for such Germans and even more so for foreigners to be addressed in the familiar '*du*', as indeed I was, which is considered enough of an insult for police to take students who so address them to court. The cumulative effect of this institutionalized and personal racism can be highly demoralizing when combined with go-slow tactics, a long separation, and possibly similar prejudices from family and friends. In keeping with the research on the hierarchy of foreignness, it seems that the more different – and darker – the foreigner is and his culture is seen to be, the more resistance is met with from officials.

Although German men marrying foreign women may also be exposed to the same prejudice, anecdotally it seems to depend on where their wives come from. As noted earlier, wives from Asia and Poland tend to be considered more positively, even an asset.

P (German) was a young talented student. On an exchange programme to the United States, he met and fell in love with his Japanese wife, M, also visiting the USA on an exchange programme. They each returned to their respective countries, but after their schooling and first few years of university, they decided to get married. P wanted to marry in Germany. In the course of arranging matters with the authorities, he was at first hampered by an immigration official who asked him outright why he did not choose a German girl. P made a joke of the issue; some months later when his fiancée arrived, they returned together to the same official to complete the paperwork. The official took one look at M, who is beautiful, graceful and petite, and said, meaning to compliment P, that he understood why P should choose such a beautiful woman, who knew her place – which was in P's bed.

Foreign spouses, but especially wives from Asia who have been brokered through marriage bureaux, may be at a great disadvantage in Germany: many can speak no German at all, and therefore cannot work, or at least work only in areas where understanding is of minimal importance, such as shelf-stackers or packers. This means that they are economically dependent on their husbands. It also means that all dealings with the outside world must be brokered through their husbands, who literally become 'cultural brokers'. In case of marriage breakdown, they can seldom call on their own families for support, not only because of the impracticalities of distance and cost, but also because their families may have vested interests in keeping their daughters in Germany, and would in addition lose face if they returned. It is inevitable that the wife's total dependency on her husband's goodwill makes her particularly vulnerable.

K was one such wife from the Philippines. She had been living in Germany for two-and-a-half years, and could hardly speak German. She had one baby daughter. The relationship deteriorated; she had no access to money, and her husband (a university lecturer) sometimes beat her. She took her daughter and left him, staying with a Taiwanese friend. Quite by chance, he saw her one day, and threatened to call the police and have her deported if she did not return to him. Since she knew that her daughter would remain with him according to German law (where in such cases the welfare of the child is taken to be paramount and to depend greatly on keeping the child in the cultural environment it knows best), she obeyed. She felt she could not call the police because they would not believe her, and she would be forced to leave Germany and return to the Philippines, which she could not do because her family would not take her back if she disappointed them in this way.

Once married, the foreign partner is generally granted a residence permit. The Aliens Act of 1990 stipulates that at first it should be valid for three years, after which it can be renewed without time limit, as a permanent residence permit, as long as the couple remains together and lives in Germany, but it also allows the authorities to limit the first permit to less than three years should they feel there is reason. Under European law, European Community citizens are entitled to a first-time permit of five years. After this period, the foreign spouse is entitled to apply for – but not necessarily obtain – the right of abode, and to apply for citizenship. There is widespread lack of information about the different residence rights; many foreigners do not know that the more generous right of abode exists, or of the difference between the two rights. Many, as I did, accept with relief the granting of a permanent residence permit, and do not think of enquiring further about it until it is revoked. The IAF considers that this, too, is deliberate disinformation policy. Certainly it is up to the person concerned to inform herself about such issues, but not once in all my dealings with the *Ausländeramt* (Foreigners' Office) was I informed about its limitations or other forms of abode except naturalization: a friend of a friend, whom I met socially at times, worked for the *Ausländeramt*, and she refrained from telling me, despite our many conversations about related issues. Permanent residence applies only while living together in Germany; all residence and employment rights are immediately forfeit if the foreign partner or both partners live outside Germany for longer than a six-month period. The procedure of applying for residence and employment rights starts again on return to Germany.

Should a foreign partner commit a crime, these rights are immediately re-examined with a strong gender bias directly relating to the discourse that portrays foreign men as potentially far more dangerous than foreign women. Foreign men who commit imprisonable crimes often lose all rights and are deported, whereas, depending on the severity of the crime, foreign women are often not deported (Wolf-Almanasreh 1991).

In case of separation, divorce or death of the German spouse, the foreign spouse will be allowed to remain in Germany only under certain conditions if the marriage is less than three years old; if the pair has been living abroad immediately before the end of the marriage, the foreign spouse no longer necessarily has any right to return to Germany. Children will be given in custody to the parent who seems best fit to take them, taking into consideration where the child has its normal place of residence and 'feels at home', so a foreign divorced parent may not be allowed to renew his or her residence permit, and the children are given into the custody of the parent remaining in Germany, because that will be least disruptive to the child's life. Visiting rights from Africa, India, or the Philippines would then be meaningless. German husbands used this as a threat to coerce wives in two cases in my small sample.

German citizenship is not a right granted automatically to foreign spouses. The latter may apply for naturalization only after three years of unbroken legal abode in Germany after marriage, and the process can last several years. However, naturalization is bestowed only if the candidate is 'integrated' or 'integrable', with officials using their powers of discretion to judge each case individually. The law lays down that at the very least integration involves the ability to speak and understand the German language, interact within German culture, and an understanding and acceptance of the political principles in a democracy. This is checked on in the extensive personal interviews involved in the process of applying for citizenship, which are conducted in German. In practice, it also means that the official can include her or his own ideas. Thus, 'German culture' is set up against 'ethnic cultures' in a highly politicizing relationship, in which cultural difference is constructed as potentially dangerous. Garcia (1992) maintains that Germany has some of the most discriminatory and strictly applied rules for obtaining citizenship in Europe.

B, a German citizen resident in England, visited the German embassy in London to register his child's birth, and at the same time to enquire about the possibility of his Nigerian wife becoming naturalized. The official demanded very rudely why his wife should now, after so many years, want a German passport. He insinuated that she was trying to bring in some large, poverty-stricken family to feed off Germany's over-generous welfare system. He then asked by what right she wanted to become German; what had she to offer to the German people, the state? After all, as an African, he continued, could she even read and write? Was B even aware that a basic requirement was the ability to speak German, and to accept the laws of democracy, which were so foreign to Africa. B, furious, told the official that his wife had a doctoral degree from a German university. The official answered that her education had been at the cost of the German tax-payer [which indeed it had been, as all university tuition costs are paid for by the state], so that she was already in the habit of living off the state. He ended by stating that German citizenship was a privilege to be granted after due consideration, and not thrown away to all and sundry. That was the end of that effort to gain information.

Work, Income and Self-esteem

There is an insidious feedback effect between public stereotypes and the policies that are influenced by, and influence, them. On the broadest level, the state is saying in many ways that foreigners are undesirable, unwelcome, suspect, and it is hard not to be affected by constant reminders of this xenophobia. One of the key areas in which this occurs is employment of foreigners. Paid employment is not only an economic necessity for most of us, but in a late capitalist society, it also still provides a central means to self-recognition and public approval.

Although spouses of German citizens automatically acquire a work permit as long as they have a residence permit, that does not mean they will find the type of work they are seeking, or even find work at all: there is still the enormous issue of previous training and experience being accepted by future employers. It is in the interests of both employers and closed professional bodies to undergrade foreign qualifications. Curiously, foreign experience, achieved either by being foreign and bringing other skills into a job, or in the case of a German, by having lived abroad, still seems to be considered rather damaging to a person's career, except perhaps in higher management positions in industry, since it is considered preferable to stay at home to establish and maintain the right networks within the highly competitive German employment market. Combined with a halting command of the language, it is not surprising that the foreign spouse is at an economic dis-advantage both in the employment market and in the marital relationship: economic asymmetry or downright dependence in the marriage relationship creates a potentially conflict-laden power imbalance (see Refsing's discussion on employment and gendered roles, this volume).

The regional *Kultusministerium* grade foreign qualifications; this process can take up to two years, costs money, and the results may not be accepted by another *Bundesland*. Problems occur when there is no equivalent grade or status, or there is not seen to be one. Universities often have special measures to grade foreign students, as do large employers.

One case-study was of a German man with a wife from a New Commonwealth Country. Both had obtained first-class Masters degrees at Commonwealth universities, and wanted to have their degrees recognized by the Bavarian authorities (who are notorious for not willingly recognizing school qualifications even of other *Bundesländer*). They approached the Ludwig Maximillian University of Munich, where, after lengthy interviews, they were told that their first degrees as well as their post-graduate degrees were worthless, because Bavarian children went to school for more years than other children. In addition, they were told that if it were difficult for other, non-Bavarian German schooling to be accepted, and German schooling was amongst the best in Europe, it would be highly unlikely that schooling from 'some poor third-world country' could even be remotely comparable. Bavarian university therefore began at a higher level, and thus the Bavarian end degree was at a generally higher level than most other university degrees. The Masters degrees might perhaps be considered equivalent to a four-year diploma, but this would require a special exam committee to meet and exams to be written, since no one had ever heard of a Masters degree: they did not exist in Germany. The couple was asked if Master's degrees were a peculiarity of Commonwealth universities. As the couple left the rector's office, they saw a huge poster offering Master's courses in physics, geology and computer science at that very university. They left without any formal recognition of their qualifications and decided to obtain these through the *Kultusministerium*. It took nearly six months for all the required documents to be obtained; after waiting another eighteen months without any sign of success, they abandoned the effort. The man was employed during this period as though his highest qualification were a low-status 4-year diploma from a technical college, and not a university research degree, that is, as a technician, meaning that unlike other engineers he would not qualify for promotion to the next salary scale.

In finding jobs, foreign women have to cope with the double disadvantage of being foreign with foreign qualifications, and with being female. There are very few childcare facilities in Germany, and there is a prevalent discourse of femininity propagated by various ministers, as well as by the Catholic church, that a good mother is one who spends all her time with her children, and that the most important bond in a child's life is to its mother (cf. also Hoecklin's work, 1996, on the gender ideologies surrounding – and largely accepted and perpetuated by – housewives in Bavaria). Prospective employers still generally ask female candidates whether they have children, and what will become of them if they work.

Foreigners who wish to work in some protected professions, such as medicine, pharmacy, or in restricted areas of science where there is a fear of information and material theft, must prove there is a national need for their expertise that cannot be filled by a German citizen. This can be done only with the cooperation of the future employer, in other words if the person has already been offered a position. In addition, partners from non-EU states are not allowed to be self-employed, or to work in employed situations resembling self-employment (Wolf-Almanasreh 1991).

Retreat and Reaffirmation

The institutionalized xenophobia that defines foreigners as threatening and erects such daunting barriers plays an important role in limiting their life chances. Abdulrahim (1993), as many others before her, notes in her work on Palestinians in Berlin that rejection by the host society may lead those affected to reappraise their identity, in the process of which they form a highly idealized – and politicized – view of their ethnic identity. This they express privately, within the private and domestic sphere, where people feel they can still exert some personal control over their lives. Because it is embedded in the private sphere, it generally relates to (male) control over female behaviour, that is, it centres the core of ethnic identity in feminine behaviour (Burton et al. 1994; MacDonald 1994; Chinchaladze and Dragadze 1994; Lutz et al. 1995). In this situation, it can be very difficult for mixed couples to be welcomed and incorporated into the ethnic 'community' (whereby the 'community' may be more imagined, and far less cohesive than the term suggests).

Public-domain rejection can lead to both partners questioning the host culture. Within my sample, this was often accompanied by an over-idealization of the foreign partner's culture, involving a reaffirmation of the worth of the foreign Self, of what German law and culture reject. Where such a reaction occurred, a common strategy was to participate energetically in the appropriate ethnic 'community' where this was present, thus retreating from the majority culture. This was always presented as deliberately creating a new identity in which the relationship could exist with some self-esteem. However, there was not always ready acceptance by the ethnic group concerned. In such cases, people then often joined the religion of their foreign partner especially in cases of proselytizing sects of Islam and Buddhism, who by definition rely on bringing strangers into the fold and incorporating them.

> For example, many German–Japanese couples participated in Buddhist meetings. One such couple lived in Düsseldorf where there is a small but economically powerful Japanese business community. They were not accepted into it, although E (the Japanese husband) worked for one of the Japanese multinationals situated there. Instead, they found acceptance and social and self-esteem within the very active multicultural Nichiren Daishonin Buddhist group. There were many Japanese–German couples in this group, where the ability of the Japanese partner to read Japanese and to have some deeper understanding of Buddhist thought was considered by those with no knowledge of either to be vitally important in conveying to newcomers the essential message of the sect. In this way, that which is 'foreign' [here, being Japanese] is defined as crucially important.

Another alternative was for mixed couples to join or form societies for mixed partnerships. For example, the Foreign Students' Club at my university was dominated by such couples from many different countries, and there was an explicit, well articulated feeling of being rejected or marginalized by other student bodies.

A variation of this is the formation of women's self-help groups. These exist in many countries, formed by women in mixed marriages rather than their menfolk. This means that they are sometimes formed by indigenous wives of foreign men, as in Japan, or the IAF in Germany which is a (legally registered) society formed by German women married to foreigners (Wolf-Almanasreh 1991, see above), or by the foreign wives of indigenous men, such as the foreign wives' associations in Nigeria, France and Japan (Cottrell 1990; Imamura 1990). They can be local or national, informal, or formally registered. At my German university, there was an informal group which met weekly of foreign women married to Germans, led by German women (most of whom were married to Germans in this case) within the

Protestant mission at the university. These groups all tend to serve not only social needs, but to cope with practical, employment and legal issues, such as foreign-language learning, residence and employment rights, visas and citizenship issues, property ownership, divorce and inheritance issues. The objectives of these associations tend to revolve around providing their members with friendship, support, mutual help, in general helping each other to cope with these sorts of practical issues that directly affect themselves or their husbands, and their children.

It is easy to understand why marginalized foreigners would form such associations under disadvantaged conditions. What is interesting to note, however, is that even when the husbands are (disadvantaged) foreigners, while their wives are not, it is the women who form these societies and not the men. Naïve feminist answers maintain that women form these associations because they are excluded from so-called malestream society; this ignores that in many of these situations it is the husbands and not the wives who are marginalized. While no one would argue that women do not suffer discrimination in their own home countries, in this situation their foreign husbands may very probably be even more marginalized than they are.

Essed (1995) gives some insight into the structures and types of ethnic associations based on her own personal experiences in the Netherlands, although she does not look at the specific case of cross-cultural spouses and foreign wives' associations. She claims that ethnic associations tend to be gendered, with ethnic men holding most of the positions of power within them. Therefore ethnic women tend to form their own gendered groups either within the ethnic organizations, or across them, which deal broadly with issues of discrimination common to women. She maintains that ethnic women's exclusion from power within their own organizations in fact helps to free them from cross-ethnic rivalries. Ethnic men, on the other hand, have a stake in maintaining their ethnic identity, therefore they are less willing to form cross-ethnic alliances to lobby for common causes. Essed does not go on to ask whether women would behave differently if they, too, had positions of power to protect within the ethnic 'community'.

So while this explanation might shed light on ethnic women's associations within an excluding society, it does not (set out to) explain why indigenous women married to foreigners also form such associations, whereas their marginalized foreign husbands do not. I would suggest tentatively that where women and not men bear most of the responsibility of domestic reproduction and all it entails in a potentially hostile society, then it makes sense to form alliances in order to share resources and to lobby for issues important to them. Furthermore, perhaps one could examine in future research whether it holds that where cultural definitions of masculinity emphasize men's provider role, then perhaps male constructions of honour and shame might mitigate against them openly admitting to others that they have failed in this role, and thereby prevent them forming such pragmatically based associations.

Another common reaction was for people to withdraw from what they perceived to be a hostile society, avoiding contact with all groups. This can lead to isolation and depression, and the self-reinforcing feeling of not coping.

S, a Canadian, had such low self-esteem after her qualifications were down-graded and no job application succeeded, that she virtually stopped leaving the apartment at all, and for weeks on end her only contact would be with her husband. Many people, especially the foreign *wives*, experienced such depression, which formed a central recurrent topic at the women's group (consisting of foreign women married to Germans, German women married to foreigners, and German women concerned by the plight of foreigners in Germany) of which I was a member. It of course places almost unbearable stress on the marital relationship, since the one partner is almost totally dependent on the other not only for companionship, but also to perform all the tasks of contact with the outside world, like shopping, dealings with banks, repair men, and so on. They became less and less capable of coping. This is what happened to S, who no longer trusted herself even to go to the post office. Everything of meaning in her life became invested in her relationship with her husband, which she idealized more and more, beyond the bounds of ability and reality. In time, the relationship became untenable, especially for him. She packed her bags to leave; the lack of somewhere to go and the financial means to support herself drew her back after a long day wandering about the town. This couple weathered the storm.

Conclusion: Crossing Boundaries

The various experiences related above illustrate how much state attitudes to outsiders can influence on a private level the relationships within a mixed marriage. On a broader, public level they also show how these attitudes can serve to justify intolerance or even racism by perpetuating and legitimizing concepts of outsiders as undesirable and of lesser value, marking them as different by limiting their rights. Nevertheless, the number of mixed marriages in Germany continues to rise; sadly, so do the numbers of neo-fascist attacks against foreigners and mixed couples, as the case of the German neo-Nazi participation in the plot to send letter bombs to people in mixed marriages in England, cited in the Introduction shows. From my informants as well as from my own experiences, however, it seems that those mixed marriages that manage to survive both private and public harrassment seem indeed to be strong; overcoming difficulties empowers, the people concerned take action to circumvent problems, apply their talents, move on.

References

Abdulrahim, D. (1993), 'Defining Gender in a Second Exile: Palestinian Women in West Berlin', in G. Buijs (ed.), *Migrant women: Crossing Boundaries and Changing Identities*, Oxford: Berg.

Ardener, S. (ed.) (1977, 1975), *Perceiving Women*, London: Dent.

——, (1978), 'Introduction: The Nature of Women in Society', in S. Ardener (ed.), *Defining Females: The Nature of Women in Society*, London: Croom Helm.

Barbara, A. (1989), *Marriage across Frontiers*, transl. D. Kennard, Clevedon: Multilingual Matters.

Barker, D. (1978), 'The Regulation of Marriage: Repressive Benevolence', in G. Littlejohn, B. Smart, J. Wakeford and N. Yuval-Davis (eds), *Power and the State*, London: Croom Helm.

Breger, R. (1990), *Myth and Stereotype. Images of Japan in the German Press and in Japanese Self-Presentation*, European University Studies, Frankfurt: Peter Lang.

——, (1992), 'The Discourse on Japan in the German Press: Images of Economic Competition', in R. Goodman and K. Refsing (eds), *Ideology and Praxis in Modern Japan*, London: Routledge.

Burke, J. (1972), 'The Wild Man's Pedigree: Scientific Method and Racial Anthropology', in E. Dudley and M. Novak (eds), *The Wild Man Within. An Image in Western Thought from the Renaissance to Romanticism*, Pittsburgh: University of Pittsburgh Press.

Burton, P., Kushari Dyson, K., and Ardener, S. (eds) (1994), *Bilingual Women: Anthropological Approaches to Second Language Use*, Oxford: Berg.

Chinchaladze, N., and Dragadze, T. (1994), 'Women and Second-Language Knowledge in Rural Soviet Georgia', in P. Burton, K. Kushari Dyson, and S. Ardener (eds), *Bilingual Women: Anthropological Approaches to Second Language Use*, Oxford: Berg.

Cohen, R. (1993), 'International Labour Migration post 1945', in M. O'Donnell (ed.), *New Introductory Reader in Sociology*, Walton-on-Thames: Nelson.

Cottrell, A. Baker (1990), 'Cross-National Marriages: A Review of the Literature', *Journal of Comparative Family Studies*, XXI, no.2, pp.151–69.

Crester, G. (1990), 'Intermarriage between "white" Britons and Immigrants from the New Commonwealth Countries', *Journal of Comparative Family Studies*, XXI, no.2, pp.227–38.

Dower, J. (1986), *War without Mercy. Race and Power in the Pacific War*, London: Faber and Faber.

Essed, P. (1995), 'Gender, Migration and Cross-Ethnic Coalition Building', in H. Lutz, A. Phoenix, and N. Yuval-Davis (eds), *Crossfires: Nationalism, Racism and Gender in Europe*, London: Pluto.

Evans, D. (1993), *Sexual Citizenship. The Material Construction of Sexualities*, London: Routledge.

Foucault, M. (1980), *Power/Knowledge. Selected Interviews and Other Writings 1972–1977*, transl. C. Gordon, L. Marshall, J. Mepham and K. Soper, Brighton: Harvester.

Gamson, W. and Modigliani, A. (1989), 'Media Discourse and Public Opinion on Nuclear Power: A Constructionist Approach', *American Journal of Sociology*, 95, no.1, pp.1–37.

Garcia, S. (1992), *Europe's Fragmented Identities and the Frontiers of Citizenship*, London: Royal Institute of International Affairs, Discussion Papers, 45.

Gluck, C. (1985), *Japan's Modern Myths. Ideology in the late Meiji Period*, Princeton: Princeton University Press.

Götze, L. (1985), 'interkulturelles lernen-konkrete utopie oder pedagogische spielweise?', *kultuRRevolution*, 10, pp.23–6.

Gouldbourne, H. (1991), *Ethnicity and Nationalism in Post-Imperial Britain*, Cambridge: Cambridge University Press.

Harrison, M.L. (1991), 'Citizenship, Consumption and Rights: A Comment on B.S. Turner's Theory of Citizenship', *Sociology*, 25, no.2, pp.209–13.

Heckmann, F. (1981), *Die Bundesrepublik: ein Einwanderungsland?*, Stuttgart: Klett-Cotta.

Hobsbawm, E. and Ranger, T. (eds) (1983), *The Invention of Tradition*, Cambridge: Cambridge University Press.

Hoecklin, L. (1996), 'Reconstructing "Hausfrauen": Gender Ideology, the Family and Social Welfare Policies in Southern Germany', unpub. paper presented at the Centre for Cross-Cultural Research on Women, University of Oxford, Research Seminar on 'Gender and Development – Protest and Politics', Trinity term 1996, to be published.

Höllinger and Haller (1990), cited in M. Haralambos and M. Holborn, *Sociology. Themes and Perspectives*, London: Collins Educational.

Hübner, E. and Rohlfs, H.-H. (1987), *Jahrbuch der Bundesrepublik Deutschland 1987/1988*, Munich: Beck/Deutscher Taschenbuch Verlag.

Imamura, A. (1990), 'Strangers in a Strange Land: Coping with Marginality in International Marriage', *Journal of Comparative Family Studies*, XXI, no.2, pp.171–91.

Korte, H. (1987), 'Guest-Worker Question or Immigration Issue? Social Sciences and Public Debate in the Federal Republic of Germany', in K. Bade (ed.), *Population, Labour and Migration in Nineteenth and Twentieth Century Europe*, Leamington: Berg.

Kreiner, J. (1984), 'Das Deutschland-Bild der Japaner und das deutsche Japan-Bild', in Klaus Kracht, Bruno Lewin, and Klaus Miller, *Japan und Deutschland im 20. Jahrhundert*, Ostasien Institut, Ruhr Universität Bochum, Wiesbaden: Harrassowitz.

Lee, S. and Yamanaka, K. (1990), 'Patterns of Asian American Intermarriage and Marital Assimilation', *Journal of Comparative Family Studies*, XXI, no.2, pp.287–305.

Lee Sung, B. (1990), 'Chinese American Intermarriage', *Journal of Comparative Family Studies*, XXI, no.3, pp.337–52.

Link, J. (1985), 'multikulturen: auf verlorenem posten gegen den nationalismus?', *kultuRRevolution*, 10, pp.6–12.

Lutz, H., Phoenix, A., and Yuval-Davis, N. (eds) (1995), *Crossfires: Nationalism, Racism and Gender in Europe*, London: Pluto Press.

MacDonald, M. (1994), 'Women and Linguistic Innovation in Brittany', in P. Burton, K. Kushari Dyson, and S. Ardener (eds), *Bilingual Women. Anthropological Approaches to Second Language Use*, Oxford: Berg.

Merten, K. (1986), *Das Bild der Ausländer in der deutschen Presse*, Zentrum für Turkeistudien, Frankfurt: Dagyeli.

Miller, R. (1982), *Japan's Modern Myth: Language and Beyond*, New York: Weatherhill.

152 | **Rosemary Breger**

Mouer, R. and Sugimoto, Y. (1986), *Images of Japanese Society. A Study in the Social Construction of Reality*, London: KPI.

Räthzel, N. (1995), 'Nationalism and Gender in West Europe: The German Case', in H. Lutz, A. Phoenix and N. Yuval-Davis (eds), *Crossfires: Nationalism, Racism and Gender in Europe*, London: Pluto Press.

Said, E. (1978), *Orientalism*, London: Routledge and Kegan Paul.

Scheuch, E. (1982),'Ausländer, "Bindestrich-Deutsch" oder Integration', paper presented at the CDU conference 'Ausländer in Deutschland. Für eine gemeinsame Zukunft', Bonn, 20–21 October 1982.

Smith, A. (1986), *The Ethnic Origin of Nations*, Oxford: Blackwell.

Snyder, L. (1978), *Roots of German Nationalism*, Bloomington: Indiana University Press.

Spickard, P. (1989), *'Mixed Blood': Intermarriage and Ethnic Identity in Twentieth Century America*, Wisconsin: University of Wisconsin Press.

Spiering, M. (1996), 'National Identity and European Unity', in M. Winter (ed.), *Culture and Identity in Europe. Perceptions of Divergence and Unity in Past and Present*, Avebury: Contemporary Interdisciplinary Research.

Thränhardt, D. (1985), 'mythos des fremden – deutsche angst und deutsche lust', *kultuRRevolution*, 10, pp.35–8.

Treibel, A. (1990), *Migration in modernen Gesellschaften. Soziale Folgen von Einwanderung and Gastarbeit*, Weinheim: Juventa Verlag.

Turner, B. (1990), 'Outline of a Theory of Citizenship', *Sociology*, 24, no.2, pp.189–217.

——, (1991), 'Further Specification of the Citizenship Concept: A Reply to M.L. Harrison', *Sociology*, 25, no.2, pp.215–18.

Walby, S. (1994), 'Is Citizenship Gendered?', *Sociology*, 28, pp.379–95.

Wobbe, T. (1995), 'The Boundaries of Community: Gender Relations and Racial Violence', in H. Lutz, A. Phoenix and N. Yuval-Davis (eds), *Crossfires: Nationalism, Racism and Gender in Europe*, London: Pluto.

Wolf-Almanasreh, R. (1991), *Mein Partner oder Partnerin kommt aus einem anderen Land. Inter-kulturelle Ehen, Familien und Partnerschaften. Ein Wegweiser für die Selbsthilfe*, IAF, Verband bi-nationaler Familien und Partnerschaften, Frankfurt: Interessengemeinschaft der mit Ausländern verheirateten Frauen e.V.

9

Cross-Cultural Marriage within Islam: Ideals and Reality

Mai Yamani

This chapter reviews a variety of legal aspects within the marriage ideal in Islam, presenting some of the special characteristics of Islamic marriage and seeing how they relate to cross-cultural unions. The chapter then specifically addresses the diversity within the international Muslim community in respect of marriage practices and traditions. The roles of patriarchy, culture and status are discussed and the interaction of cultural norms with Islamic precepts. Some of the practical problems that can arise from a contemporary cross-cultural Muslim marriage are illustrated by the personal experiences related in a single example of a marriage between a Saudi Arabian woman and a Pakistani man, both Sunni Muslims. Finally, the question is asked as to how harmony may be sought within nuclear and extended families of a cross-cultural union.

It should be borne in mind that from the beginning of Islam, cross-cultural marriage has been a significant agent of Islamization, not only in areas that were conquered militarily, but also in the outlying areas of the Muslim world which were not subject to military conquest.

The Marriage Ideal in Islam

Ideally, the spirit of Islam is supposed to promote cohesion between Muslims despite any racial or cultural differences that may exist. A verse of the Qur'an states: 'Oh Mankind! We created you from a single (pair) of a male and a female, and made you into nations and tribes, that ye may know each other. Verily the most honoured of you in the sight of God is the most pious of you'.[1] Piety, then, is of great import in the eyes of Allah and cross-cultural marriage is a Qur'anic injunction sent down to encourage interracial, and by extension cultural, harmony.

The Qur'an acts as the basic statement of Islamic principles and ethics, according to which Muslims should live their lives. But even in Islamic countries, there is some distinction between the (ongoing) formulation of Islamic law and jurisprudence within different Muslim countries, and the ideals laid down in the Qur'an (see Coulson and Hinchcliffe 1978 for a discussion of how women are affected by this process). Islam permits Muslim *men* to marry non-Muslim women provided they are 'people of the Book', *ahl al-kitāb*, meaning Jewish or Christian women. The Qur'an says 'lawful for you are the chaste women from among those who have been given the Book'.[2] Muslim *women*, on the other hand, are prohibited from marrying non-Muslim men. A Muslim woman's marriage to a non-Muslim would be considered a form of illegal intercourse and any offspring from that marriage would be considered illegitimate. This is justified by the predominant rule of patrilineal descent providing the child with its name and religion. In addition, as in similar (conservative) Jewish practice, a mother is supposed to be the main source of religious and moral education for young children, so that it is considered important that she belongs to (and practises) the religion to which the children should belong. It is noteworthy that Muslim women do not legally change their patronymic after marriage. However, after the colonial experience and European–American influence on some societies, women have adopted the westernized tradition of changing their names to those of their husbands. In addition, it has become increasingly common for Muslim women to draw up a legally binding marriage contract safeguarding their dower and specifying their objection to polygyny (Coulson and Hinchcliffe 1978).

In fact, Islamic marriage in general could be said to have a distinct patriarchal and patrilineal bias. In most Islamic Sunni societies a woman cannot contract a marriage on her own account but has to be given in marriage by a male guardian (Coulson and Hinchcliffe 1978). The Qur'an states: 'Marry them with the permission of their guardians and give them dowries justly, so they become chaste women'.[3] The woman is therefore formally a third party, an outsider in the contract. In another chapter the Qur'an states: 'Men are the maintainers of women because Allah has given the one more (strength) than the other, and because they support them from their means'.[4] The husband has to pay the wife a dower, *mahr*. In Islamic law this is specifically the money a husband gives to his wife upon the contraction of their marriage. It should be noted that the dower belongs entirely to the wife who disposes of it as she wishes; it is the duty of the husband to bear all the living expenses of the wife according to the concept of *iltizām*. Furthermore, she is entitled to maintenance, *nafaqa*, in the case of divorce or separation as long as she remains the guardian of his children (Esposito 1982; Maudoodi 1983; Nasir 1990). The size of the dower is determined by the economic standards of the country alongside those of the particular class or section of society involved.

There is no concept of joint property in Islam. A woman's dower constitutes part of her private wealth together with other sources from inheritance or gifts of money. Even though family law works within a rigid patriarchal structure, the woman still should inherit according to the Qur'anic command: 'Unto the men (of a family) belongeth a share of that which parents and near kindred leave, and unto women a share of that which parents and near kindred leave, whether it be little or much – a legal share.'[5]

Divorce is permitted in Islam. The Qur'anic rule enjoins men to keep their wives in good fellowship or release them with kindness. Divorce is generally a right available exclusively to the husband; however, the *Hanbali* school (one of the Sunni Schools of Islamic Law, and dominant in Saudi Arabia) allows the wife to have the *işma*, the right to divorce. Certain conditions pertaining to divorce can also be stipulated in the marriage contract. These could be asking for the right to work or the right to divorce if he takes another wife. However, although Islam allows divorce, there is a well-known *hadīth* (saying of the Prophet Muhammad) that states: 'Of all things that Islam has permitted, divorce is the most hated by Allah.' There is also a popular *hadīth* stating that the throne of the Lord shakes on the occasion of a divorce. Divorce is morally reprehensible, *makrūh*, if it is done without a valid reason but this is a matter for the man's conscience. Although a man can divorce his wife for any reason, divorce on grounds of infidelity is more acceptable in the eyes of society than divorce due to minor faults on her part. In Arabia, the nomadic Bedouin tribes[6] have always been more tolerant of divorce than the urban dwellers. Many tribal women have married more than once without any stigma being attached to them. However, in other Muslim countries, such as Pakistan, the social stigma attached to divorce is greater than in Saudi Arabia. In this particular example, this is said to be due to the influence of a Hindu Indian heritage which stresses that a woman belongs to her husband for life, even after death. In the case of Pakistan and Islamic India, the subsequent Christian colonial experience will also have influenced notions of marriage and divorce somewhat differently to those in Saudi Arabia (Doi 1989; Afshar 1993).

In marriage, as in every other aspect of life, the practice of the prophet Muhammad provides the example that all Muslims are expected to follow. However, unlike other aspects of the message, it is not such an easy matter to draw conclusions from the matrimonial life of the Prophet. The first twenty-eight years of his married life were monogamous; the following period was marked by matrimonial alliances undertaken to consolidate the political position of the fledgling Islamic state. These alliances of the Prophet were one of the ways of integrating the newly formed state.

Khadija, Muhammad's first wife, was a widow and a wealthy business woman. She first employed the Prophet and then proposed to and married him when he was twenty-five and she was forty. She remained his only wife until her death at about sixty-five. The Prophet remained celibate for three years after her death. After this he married daughters of some of his supporters as well as a Christian woman, Maria al-Qubtia, and a Jewish woman from the tribe of bani Quraida. There were a total of nine wives;[7] most were widowed women who had lost their husbands during the early battles of the Muslims. One of the Prophet's wives,

Aisha, daughter of the future Caliph Abu Bakr, was distinguished from all the others in that she was a virgin and married the Prophet at the age of nine. Aisha was known as 'the beloved of the Prophet'. She was renowned for her religious knowledge and political skills. Following the death of the Prophet, there are many examples of cross-cultural marriage for political and economic reasons, since several Caliphs married Muslim but non-Arab women, for example Berber or Persian.

The exchange of women, in most cultures and throughout history, has been used to cement political and economic ties between groups of people. As Lévi-Strauss (1969) has observed, women have unsurprisingly been the most precious category of goods exchanged. Although marriage is considered a contract, it is important to note that Islamic law distinguishes between a contract of sale and a contract of marriage (Haeri 1989).

Polygamy, or more precisely in this case polygyny, although permitted, has been a much debated phenomenon in Islam. As Leila Ahmed (1992: 91) notes, '. . . the injunctions on marriage in the Quran are open to radically different interpretations even by individuals who share the assumptions, worldview, and perspective on the nature and meaning of gender typical of Muslim society in the Abbasid period.' The only Qur'anic verse that refers to polygyny can be translated as follows, 'Marry the women of your choice, two or three or four. But if you fear that you may not be able to deal justly with them, then marry only one.'[8] Many Muslims believe that the stress on complete equality for each wife acts as a limiting factor since no husband can treat all his wives absolutely equally: strictly speaking, it would not be humanly possible. Therefore, according to modernist interpretations, polygyny is impossible in principle, while to fundamentalists it is still an option. The interpretation of this verse has affected modern legal codes in different ways, so laws on polygyny vary from one Muslim country to another. Polygyny was pro-hibited in Tunisia in 1957, while in Morocco (in 1958) conditions were imposed by the courts prohibiting polygyny in practice. Similarly, in Iraq restrictions on polygyny were imposed in 1959 (Anderson 1976). In some Muslim countries, including Iraq, Singapore and Pakistan, polygyny is permitted only with court permission, which takes into account the views of the first wife. However, if a second marriage occurs without this permission, the union is still seen to be legally valid; in this case, the first wife is then allowed to petition for divorce (Coulson and Hinchcliffe 1978: 40). In many Muslim countries, a wife is allowed to stipulate in a legally binding marriage contract that her husband will not take a second wife (see also Haeri 1989 on temporary marriages in Iran).

Even in countries such as Saudi Arabia, where polygyny is legally permitted and assumed to be socially acceptable, many Muslim women dislike the practice, finding it emotionally difficult to tolerate the idea of a co-wife. In Saudi Arabia it is perceived by most women and their extended families as an insult or rejection if their husbands take second wives. But, again, the emotional attitude towards this practice is socially determined and differs according to region, class and personal inclinations. Reactions vary from the extreme of the co-wives siding with each other to subjugate their husband as an expression of anger, to submitting to the fact. The most common reaction in Saudi Arabia is for a wife to ask for a divorce, though it is by no means the most common result (see also Altorki 1986; Tucker 1993).

Marriage in Practice: The Case of Saudi Arabia

One of the main objectives of Islam is internal unity, so it would therefore be expected that cross-cultural marriage between Muslims would be favoured. Islamic ideology on marriage and sexuality reflects the recognition of human needs. This is the ideal; however, in practice local tribal customs take precedence. Muslim marriages – as marriage elsewhere in the world – tend to take place not only between people from the same country but also from the same social stratum or class. This departure from the teachings of the Qur'an is justified by some people's reference to the Islamic legal principle of *kafā'a*, 'equality or compatibility in marriage'.[9] *Kafā'a* enshrines principles by which compatibility of the status of the couple can be judged. Its main categories are lineage, *aṣl*, wealth, *māl*, and religion, *dīn*. Despite the popular quote from the Prophet, 'If a man whose religion and character are acceptable comes to you [for your daughter's hand] give her to him in marriage', which indicates that ideally, being Muslim and of good character should rank higher than wealth or lineage, the practice of some Muslims in many instances is completely contrary to the spirit of this *ḥadīth*.

Marriage in the Arabian peninsula before Islam, during the period of the *Jāhilīya* (age of ignorance), was between tribes; then, after the arrival of Islam, marriage became an alliance between two (extended) families (Keddie and Baron 1989). A father has the right to refuse to give his daughter in marriage on the basis of *kafā'a*, the Islamic legal principle of equal social status. This is because marriage has the objective of creating large and long-lasting family groups. In Saudi Arabia patronymic groups generally seek *musāhara*, a marriage alliance as a result of which a relationship with another patronymic group is formed which will honour them and 'whiten their face' in the eyes of society. A woman from a 'good family' (a family that has the required social criteria for high status) should be married only into an extended family of similar socio-economic background, preferably a family with a long-established reputation in that community. The rule is less strict for men, since the patrilineal system that exists ensures that all his offspring carry his name, hence, his family's position would not be affected by marrying someone of lower status. According to Islamic jurisprudence, men can raise the status of women, but women can never raise the status of men. However, in practice, the social status of a woman does have some impact on that of her husband.

Social status is generally defined in relation to the group – the way a person stands or is regarded vis-à-vis others in the community. In Saudi Arabia, among the people studied, social status is defined according to several criteria. These are: origin or lineage (purity of blood, that is, blood not mixed with non-Arab blood), reputation, wealth, correct conduct, observance of 'tradition' and Islamic behaviour, political connections, and education. These distinctions are based on regional tribal concepts as well as economic and political competition. Among the merchant elite in Saudi Arabia there has been an increase in social mobility, and some families have recently acquired substantial wealth. Despite the fact that they are regarded as *arrivistes*, they can further strengthen their status by marrying into 'good families', families of old status and wealth. Conversely, good families of respected lineage who are not wealthy can marry into newly rich families because for this latter group status is intrinsically linked to wealth. This phenomenon has been a universal factor affecting relationships throughout history: religion, wealth and politics are closely intertwined, affecting people's decisions and alliances.

These criteria are defined by members of the community and serve as a means of exclusion and inclusion. It is noteworthy that the criteria particular to one community do not necessarily mean much to another social group. This is because each society historically has its own geo-political structure. Interestingly, the order of importance or ranking of the criteria within the same community, for example wealth, descent or education, changes from one period of history to another.

Social competition, of course, is a phenomenon that occurs not only within one society but also between different cultures or societies. Countries in a region will compete with each other for economic and political dominance; an extreme example can be seen in the phenomenon of war between Muslim states, despite their aspirations to Islamic brotherhood. Examples of cultural differences within the same religion, both between and within Arab and non-Arab Muslim groups, have been seen between Iran and Iraq, Kuwait and Iraq, Pakistan and Bangladesh, all of which have fought wars for economic and political reasons, notwithstanding their shared Islamic identity.

Islam definitely provides a unifying aspect of identity, but only at certain ideological levels. Indeed, in June 1997, Islam served as the *raison d'être* in a new political and economic alliance of Muslim countries, called the Developing Eight, formed by Nigeria, Egypt, Iran, Pakistan, Bangladesh, Malaysia, Indonesia and Turkey to counterbalance the power of the G7 states. Social identity is a complex matter; it is expressed at different levels and in different ways depending on the context. There are other, cross-cutting, forms of identity such as nationality, locality and, at the most pervasive level, family. Additionally, Islamic identity is less significant in secular countries, but it is expressed more strongly in countries such as Saudi Arabia where Islam serves to legitimize political, economic and social activities.

The Heterogeneity of the Islamic World: Ethnocentricity and Feelings of Superiority

Interpretation of, and degree of adherence to, religious and legal precepts vary according to how they interrelate with other familial and social values as well as with political and economic circumstances. Despite the fact that, ideally, cross-cultural marriage is allowed in Islam, in practice different attitudes to issues such as polygyny, dowry and socio-economic compatibility and other aspects of cultural variation such as modes of dress, celebratory ritual, not to mention language, may become enormous points of contention for the couple involved in a mixed marriage and their extended families. This problem can become magnified when extended families have traditions of reciprocal formal obligations that are totally different (see Sissons Joshi and Krishna, this volume).

People tend to be ethnocentric and Muslims are no exception. Different Islamic countries not only define and emphasize their cultural distinctiveness, but will sometimes promote what they perceive as their economic, political or racial superiority (cf. Shibata, this volume). For example, the use of the term 'Persian' by Iranians emphasizes the long and rich Islamic cultural traditions associated with certain periods of creative arts and political and economic strength. It also has a racial connotation, as opposed to 'Iranian', which merely identifies the modern nation. The use of 'Persian' thus enables Iranians to feel superior to Arabs because they perceive their culture to be richer in terms of poetry, philosophy and the arts. The Arabs, on the other hand, consider the Persians to be *ajam*, a pejorative term implying inferiority of lineage, meaning not from the same race that gave birth to the great Prophet Muhammad. The Persian language has, over time, borrowed heavily from the Arabic language, a practice which, in fact, was seen by Persian cultural purists as somehow shameful or polluting. Indeed, under the Shah of Iran's rule Persian was officially purged of Arabic words which were replaced by largely English or French words or their Persian translations (the Shah, being educated in Europe, and accepting European visions of modernization and nationalistic self-determination, wished to associate his nation with what he perceived to be a more developed society and link it to Persia's great pre-Islamic past). On the other hand, historically, Arabs have boasted about the Caliphate, the Caliphs being those who were elected as leaders of the Muslims after the death of the Prophet, and those who were responsible for consolidating the message of

Islam and taking it to the rest of the world via the expansion of the Muslim empire.

Social boundaries are expressed in a multiplicity of ways: how people practise religion, the way they dress, what they eat and their culinary mannerisms, the names they call each other and, especially, through non inter-marriage. The ultimate test of toleration of the other is to give one's daughter to a man from another community or country.

Cross-cultural marriage is like a microcosm of larger competitions, a unit where perceived cultural superiorities push up against each other, in addition to local class competition, on a personal level. This is particularly true if there is an imbalance within a marital relationship; for example, if one partner is more wealthy or perhaps better educated, the other might claim cultural superiority, depending on the local ranking criteria. These could range from one family's feeling of moral superiority expressed in the chastity of their women, to the value of the grandmother's priceless jewels as a symbol of another family's old standing. Cultural superiority may thus become a battleground for the couple, although such competition is more likely to take place between the extended families, particularly if their union was formed on the basis of commitment to religious belief. If personal insecurities develop within the marriage, 'culture' can become a weapon with which the person promotes him or her self. For example, in a marital dispute between Arabs from different regions, one party may call upon the superiority of their homeland, referring to fertile crescents of river civilizations continuously inhabited for thousands of years, as opposed to the partner's arid desert culture only recently rich from oil wealth. In this situation, highly charged stereotypes of groups of people and their culture are both maintained and reconstructed (cf. Shibata and Breger, this volume).

Social Status and Locality

Since social status is defined in relation to the *local* group, the marriage partner who moves in to live in the society of the other is in many ways 'status-less'. His or her origins cannot be traced back within the society to ensure or establish status. It appears that women tend to (be expected to) move more easily over cultural boundaries with marriage, while men tend to be more confined and restricted in political and social associations. Perhaps this is most easily explained by inheritance practices that tend to exclude women from property rights, whilst keeping men tied to their native local communities.

In Saudi Arabia, the criteria for selecting marriage partners are influenced more by the status of the extended family than by the individual's own attributes. Hence, the lineage, the wealth and the reputation of the groom's extended family should first be compatible with those of the bride's extended family, and only then will his own social achievements be taken into account. People will first ask: 'Who is so-and-so family marrying into?' A person's worth is socially evaluated on the basis of the extended family. Without a family background that meets such criteria, individual achievements count for nothing; outside the context of his or her family, the individual has no social identity.

Following her marriage, a woman retains her association with her own natal family and is known by their surname. Whom she marries is important to her continued status. It is more likely that when someone asks to whom she is married, the question would be formulated thus: 'From which family is your husband?', rather than, 'Who is your husband?' or 'What is your husband's name?'

From ancient times and in many different cultures marriage has always been linked with materialistic interest. Recently, however, and especially in Saudi Arabia and the Gulf states, and other parts of the Muslim world where great wealth has arisen within a very short period of time, criteria for choosing marriage partners have become overwhelmingly concerned with materialistic considerations such as wealth and social status at the expense of other factors such as piety and good character.

A Personal Narrative

In the example discussed here, a Saudi Arabian Muslim woman from a wealthy elite family married a Pakistani Muslim (rather than a Saudi Arabian from her own community), who came from an educated and respected but not particularly wealthy family. Here, the usual questions designed to establish social identity could not be asked because the groom's family belonged to a completely different, foreign cultural context. Their marriage took place at a time when the impact of growing numbers of foreigners in Saudi Arabia was becoming a cause of public concern. The Saudi Arabian woman was from an upper-class family very much concerned with the question of lineage and 'purity of blood', specifically, their claim of descent from the tribe of Quraysh (the tribe of the Prophet), and the reputation of the family was of primary importance, wealth being a secondary consideration in judging the compatibility of any suitor.

The husband's family were a landed military family with little wealth, especially when compared with the grand scale of Saudi oil wealth. The military background of the groom did not heighten his status or even make any sense to the Hijazi Saudi Arabian family in question because there was no comparable meaningful historical military tradition in Saudi Arabia. Since the establishment of the kingdom in 1932, the military forces had been drawn from other tribes, not the Hijazis.

This was not a common type of cross-cultural marriage. Marriages of Saudi women to other Arabs, Egyptians, Lebanese or Palestinians, or, even closer, to other Gulf Arabs from perhaps Bahrain or Kuwait occur, but this marriage of an Arab woman to a non-Arab man, even if both were Muslims, was considered a case of extreme cultural, racial and linguistic differences. These differences were perceived by the extended families to be problematic, rather than enriching.

The Reaction of Individuals: Judging Suitability

To the couple, the fact that they were both Muslims was enough to unite them, especially in the light of their compatibility based on education, both Islamic and European, received outside their home countries in a third, non-Muslim country.

The bride's family, however, felt they could not establish to their satisfaction the character of the groom. His family could not be identified, nor their social status established, as they were culturally out of context. The groom, when outside the context of a family, becomes an unknown quantity, and equally so a family when appraised outside the context of its culture. Although Islam offers the potential of a common bond between cultures, it is ultimately not the piety of the groom, but the groom in his cultural/tribal background that provides the yardstick. This disturbed members of the bride's extended family and made them hostile, aloof and discouraging. This caused confusion and malaise in the groom's family, which in turn generated social *faux pas*. Additionally, the scales on which suitability is measured in both cultures is so different that no common point for assessment could be clearly identified. The issue was possibly made easier for the groom's family, due to the fact that beauty is always a desirable criterion for a good bride, and in this case the bride was not only physically pleasing to his family, but wealthy too.

The Danger of Love

The concept of marital love and compassion is underlined in the Qur'anic verse: 'And among His Signs is that He created you mates from among yourselves, that you may dwell in tranquillity with them and He put love and mercy between your hearts. Undoubtedly in these are Signs for those who reflect.'[10] Although the concept of love and compassion is a common religious ideal, it has different forms of expression within Islam. There are particular Islamic rules of behaviour that married men and women should maintain, for example concepts of conjugal intimacy and marital decorum that express the love and compassion existing between them. However, despite the concept of mutual respect, the command exists for the woman to obey her husband. This is known as *tamkīn*, obedience, as opposed to *nushūz*, disobedience (see also Maudoodi 1983; Doi 1989; Mir-Hosseini 1993).

Love, however, does not conform to the concept of *kafā 'a,* equality or compatibility. 'Love' is criticized if it conflicts with the idea of the maintenance of a well-integrated family unit. By definition, it implies putting one's own individual interests above those of the well-being of the extended family.

The circumstances in which the couple met (at university in England) implied that 'love' had been the cause of marriage. In Saudi Arabia, marriage based on overt 'love' is considered shameful, *'ayb,* a social taboo, as opposed to *harām,* a religious taboo. It is unusual for someone to admit to love for it implies a clandestine relationship before marriage in a society which strictly stresses the importance of the sexual 'purity' and unimpugned honour of the bride. In Saudi Arabia, the segregation of the sexes is strictly imposed in all public spaces including government and business areas, in restaurants, in mosques and even to the extreme of separate elevators in buildings. Young men and women therefore have limited places to meet except when introduced 'properly' by their relatives under chaperoned conditions with the intention of getting married.

The norm is that after the marriage contract has been discussed between the respective families, the *Fatiha* (the opening chapter of the Qur'an) is read by the close kin of the future spouses. This ceremony does not establish a legal tie between them, but rather 'reserves' the bride by good intentions, *mahabba.* In other words, it is comparable to engagement in other Muslim societies. However, until the marriage contract is signed in the mosque the future bride meets her husband only when chaperoned by relatives, and the only un-chaperoned conversations allowed from then on until the marriage are over the telephone.

State Control of Marriage Partners

The nationalistic ideals of the modern nation-state have impinged on Saudi Arabian legal practice (see also Breger, this volume; Anderson 1976; Beck and Keddie 1978). For the couple in the example here, the marriage procedures became more complicated when the Pakistani husband had to change his nationality and acquire a Saudi Arabian one. This entailed giving up his original nationality since in Saudi Arabia it is forbidden to have dual nationality. This procedure was necessary because it is illegal for Saudi women to marry non-Saudi citizens. In the case of men, however, permission from the Ministry of Interior is necessary in order to marry foreigners. This came into effect following a general decree issued by the government at the end of the 1970s in an attempt to control the marriage process and choice of partner.

A new phase marking a resurgence of cross-cultural marriages was evident in the 1970s: in Saudi Arabia this was a period of openness to change and the exposure of young Saudis at an impressionable age to foreign influences. This came about through higher education for both women and men, mainly in other Arab countries, as well as Europe and the United States. But at the end of the 1970s the Saudi government discouraged Saudis, especially women, from studying abroad, primarily by stopping scholarships. This was in line with a return to conservative tradition alongside a general Islamic revival triggered by the Islamic revolution in Iran.

The ban on marrying foreigners can be explained in the following manner. The dower of Saudi women, after the oil booms of the 1970s, increased phenomenally. This led Saudi men to seek 'cheaper' wives from Syria, Egypt or other poorer Arab states. The dower offered by a man can be very high, reaching hundreds of thousands of rials among the wealthier families. In addition, Saudi men consider the lifestyle of local women materially demanding, while Muslim women from poorer countries such as Egypt or Morocco are perceived to be more easily satisfied. This post-colonial phenomenon is associated with the rise of nationalism and the strict enforcement of border and immigration controls, exacerbated by the huge disparities in wealth that have emerged between different Muslim countries as a result of the discovery of oil in some Muslim states and not others. Indeed, the problem of the 'inflation of dowries' has been discussed in the press.

The decree forbidding Saudis to marry foreigners remains somewhat ambiguous. Permission is granted or withheld according to the man's profession or socio-political position. For example, those working in the military are not granted permission to marry foreigners. The marriage of a Saudi woman to a foreigner would be socially frowned upon, even feared. It is generally perceived that if a woman marries a foreign man she will adapt or conform to his social and familial situation or background, since women are generally expected to change their family, adopt their husbands' names and bring up children to conform to the expectations of their husbands' patrilineal kin. It is perceived that a woman cannot expect her foreign husband to adapt or conform, but instead she must follow him and gain or maintain his consent or approval, *ridā*, throughout the marriage. Children carry the name, social and legal identity of their fathers. It is therefore due to this strong patrilineal concept and patrilocal residence practice that Saudi families are reluctant to give their daughters away to foreigners. Ultimately, men appear to have more freedom to reject the decree, whilst the patrilineal nature of society works against the woman in the realm of law, using the obscurity of the decrees to subvert any different plans she may have (Yamani 1996).

Descent: Purity and Control

In Saudi Arabia, the concept of 'purity of blood' remains a central, status-related ideological issue. Saudi Arabians generally, and Meccans particularly, feel pride in this, justifying thereby their perceived superiority over other non-Arab Muslims. In the case of the couple under discussion, an elderly uncle of the bride, trying to resolve the ambiguities, declared that 'the husband of our daughter has Arab "blood", for he is a descendant of Muhammad bin Qasim, the founder of Islam in India'. The preoccupation with improving or preserving 'blood line' is also common amongst families who consider themselves elites in other societies worldwide.

Over the years there has been an obvious change in attitudes towards cross-cultural marriage between Muslims in Mecca, a city described as 'the capital of Muslims'. From accounts of those who lived in the late nineteenth and early twentieth centuries (see, for example, Hurgronje 1970), Mecca was the melting pot of the Islamic world and mixed marriages were the order of the day. Ironically, in modern Mecca the descendants of mixed marriages are at the forefront of efforts to maintain 'purity of blood' in the construction of national identity, linking biology with culture in this, in historical terms, newly founded state.

Wedding Ceremonies: Symbols of Unity or Difference

Aside from the essential religious elements of the marriage rite, the ceremonial rituals and social mores that surround a wedding can differ significantly within the Islamic world, as our example reveals.

In this case the wedding ceremonies took place in both countries, following the different local practices. The first set of ceremonies was held in Saudi Arabia, and consisted of a religious ceremony, the 'aqd al-qirān, as well as a social celebration. It was rife with misunderstanding. The groom's family came from a different country, speaking a different language, wearing different clothes and with different expectations of these rituals and ceremonies. In Saudi Arabia the bride conventionally wears white on her wedding day while in Pakistan traditional colourful dress is worn. The music at the Saudi Arabian festivities was not enjoyed by the visiting parties, and by the spicy standards of Pakistani cuisine the local food seemed bland. The ceremonies in Saudi Arabia are segregated according to sex and age, which tends not to be the case in Pakistan, where men, women and their children celebrate together, albeit in different sections of a room. These and other differing cultural practices made the wedding celebrations only partly understood by the visiting party. The one ceremony familiar to both parties was the religious wedding contract, 'aqd al-qirān, which took place on the first evening.

Although all belonged to the same religion, these differing customs and expectations made communication limited and full of misunderstandings. For example, the older Pakistani female relatives, thinking that the Saudi bride was worried about polygyny, tried to reassure her that the Pakistani groom would not marry other wives, as they assumed Bedouins did. This advice, however, had just the opposite effect of deeply insulting the Saudi family, since the Saudis interpreted it to mean that their daughter was viewed inadequate as a wife, and that as a family they were not of sufficiently high status to protest against and prevent a second marriage. A high-status Saudi family would never consent to their daughter entering into or remaining in a polygynous marriage.

After the festivities in Saudi Arabia another set of wedding ceremonies took place in Pakistan in order to satisfy the groom's cultural practices. These lasted another four days and followed the traditional Pakistani format. Although the bride had already been married for a week, she had to act as if she was just married, exhibiting the traditionally expected shyness, that is, her head bent and gaze lowered according to local custom. However, the family of the bride considered that the wedding celebrations had been concluded in Saudi, the heart of Islam, so they did not attend these celebrations.

The accumulation of misunderstandings and tensions in this example of cross-cultural marriage added greatly to the difficulties with which the couple were faced in establishing a life together. Here we see a clear example of what happens when the spirit of Islam does not successfully cut across cultural boundaries; instead, socio-economic criteria predominated.

The situation of cross-cultural marriage in Islam remains ambivalent because, while differences between the cultures of Muslim countries do indeed exist, their significance is frequently denied, to the detriment of all concerned, for fear of not fulfilling the ideals of Islamic unity. Although the marriage of Muslims to one another cross-culturally is very rare because of patriarchal norms, it is more likely that a woman of high status would venture out of her culture to marry than a woman of lower social status, partly due to exposure to the outside world achieved through the privileges of wealth and education, and also due to the degree of confidence she would acquire from this experience (see also Breger and Hill; Khatib-Chahidi et al., this volume). Her education and knowledge of Islam would enable her to realize that a cross-cultural union was within permitted religious boundaries. She would be aware that ignorance of Islamic precepts allows the blind acceptance of local cultural practice disguised as universal Islam. The code of moral conduct prescribed in Islam, in fact, offers political, social and economic rights that aim to overcome cultural differences and transcend cultural norms (cf. Fawzi El-Solh and Mabro 1994: 1–32, and see Beck and Keddie 1978 for discussions on variations between ideals and praxis).

Neutral Space and Coping

The case described here is by no means typical or representative of cross-cultural marriage within the vast world of Islam. But in similar cases in this day and age, frequently the only way a couple can deflate the pressures of cultural and economic differences is by removing themselves from the particular cultural context to a more neutral one. In any culturally mixed marriage, when one partner moves into the cultural milieu of the other, the pressure on the incomer to adapt to the foreign community is greater than for the other partner. It is unavoidable that one culture would predominate in such a marriage. No matter how hard the partners may try, the incomer would always remain an outsider to some extent. This results in imbalances in the power relationship within the marriage, especially in an era when the growing consciousness of gender relations is promoting a degree of equality between husband and wife (see Refsing, this volume). In the case of women moving to their husbands' country this was perhaps considered acceptable in the past because women were perceived as appendages to their husbands, and the value of the marriage alliance was seen to outweigh any personal problems.

Changes in the socio-economic context of marriage mean that other options for organizing families are becoming available, in particular, the nuclear family as opposed to the extended. The model of the nuclear family so well established in the developed world is becoming a trend in the developing world. By changing their social context – either by moving away or establishing their own nuclear unit – couples in a cross-cultural marriage can thus neutralize to some degree the pressures they face, which creates a more relaxed atmosphere for raising their children.

In cultures where racial and economic background are important, the children of a cross-cultural marriage can become victims of criteria imposed by that particular society. In our example, the children of the Pakistani man are not perceived as pure Arabs in a country where purity of Arab blood is a basic requirement for status and upward social mobility. This does not mean to say, however, that the same children growing up in a country not common to either parent might not also encounter racism and prejudice.

In a cross-cultural marriage, the nuclear family becomes the new focus as it did for the couple here. They established a common bond and overriding identity by emphasizing a sense of shared religion, establishing a sense of religious unity for their children. At the same time, this particular couple adopted and adapted various aspects of their different cultural inheritances, such as cuisine, clothing, lay celebrations, in an enriching negotiated amalgamation of cultures. In this particular family, English became their first home language, as the language of the society where they were living and as the (second) language in which both partners were fluent. Their native languages played a secondary role. Thus the heritage of culture and language of both parents can be passed on, beyond the controlling proximity of extended kin.

In the past, cross-cultural marriage within the world of Islam served to cement tribal and racial ties and contributed to the process of Islamization. Where culturally specific social norms prevail over religious ones, however, cross-cultural marriage can be perceived as a threat and a challenge to the integrity and continuity of the extended families involved. This applies particularly in modern times where social identity can be shaped to a large extent by nationalistic ideals and other social considerations. Cross-cultural marriage, however, continues to be a source of renewal of the Islamic world.

Notes

1. Qur'an, chap.49, *al-Ḥujurāt* (The Inner Apartments), verse 13. Trans. Yusuf Ali. This Qur'anic verse is printed on every wedding invitation card among the elite families in Saudi Arabia.
2. Qur'an, chap.5, *al-Mā'ida* (The Food), verse 6.
3. Ibid., chap.4, *al-Nisā'* (The Women), verse 25.
4. Ibid., verse 34.
5. Ibid., verse 7.
6. Prior to the unification of the country in 1932, there were four provinces: the tribal Najd, the coastal Ahsa, the Hijaz with its urban centres of Mecca and Medina, and the mountainous Asir.
7. Some say fourteen; see Freyer Stowasser 1994.
8. Qur'an, chap.4, *al-Nisā'* (The Women), verse 3.
9. See Anderson 1976 and also Sidiqqi 1996.
10. Qur'an, chap.30, *Rūm* (The Romans), verse 21.

References

Abu-Lughod, L. (1986), *Veiled Sentiments*, Berkeley, Los Angeles and London: University of California Press.
Afshar, H. (1993), *Women in the Middle East*, London: MacMillan Press.
Ahmed, L. (1992), *Women and Gender in Islam*, New Haven and London: Yale University Press.
Ali, Y., (trans.) *The Holy Quran*, Delhi: Kutub Khana Ishayat-ul-Islam.
Alireza, M. (1971), *At the Drop of a Veil*, Boston: Houghton Mifflin Company.
Altorki, S. (1986), *Women in Saudi Arabia: Ideology and Behaviour Among the Elite*, New York: Columbia University Press.

Anderson, N. (1976), *Law Reform in the Muslim World*, University of London: Athlone Press.

Beck, L. and Keddie, N. (eds) (1978), *Women in the Muslim World*, Cambridge, Massachusetts: Harvard University Press.

Coulson, N. and Hinchcliffe, D. (1978), 'Women and Law Reform in Contemporary Islam', in L. Beck and N. Keddie (eds), *Women in the Muslim World*, Cambridge, Massachusetts: Harvard University Press.

Doi, A.R.I. (1989), *Women in Shari'a'*, London: Ta-Ha Publishers.

Du Pasquier, R. (1992), *Unveiling Islam*, Cambridge: The Islamic Texts Society.

Esposito, J.L. (1982), *Women in Muslim Family Law*, Syracuse New York: Syracuse University Press.

Fawzi El-Solh, C. and Mabro, J. (eds) (1994), *Muslim Women's Choices*, Oxford: Berg.

Freyer Stowasser, B. (1994), *Women in the Qur'an, Traditions, and Interpretation*, Oxford: Oxford University Press.

Haeri, S. (1989), *Law of Desire – Temporary Marriage in Iran*, London: I.B. Tauris.

Hurgronje, S. (1970), *Mekka in the Latter Part of the Nineteenth Century*, Leiden: Brill.

Keddie, N.R. and Baron, B. (eds) (1989), *Women in Middle Eastern History*, New Haven and London: Yale University Press.

Lévi-Strauss, C. (1969), *The Elementary Structure of Kinship*, Boston: Beacon Press.

Maudoodi, M.A.A. (1983), *The Laws of Marriage and Divorce in Islam*, Safat Kuwait: Islamic Book Publishers.

Mir-Hosseini, Z. (1993), *Marriage on Trial*, London: I.B. Tauris.

Nasir, J.J. (1990), *The Status of Women under Islamic Law*, London, Dordrecht and Boston: Graham & Trotman.

Sidiqqi, M. (1996), 'Law and the Desire for Social Control: An Insight into the Hanafi Concept of Kafa'a with Reference to the Fatawa Alamgiri, 1664–1672', in M. Yamani (ed.), *Feminism and Islam: Legal and Literary Perspectives*, Reading: Ithaca Press.

Tucker, J.E. (1993), *Arab Women: Old Boundaries, New Frontiers*, Bloomington and Indianapolis: Indiana University Press.

Yamani, M. (ed.) (1996), *Feminism and Islam: Legal and Literary Perspectives*, Reading: Ithaca Press.

10

English and North American Daughters-in-Law in the Hindu Joint Family

Mary Sissons Joshi and Meena Krishna

People in all cultures have fathers, mothers, sons and daughters. But the relations between them are not culture free.

A. Ramanujan

He had explained once that to be born into a strong tradition was to know the steps to an intricate dance which started with birth and ended with death. 'When you know all the steps by heart, you don't have to think any more – you are the dancer and the dance' he said and she had loved the mystery, the poetry of it. It hadn't occurred to her to ask him what happened when a dancer found himself alone on the floor of a different tradition. Could the steps of one dance fit the music of another?

Manjula Padmanabhan, *Stains*

In a world of ever-increasing travel opportunity and economic interdependence between nations, practical advice is frequently offered to those who interact across cultural boundaries. 'Cultural guides' for investors are common-place (Dunung 1995), and there is a growing demand for anthropologists to interpret one culture to another (Hoecklin 1995). Attention is drawn to the nuances of language use (Gumperz et al. 1979), the subtleties of non-verbal communication, and the explicit social rules and conventions which differentiate cultures (Argyle 1982). It is normally assumed that those who marry across cultures do not need advice on intercultural communication since, by virtue of their relationship, they have shown the ability to cross cultural boundaries. However, the pathway of an intercultural marriage is not always a smooth one (q.v. Alibhai-Brown and Montague 1992).

'Virtually everyone, in all societies, is brought up in a family context: and in every society the vast majority of adults are, or have been married' (Giddens 1989: 383). However, cultures differ markedly with respect to the conventions and social construction of marriage, and it is the perceptions of these differences which enrich and challenge those who marry across cultures. In this chapter we shall consider the experiences of women who have been reared in nuclear families but through marriage have lived in joint families. Specifically, we interviewed twenty English and ten North American women graduates who had married Indian professional men. The transcripts of the interviews were discussed with thirty Indian graduate/ professional women of whom fifteen were currently living in Britain, Canada or the USA, and fifteen were currently living in India. It is the English, North American and Indian women's comments on female identity and their inter- pretations of their experiences within joint households which form the basis of this chapter.

The English and North American women in our sample have the following characteristics:

1. They grew up in middle- and upper-middle-class nuclear households, which were linked to kin through economic and social relationships, but primarily organized around the relationship between husband and wife (q.v. Allan 1989; Ribbens 1994). In such families it is customary for a new couple to set up a separate residence from the older generation upon – or before – marriage (Kiernan 1989; Cunningham and Antill 1995; Goody 1996).
2. They had married Hindu Maharashtrian or Gujarati men, from the professional and business classes, who had been brought up in extended or joint patrilineal households.[1]
3. The majority of women interviewed were aged forty to fifty, and were reflecting on marriages begun some fifteen to twenty years ago in the mid-1970s.
4. Upon marriage, the women had resided in the joint family – that is to say, in their husband's parents' household.

The interviews can be contextualized by the contemporaneous Government of India's *Committee on the Status of Women* which reported that 'very few women start their married life independently in a simple household' (1974: 60). Further- more, a foreigner who marries into an affluent urban Indian family is more likely to confront the realities of joint family life than a foreigner who marries into a poorer or rural family since while the extended or joint family is an *ideal* for the whole society, it is more likely to be a *reality* for the wealthier and urban (Shah 1974; Nanda 1991). Furthermore, recent high housing costs in cities 'have provided the joint family with a new lease of life' (Jain 1994: 74).

Arranged and Non-arranged Marriages: The Issue of Acceptance

Barbara (1989: 23) has commented that, 'Marriage to a foreigner always upsets the existing equilibrium in a family.' When a marriage takes place between indi- viduals who come from cultures with different marriage practices, such a marriage confronts more than incipient ethnocentrism in both societies, challenging the very notion of what constitutes a 'proper' marriage. 'In India, almost all marriages are arranged. So customary is the practice of arranged marriage that there is a special name for marriage that is not arranged: it is called a "love-match"' (Nanda 1991: 224).[2] An intercultural marriage, by definition, cannot have been arranged since marriages are arranged along strict community, caste, and sub-caste lines. The challenge to the approved marriage system is evident every time the couple appear in public since a non-Asian cannot 'pass' (Goffman 1969) as an Asian. One informant spoke of her embarrassment on a holiday in the small town of Aurangabad where teenage youths followed the couple down the street chanting, in English, 'love-marriage, love-marriage'.

Amongst middle-class families, foreign wives rarely face direct rejection, but the husband's family may nevertheless signal disapproval or disappointment in indirect ways. Several informants reported that their mothers-in-law would comment disparagingly on other mixed marriages where men were to be pitied, partly on account of the assumed inability of foreign wives to cook 'proper home food'. Appearance can form the basis for negative comment for although advertisements in the arranged marriage columns make clear the high value which middle-class Indians place on fair skin, it is the ivory skin of pale Indians which is valued rather than the pink complexion common amongst Northern Europeans. Further, since Northern European women tend to be taller and larger than women in the west of India, foreign daughters-in-law were frequently regarded as lacking in femininity/delicacy. Size can have consequences beyond the aesthetic: several informants reported that their mothers-in-law were upset by not being able to pass on their bangles on account of the outsize wrists of their foreign daughters-in-law. Meanwhile, through ignorance, a foreign wife's own mother will disappoint the Indian family by failing to present a sari to the son-in-law's mother on appropriate life-cycle occasions (e.g. at a grandson's naming or thread ceremonies).

Acceptance is not only relevant in the early years of marriage. An English woman commented that although her husband's parents initially seemed to accept her, when a nephew showed signs of wanting to prolong a period of study abroad, the family made their objections clear on the grounds that foreign study equalled foreign marriage which 'would be a disaster'. Many parents of those who marry cross-culturally and cross-racially have reservations about the wisdom of their child's choice (q.v. Alibhai-Brown and Montague 1992). But when an outsider marries into a culture whose rules explicitly favour *arranged* marriage, family reservations can form the basis for direct 'up-front' comments which will hurt the incomer unless and until she is able to construe these statements as a compliment marking her successful transition from outsider to insider.

Everyday Ritual: Culture and Gender

Much of Erving Goffman's work (e.g. *Interaction Ritual* 1967) attests to the importance of ritual in everyday life – the significance of which may only become apparent to the players when unspoken expectations are not fulfilled. A lack of fit of cultural expectations may lead to problems, as indicated by the comments of an Indian man about the arrangements surrounding his wedding in London to an English woman:

> . . . the day we got married Catherine and I left with my brother, mother and cousin in the car. It didn't seem incongruous to me, but to Catherine it was a violation of all that she had been brought up to expect . . . The next morning, just after our marriage, I took my cousin to the airport and saw him off. It was really hurtful to Catherine, but I didn't realise that. Then we went on our honeymoon for a few days and came back to London because my mother had a throat problem. It wasn't incongruous to me to break up the honeymoon and then go back again, but to Catherine it was (Alibhai-Brown and Montague 1992: 181).

In this interview it can be inferred that the English woman felt that during their honeymoon her husband should give her precedence over his mother – both in terms of time spent, but also in the public demonstration of affection. Indeed, there is an obligation, in North American middle-class society, for a newly married man 'to treat his bride with affectional deference (and) whenever it is possible to twist ordinary behaviour into a display of this kind' (Goffman 1967: 59). However societies differ with respect to such rules of conduct, and married couples in India rarely engage in public demonstrations of affection (Das 1979; Trawick 1990; Desai 1995).

In his paper 'The arrangement between the sexes', Goffman (1977) suggests that women in America and Europe are subjugated and treated as second-class citizens and at the same time are idealized and treated as fragile objects worthy of respect. Men accord this fragility to women by rituals such as allowing them to pass through doors first and relieving them of heavy items. These particular rituals are not associated with gender roles in Hindu society and some English informants were distressed to see their elderly mothers-in-law insist on carrying suitcases rather than letting their sons help.

Cultural practices associated with gender and food can be particularly compelling for, as Appadurai (1981: 494) has written, food has 'the capacity to mobilize strong emotions'. An American informant was startled by her husband's adoption of what she saw as the 'child's role' at his mother's table – expecting to be served, and oblivious to the needs of his own wife and child. Another informant commented:

In my own family in England, either my mother or father serves the food, and the women are served before the men, and the girls before the boys. My brother's wife is served first as she is both female and a 'guest'. But in India my mother-in-law serves the men first and won't herself sit down to eat until they have virtually finished eating. Daughters and daughters-in-law – whether they live there or are visiting – are last-in-line.

When food is not plentiful such habits can have deleterious consequences for the nutritional status of women (Agarwal 1994). Our English and North American interviewees were also concerned with the symbolism involved. For instance:

It saddened me to see my mother-in-law put up with eating cold chappatis and only the remnants of the vegetables. And, truthfully, I used to feel rather annoyed when at breakfast, she would expect me to eat yesterday's bread, along with her and the servants, while the men in the family were always given fresh bread. My husband appeared not to notice these little inequalities – and if I pointed them out, he would say: 'Don't raise these issues. It's not worth it. Anyway, she likes it like that.'[3]

Rituals surrounding the preparation and eating of food are important in all cultures (Douglas 1966), but they are of immense significance in India (Khare 1976; Appadurai 1981). Castes are partly defined by the type of food eaten and the offering of food is a crucial component of deity worship (Ferro-Luzzi 1977). Foreign wives told of their husband's anger when they inadvertently placed vegetables on the wrong area of the *thali* (plate), or used the tableware in a potentially ritually polluting manner. Indian women reported that the early years of marriage are an apprenticeship to the mother-in-law with the explicit goal of cooking appropriate food for the son. One informant reported: 'Even if you come from the same caste as your husband, each family has a different way of cooking things – *dal* and so on – so your mother-in-law instructs you.' An American woman commented that when she cooked an excellent *masala dosa* she was praised by the family not as a good cook but as a good daughter-in-law. For English and North American women coming from cultures which emphasize the abstract person as a causal category (Shweder and Bourne 1982; Miller 1984), and where self-perception is in terms of psychological traits rather than role (Dhawan et al. 1995), invocations of role or context as the explanation of 'good' behaviour may be experienced as impersonal and potentially insulting.

The Negotiation of Privacy and Intimacy

Sciama (1993: 93) notes that 'in suburban England, a son's or daughter's room in their parents' home is private in relation to the house (or he or she may so regard it)'. But as Anandalakshmy (1981: 15) has written: 'In India . . . privacy is treated as secrecy. In an extended family in India, closing a door inside a house is almost an act of hostility.' Different cultural attitudes to space and privacy were frequently reported as problematic by our informants. An American woman married to a Maharashtrian business man commented:

I didn't mind at all when we were first married – living with my husband's parents in Bombay. The flat was large and we had our own room. But after our first child was born, I really began to resent it. Family members would just walk in and out of our room and I felt we had no privacy at all. It was then that the marriage ran into difficulties.

Another American informant, upon arriving as a new bride in Bombay, felt her privacy violated when her sisters-in-law not only felt free to wander into the bedroom but also 'ransacked' her luggage and took away personal items assuming them to be gifts for the women of the family.

It is important to understand the control of space (Ardener 1993) and the use to which space is put. English and North American informants stated that lack of private space primarily deprived them of opportunity for secluded conversation with their spouses. A woman from a nuclear family is likely to view marriage as a partnership (Moore 1988) and expect the marital unit to be her key emotional relationship (Reibstein and Richards 1992). Critical to such a notion of marriage is 'affective individualism', where the formation of marriage ties is based on personal selection which is in turn guided by norms of sexual, romantic and companionate love (Giddens 1992; Tysoe 1992). In contrast, the expectation that the couple is the prior unit in all matters is inappropriate within an extended family where ties of lineality between the generations are of most importance (Nanda 1991; Harlan and Courtwright 1995). Psychoanalytic writers have commented that in Hindu families 'following the prolonged fusion of the early mother-son dyad, the son does not create a comparably intense affiliation with his wife' (Guzder and Krishna 1991). Intimacy between spouses is thus minimized, and may often even be discouraged (Davar 1995).

One informant recounted how a weekend trip she and her husband planned to take provoked cultural misunderstanding. Her father-in-law was perplexed, wondering 'Why are you going to Marve? What will you do there all alone?', and suggested that he, his wife and several grandsons should accompany the couple to alleviate their inevitable boredom. In view of their impending first-time parenthood, the couple valued their last chance to be alone, but their preference was regarded by the rest of the family as strange and excluding. Many of the British women interviewed by Alibhai-Brown and Montague (1992) talked of feeling overwhelmed by the joint family and frustrated in their desire to be alone with their husbands. For example, a Scottish social worker married to a Muslim Bengali commented:

> When I first married Nasir, I felt as if his two nephews came with the package. That was something I sometimes resented because I felt that we never had any time on our own. I remember thinking at one stage: we have never spent a night on our own in this house. We used to have to go away to be alone. If he had been an Englishman we wouldn't have had that, he would have made time for us to be on our own (Alibhai-Brown and Montague 1992: 108).

For cultural and economic reasons Indian middle-class men rarely engage in DIY activities in the home. But some of our informants commented on how lack of such 'joint domestic projects' increased their sense of isolation from their husbands.

The psychoanalyst, Sudhir Kakar (1989: 144), suggests that Indian women also long for a 'two-person universe', but only in their imagination, and that middle- and upper-middle-class wives have 'a fantasy of constituting a "couple", not in opposition to the rest of the extended family but within this wider network' (op. cit.: 22). This theme is echoed in the short story 'Bahu' by Anjana Appachana, where the narrator tries, but fails, to converse with her husband in private:

> By the time I had washed the dishes and cleaned the kitchen it was well past midnight. I went to our room and found that my husband's nephew had fallen asleep on the *diwan* next to our bed. He's so fond of his *mamaji* [uncle], my sister-in-law would say each time this happened. My husband was asleep too. So, in fact, was the whole household. I could not have it out tonight. Or any other night if things continued this way and they would continue this way as long as we lived and we would live this way forever and forever (1989: 13).

Social support is an important determinant of physical and mental health (Taylor 1995). In Brown and Harris' (1978) study of depression in a south London suburb, an intimate confiding relationship with a husband or boyfriend acted as a protective factor for women in otherwise vulnerable circumstances. If, for cultural reasons, husbands are unlikely to provide this kind of relationship, then we need to ask where their wives are able to find support. Ethnography (e.g. Wilson 1978) and literary sources (e.g. Chaudhuri 1991) suggest that Indian women gain much support from same-aged women within the joint family. Writing of middle- and upper-middle-class society in Bombay, Mitter (1991: 58) notes the priority of the kinship group and that 'to seek friends outside the network of sisters-in-law, cousins, and old family connections is a relatively new phenomenon'.

However, some English informants reported difficulties in developing friendships for a variety of reasons. Research suggests that friendship in North America and Northern Europe centres on two-person relationships based on the exchange of material and emotional support (Duck 1991; Argyle 1992). For women, much of the emotional support takes the form of self-disclosure and exchange of confidences. Since it was the joint family itself which many informants found stressful, it was difficult for them to confide in members of the family, although their not doing so meant that their husband's sisters could feel rejected. Indian women visited their natal families quite frequently, but distance rendered this kind of support only an occasional option for English and North American women. Developing friendships beyond the family also presented problems as English and North American informants felt privacy and exclusivity were required but rarely available. For example:

> When we first lived in India, my husband was out at work for ten hours a day, six days a week. Luckily I knew a few women who had babies the same age as mine. But whenever you called round, their mothers-in-law, aunts and so on were also in the room. These women were perfectly nice and extremely welcoming but I found their presence quite a barrier to making friends with the woman of my own age. For me friendship was all about getting to know another *individual*, exchanging confidences and so on – not being with a big group.

An Indian informant commented that the restrictions which her husband's parents placed on her choice of friends were equivalent to confinement within 'the inner courtyard'. In making sense of the above transcripts, an Indian woman married to a British academic commented that:

> In India, the family is the major source of support – financial and emotional – for its members. It would be inappropriate to go beyond it. Firstly – think of the family as a resource – so you mustn't use it up on outsiders, mustn't 'squander' any of its reserves – be they food, money or your own time. Secondly, a united front is essential – you mustn't ever talk negatively about the family outside the family. That would be a dishonour. So the danger if you had a friend outside, would be that you might let out some secret, some confidence.

Child-rearing

Cultures are characterized by particular socialization practices. 'Parents construct learning environments for their children that foster the acquisition of skills and virtues valued in their community' (LeVine 1990: 472). Contemporary lay models of childcare in middle-class urban Northern Europe and North America owe much to the theories of Sigmund Freud, developed by John Bowlby, and popularized in childcare manuals by writers such as Penelope Leach. The most common representation of the mother-child relationship is that of an intense and one-to-one attachment, where early dependence forms the basis for the development of the child's inner sense of security and later independence. The predominant Hindu model is very different: while the mother-infant bond is prime, babies are frequently cared for by a number of women (Seymour 1983), the child is rarely left alone (Roland 1988) and is socialized to be a member of the larger family group. Independence is expected at a later age (Lazar 1979; Sissons Joshi and MacLean 1997) or, in certain aspects, not at all (Kakar 1978).

Some informants delighted in shared care and the extended family's 'protective circles' (Alibhai 1989), which enabled them to work beyond the home while relatives took care of their children. A joint family, particularly with servants, can provide virtually twenty-four-hour baby-sitting. The strength of such a system is that it can tolerate the absence of the child's mother, but some English and North American informants felt that the interchangeability of nurturing women in the family diminished the 'special' relationship they expected to have with their child. Furthermore, if childcare was shared, so too was authority and there was potential for conflict concerning views on child-rearing. As one informant put it:

My friends in England say they envy me all the help with childcare in India. But they have a rather romantic picture of what it's like. I tell them to think about all the rather annoying bits of advice they get about bringing up children when their mother or mother-in-law comes to stay – and then imagine all that advice not just for a day or two at a time, but all day every day and no walking away from it!

One area of conflict surrounded sleeping arrangements. As Shweder, Jensen and Goldstein (1995: 21) have commented 'the universal practice of determining "who sleeps by whom" in a family household is a symbolic action . . . that both expresses and realizes some of the deepest moral ideals of a cultural community'. When English women wanted toddlers to sleep alone in a separate room, Indian families regarded this as irresponsible and unfeeling. In contrast, within Indian families, intergenerational squabbles were reported over *with whom* the children should sleep – grandmothers often criticizing their 'modern' Indian daughters-in-law for 'keeping their children to themselves' as opposed to sending them to sleep in their grandparents' room. Roland's (1988: 232) interpretation of Hindu family sleeping practices is that they are by no means simply related to shortage of space but that 'Separation and aloneness are to be avoided at all costs in Indian family relationships. Dependence and interdependence are far more valued and cultivated than autonomy and separation.'

Accounts of Deference

While it may be argued that women in North America and England are socially constructed in terms of their familial roles (Delphy and Leonard 1992), increasingly girls are brought up to think of themselves as independent, to expect equality in many aspects of their relationships and a certain spatial and psychological distance from the older generation (Varenne 1996). Although a close relationship frequently exists between young parents and grandparents in England (Warnes 1986; Finch 1989), from the point of view of the present study, it is crucial to recognize that (1) the marital residence itself is usually separate, (2) such contact as there is between generations is likely to be with the maternal, not paternal, grandmother, and that (3) even where there is a lot of contact, studies suggest that all concerned subscribe 'to the ideology that mothers-in-law should keep their distance in deference to the primacy of the nuclear family' (Ribbens 1994: 80). In contrast, in Hindu society, the ideals are of interdependence rather than individuality (Hofstede 1980; Markus and Kitayama 1991; Kâğitçibaşi 1996), and girls are prepared thoughout their childhood for an accommodating role in an explicitly hierarchical society (Nabar 1995). In a joint family, (1) residence is not separate, (2) the young wife joins an existing household managed by her husband's mother, and (3) the primary relationship of a married woman is with her mother-in-law not her husband (Mies 1980).

In their review of the status of women, the Government of India (1974: 60) reported that a young married woman's behaviour

> . . . is governed by the norms of a subordinate and submissive role appropriate for a daughter-in-law. She has very little hand in any kind of decision making, and has to start her new life under severe restrictions. These are more onerous in certain regions and in the well-to-do and middle classes than in the poorer sections.

The report notes that in the authority pattern of the joint family, the daughter-in-law is directly subordinate to the mother-in-law. In her Udaipur study, Mehta (1976: 127) observed that while the education of women beyond the home revolutionized some aspects of their lives, it had not changed the basic hierarchy – young women in India are still 'mindful of joint-family etiquette' and so abide by the usual rituals afforded to elder members of the family. Thus the younger woman covers her head with a sari in the presence of her elders, touches their feet in greeting, and consults them in all important decisions. Many of our English and North American informants, although culturally entirely at ease with the notions of politeness and respect towards elders, did speak of difficulty in performing certain deferential behaviours. In particular, they found it inappropriate to consult the elder members of the family on issues which they considered either too 'trivial' (e.g. when and where to go shopping), or too 'personal' and/or 'important' (e.g. seeking an appointment with a doctor or choosing a child's school). Such 'individualistic' behaviour was not greeted favourably by older members of the family who, in India, expect to be consulted, heeded and obeyed (Vatuk 1990). One English woman reported feeling very upset when excluded from discussions concerning arrangements to celebrate her baby son's first birthday. When challenged, the mother-in-law said that 'things had come to a fine state when she couldn't plan her own grandson's birthday without interference from her son's wife'. The young wife felt impelled to assert her 'rightful' place as the child's mother, but her insistence contravened gender and hierarchy codes and was perceived as inappropriate and 'argumentative'.

Many of our English and North American informants found it hard to adjust to the degree of control which their Indian mothers-in-law expected to exercise over the joint household – the 'rights' of the mother-in-law to examine letters, monitor telephone calls, control family finances, redecorate the younger couple's bedroom without consulting them, and specify which clothes and jewellery were to be worn on which occasion. As one interviewee put it,

As a young wife in a joint household, you have no control over anything. The choice of food and how it is prepared, the lay-out of the flat, how and when the clothes are washed, how your children are to be brought up. It wasn't my idea of marriage – I expected to make a new home of my own, make my own decisions. I needed independence when I was twenty-five. That's what I thought marriage was about. Now – at forty-five – I *could* envisage living in the joint family at this stage of life – but not then.

Family roles in India are sharply differentiated according to hierarchy (Kakar 1978; Nabar 1995). One informant recounted how her eight-year-old son, who had spent his early years in Canada, disliked being expected to call his Indian cousins – only one or two years his senior – by respectful titles such as *dada* (older cousin/ brother) or *tai* (older cousin/sister). Other women, migrating back to India at a later stage in the life cycle, noticed how their teenage children were encouraged to express their own ideas on social and political matters when in the USA but were reprimanded if they expressed these views in front of their elders in India. Some informants were perplexed by how their husbands' behaviour changed upon reaching India. For example, one woman reported how in the USA she and her husband talked freely about business matters and how it was open to her to comment critically on decisions her husband made. But in India she was not permitted to discuss such matters – either in front of her in-laws or even with her husband who now deferred to his parents' views and authority. Another informant commented on how her 48-year-old husband never drank alcohol or smoked in front of his parents – she regarded his behaviour as hypocritical, but recognized that he regarded it as respectful.

Many informants commented on unspoken ground rules concerning who could communicate what and to whom. If some arrangement fell through – such as the loan of a car and driver by an older to a younger member of the family – then the younger member was not permitted to reveal her or his disappointment as such a reaction constituted disrespect. Daughters-in-law were expected to defer not only to their elders but also to males of their own age. An informant recounted an incident, taking place in England, which had upset her:

> We had been living together for some years and his family were probably relieved when we actually got married. What I didn't expect, however, was that the act of marriage would instantly transform the way in which certain relations treated me. On our wedding day we threw an impromptu party for sixty or so people and the next morning the house was littered with flowers, wine glasses and dirty dishes. My brother-in-law, visiting from India, who up until that day had treated me very courteously, looked askance at the debris and shouted, 'What a mess this is – get on and clear it up!' I was completely taken aback that he now felt he had the right to order me about in what I regarded as my own house.

The brother-in-law's use of the imperative, while not necessarily signifying rudeness in Marathi or Hindi (Gumperz et al. 1979), added to the offence caused to his English sister-in-law.

Since authors such as Bhasin (1972) have suggested that the majority of middle-class Indian women live in 'perpetual subservience, self-denial and self-sacrifice', it was not surprising that many Indian women informants also reported difficulties juggling their own desire for independence with the family's expectations of interdependence. In Gujarat, Maharashtra and other parts of India, a wife receives not only a new surname, as is customary in many societies, but a new first name chosen by her parents-in-law and signifying the end of her previous identity.[4] A management consultant recounted: 'After years of living independently – studying abroad – when my husband and I came to live in India, his parents wouldn't even give me a front-door key.' There were accounts of conflicts over jewellery, with younger women wanting to wear items they regarded as personally attractive while being pressured to wear more elaborate items which would publicly signify the family's wealth and status. A lawyer complained how it was only after ten years of marriage that she was 'permitted' by her mother-in-law to buy a night-dress and not follow the more traditional custom of sleeping in a sari.[5]

In their study of professional women in India, Liddle and Joshi (1986: 143) document the existence of 'new' joint families where communal structures are replacing autocratic ones, but note that many women live in 'traditional' joint families where 'the new wife has to adapt to the existing organization of the household and . . . has little power to demand reciprocal adjustments from the family'. Since, as we and others (e.g. Kapur 1979) have shown, strong objections to the conventional order come from Indian women themselves, an obvious question to ask is how women manage to tolerate their perceived lack of freedom. Indian women's views about their structural inequality have been the subject of much debate. Some authors have focused on 'false consciousness' (Sen 1990). Others have argued that compliance is not to be equated with complicity: women are fully aware of their position but recognize external constraints and see little room for manoeuvre (Agarwal 1994). Yet other authors have pointed to female discourses of power and resistance (Raheja and Gold 1994). In response to questions about their apparent subservience, many women reported to us that 'you just have to act in that way – for the sake of family relations'. Lannoy (1971: 126) has written that no other nation in the 'non-Western' developing world has 'such complex traditional institutions, the flaunting and open defiance of which constitutes such a high element of risk'. What seems to be at risk in gender relations is harmony in the joint family. One Indian woman reflected on her behaviour in this way:

> You have to think of being a daughter-in-law as a job. Like being at work. If you are cross with someone at work – you don't go up to them and tell them what a dreadful person they are – you bear it . You don't want a show-down because you might have to go on having an office next to that person for years. It's like that in the joint family. You are going to be there for ever. So you had better not row with them. Harmony is the essence.

Discourse of this kind suggests that Indian women value harmony in the family above the assertion of individual needs and wants. In contrast, English and North American women, unexpectedly finding themselves in a joint-family setting for which their culture has ill-prepared them, give the impression of valuing their sense of independence more than they value harmony in the family.

It is also worth considering women's short-term versus long-term goals. English and North American informants reported frustration in their desire for both status and autonomy in the early years of their marriage. Ardener (1978) has suggested that societies divide and 'mark' categories of women in different ways, and that in contrast to some other places, in England, the 'young mother' is a valued role.

Many of our English and North American respondents had felt undervalued by their Indian families at this stage. Indian society, in contrast, accords status and autonomy at a later age (Mines 1988) and thus women will feel valued in their middle or later years when they themselves become mothers-in-law. A series of early marriages and early child-bearing across generations can, however, delay a woman's ascendancy. In a four-generation joint family in suburban Bombay, a 63-year-old woman told of how she still was not able to run the home according to her own preferences as her eighty-year-old mother-in-law still presided over the details of household management. However, many of our Indian informants stated that loss of autonomy in their twenties was a price worth paying for the security which a joint family would accord them in their old age. This accords with the cultural theme, prominent amongst Hindus, that parent-child reciprocity involves a life-span calculus (Vatuk 1990). One English informant reported tolerating her loss of freedom in order that her son maintain his 'proper place' within her husband's family. Indian women may sacrifice some of their own immediate needs in favour of their sons' needs because they see their sons as their best investment in the future (Agarwal 1994). The majority of our English and North American informants either lacked the patience required or did not focus on the long term.

Ritual and the Constitution of Identity

Many English and North American women suggested that they could not play the deferential role without feeling damaged. They felt distressed at observing their own subservient behaviour to their husband or his family as it offended not only their ideology of equality but also their sense of integrity and self. As one woman said: 'It upsets me to see myself behaving in ways that aren't me – there are certain things I just can't be strategic about.'

Some English and North American informants were perplexed to see Indian women act so powerfully in their work situations and so apparently meekly in their home settings. When interviewed on this topic, some Indian woman maintained that deference to husband and parents-in-law 'doesn't mean anything, it's just a part'. A participant's account that an action is *just what's done* or *just a role* raises issues about the meaning of ritual and the constitution of identity. In Hindu society, ritual cannot be understood without reference to hierarchical inequality (Fuller 1992). Thus when a woman enacts certain rituals, her behaviour tells us about the role of women in the society, but also could be taken to indicate something about her own *relation* to gender roles and rules in that society. Indeed Goffman's (1967: 51) view is that when an individual becomes involved in the maintenance of a rule, he or she 'tends also to become committed to a particular image of self'.

However some of our Indian informants did not follow this construction in that they appeared to distance their sense of self from their performance of deferential behaviour. Mitter's (1991: 97) exploration of the relation between the self and behaviour in her analysis of Draupadi, heroine of the *Mahabharata*, is instructive:

> Draupadi is fulfilled and serene. All her chores do not make her feel like Cinderella, downtrodden and tearful, largely because she lacks ego-involvement as we would conceive it. Draupadi does not put herself on the line, swallowing her pride each time she stoops to a task. The sum of her actions does not constitute her self.

The ability to create a strong *private* sense of self within a family or public setting may be essential for both women and men if one is to 'function harmoniously within the close-knit familial hierarchical relationships from which there is no exit' (Roland 1988: 256). Ethnography in other Asian cultures has pointed to the possibility of multiple selves (Sandborg 1993), and one could speculate that Indian woman are more successful at juggling multiple selves than are English and North American women whose sense of self is more fragile because of their Weberian expectation of unity of experience.

At a general level it might seem that the construction of gender is similar in middle/upper-middle-class society in India, England and America. Women are free to leave the home, go to university, be employed, hold positions of high office in government. This implies a convergence of cultures which, along with other globalization processes, have been thought by some to be a hallmark of the late twentieth century. But this analysis ignores the crucial distinction between public and private spheres of life. Many newcomers to India are surprised by the 'Indian' aspect of friends known up until then in Western and/or public settings. An academic visitor recalled his first evening in India:

> I had spent the day with a good friend who was a film director in 'Bollywood' – his life was surrounded by modern technology, and he wore jeans. But on reaching home, the friend withdrew to don *kurta/pyjama* (a loose shirt and pyjama-style trousers), and make a *puja* (prayer) before the household arrangement of gods, and emerged 'a different man'. I had not appreciated how Indian he was.

However, perhaps only Westerners puzzle over the conjunction of 'modern' and 'traditional' for, as Sinha and Tripathi (1994) have argued, the 'coexistence of contradictions' is reflected in the various facets of Indian culture and behaviour. Such a psychic arrangement is reinforced by the role of the context as a determinant of behaviour and by contextuality as an explanation of behaviour by the participants themselves.

Endnote

In this chapter, we have concentrated on English and North American women who have married Indian men. We have not examined the same marriages from the husbands' points of view, nor have we examined in any detail the cases of Indian women who have married English or American men.[6] Some of our comments will be of relevance to therapists working across cultures. Although we have concentrated on the difficulties faced by women, there are undoubted cultural and psychodynamic benefits of cross-cultural marriage (Paris and Guzder 1989) and all but two of the thirty marriages we studied flourish. We have hinted at reframing mechanisms which enable partners to resolve differences between cultures creatively, for as Barbara (1989) has commented, cross-cultural marriages have the advantage of giving advanced warning of what every couple must eventually face – that they are different from each other.

Notes

1. The use of the terms 'nuclear' and 'extended' runs the risk of obscuring variation in family form. Within urban India, a number of complex or 'joint' domestic arrangements may be found involving lineal and/or lateral extension (Sharma 1986; Standing 1991). It is also important to note that 'jointness' may connote obligations irrespective of commensality or residence (Goody 1996).
2. Empirical research in urban India documents a growing desire amongst the younger generation to play a part in arranging their own marriages (Prakasa and Rao 1979). Young people may 'view' a series of prospective partners or invite their parents to vet the family of someone they have just met. These practices do not, however, approximate very closely to British or North American 'dating'. See Kohn (this volume) on choice within arranged marriages in Nepal.
3. The extensive psychoanalytic discussion of why Hindu men find it hard to 'defy' the authority of their mothers is beyond the scope of this chapter (Kakar 1978; Ramanujan 1983; Guzder and Krishna 1991; Cohen 1991).
4. The status of women is generally acknowledged to be higher in the south, as compared to the north of India (Karve 1953; Agarwal 1994). Furthermore, the permissibility of cross-cousin marriage means that, upon marriage, a south Indian woman may find herself

among relatives rather than strangers. However, 'the higher the caste, the more closely does the position of females resemble that accorded to them under the north Indian kinship model' (Dyson and Moore 1983: 56). In any event, from the point of view of an outsider, India will be perceived as 'on the whole, an area of comparatively low female autonomy' (Dyson and Moore 1983: 46). Also see Drèze and Sen's (1995) discussion of gender inequality and women's agency in India.

5. In Dandekar's (1981) account of constraints on sexuality in rural Maharashtra, women reported that in crowded joint households where men and women's normal sleeping arrangements were segregated by gender, their mother-in-law would decide, 'completely on whim' (p.425), where and on which days the couple could sleep together.

6. In the various communities in Britain, inter-ethnic unions are least common among those of South Asian origin. Within such unions however, those between Indian men and White women outnumber those between Indian women and White men (Berrington 1996).

References

Agarwal, B. (1994), *A Field of One's Own*, Cambridge: Cambridge University Press.

Alibhai, Y. (1989), 'Burning in the Cold', in K. Gieve (ed.), *Balancing Acts*, London: Virago.

Alibhai-Brown, Y. and Montague, A. (1992), *The Colour of Love*, London: Virago.

Allan, G. (1989), 'Insiders and Outsiders: Boundaries around the Home', in G. Allan and G. Crow (eds), *Home and Family*, Basingstoke: Macmillan.

Anandalakshmy, S. (1981), 'Learning to Live in Families: Speculations on a Holographic Image of the Indian', paper presented to *Life Courses and Family Relationships in Alternative Psychologies of South Asia*, 2nd Workshop of the Person in South Asia Project, 6–8 September 1981, Chicago.

Appachana, A. (1991), *Incantations*, New Delhi: Penguin.

Appadurai, A. (1981), 'Gastro-Politics in Hindu South Asia', *American Ethnologist*, 8, pp.494–511.

Ardener, S. (1978), 'Introduction: The Nature of Women in Society', in S. Ardener (ed.), *Defining Females*, London: Croom Helm.

——, (1993), 'Ground Rules and Social Maps for Women', in S. Ardener (ed.), *Women and Space*, Oxford: Berg.

Argyle, M. (1982), 'Inter-Cultural Communication', in S. Bochner (ed.), *Cultures in Contact*, Oxford: Pergamon.

——, (1992), *The Social Psychology of Everyday Life*, London: Routledge.

Barbara, A. (1989), *Marriage across Frontiers*, Clevedon: Multilingual Matters Ltd.

Berrington, A. (1996), 'Marriage Patterns and Inter-ethnic Unions', in D. Coleman and J. Salt (eds), *Ethnicity in the 1991 Census: Volume 1. Demographic Characteristics of the Ethnic Minority Populations*, London: HMSO.

Bhasin, K. (1972), 'The Predicament of Indian Middle-Class Women – An Inside View', in K. Bhasin (ed.), *The Position of Women in India*, Srinigar: Arvind Deshpande (cited in Liddle and Joshi 1986).

Brown, G.W. and Harris, T. (1978), *Social Origins of Depression*, London: Tavistock.

Chaudhuri, A. (1991), *A Strange and Sublime Address*, London: Minerva.

Cohen, L. (1991), 'The Wives of Ganesa', in R.L. Brown (ed.), *Ganesh*, Albany: State University of New York Press.

Cunningham, J.D. and Antill, J.K. (1995), 'Current Trends in Nonmarital Cohabitation: In Search of the POSSLQ', in J.T. Wood and S. Duck (eds), *Under-Studied Relationships*, Thousand Oaks: Sage.

Dandekar, H. (1981), 'Social and Spatial Constraints on Rural Women's Sexuality: Observations from an Indian Village', *Ekistics*, 291, pp.422–9.

Das, V. (1979), 'Reflections on the Social Construction of Adulthood', in S. Kakar (ed.), *Identity and Adulthood*, Delhi: Oxford University Press.

Davar, B.V. (1995), 'Mental Illness among Indian Women', *Economic & Political Weekly*, 11 November 1995, pp.2879–86.

Delphy, C. and Leonard, D. (1992), *Familiar Exploitation*, Oxford: Polity.

Desai, P.N. (1995), 'Personality Politics: A Psychoanalytic Perspective', in U. Baxi and B. Parekh (eds), *Crisis and Change in Contemporary India*, New Delhi: Sage.

Dhawan, N., Roseman, I.J., Naidu, R.K., Thapa, K. and Rettek, S.I. (1995), 'Self-Concepts across Two Cultures: India and the United States', *Journal of Cross-Cultural Psychology*, 26(6), pp.606–21.

Douglas, M. (1966), *Purity and Danger*, London: Routledge & Kegan Paul.

Drèze, J. and Sen, A. (1995), *India: Economic Development and Social Opportunity*, Delhi: Oxford University Press.

Duck, S.W. (1991), *Understanding Relationships*, New York: Guilford.

Dunung, S.P. (1995), *Doing Business in Asia*, New York: Lexington Books.

Dyson, T. and Moore, M. (1983), 'On Kinship Structure, Female Autonomy, and Demographic Behavior in India', *Population and Development Review*, 9(1), pp.35–60.

Ferro-Luzzi, G.E. (1977), 'Ritual as Language: The case of South Indian Food Offerings', *Current Anthropology*, 18(3), pp.507–14.

Finch, J. (1989), 'Kinship and Friendship', in R. Jowell, S. Witherspoon, and L. Brook (eds), *British Social Attitudes*, Aldershot: Gower.

Fuller, C.J. (1992), *The Camphor Flame*, Princeton: Princeton University Press.

Giddens, A. (1989), *Sociology*, Oxford: Polity.

——, (1992), *The Transformation of Intimacy*, Oxford: Polity.

Goffman, E. (1967), *Interaction Ritual*, Garden City: Doubleday Anchor.

——, (1969), *The Presentation of Self in Everyday Life*, Harmondsworth: Penguin.

——, (1977), 'The Arrangement between the Sexes', *Theory & Society*, 4, pp.301–31.

Goody, J. (1996), *The East in the West*, Cambridge: Cambridge University Press.

Government of India (1974), *Towards Equality*, Report of the Committee on the Status of Women in India, New Delhi: Government of India.

Gumperz, J.J., Jupp, T.C. and Roberts, C. (1979), *Crosstalk: An Introduction to Cross-Cultural Communication*, London: BBC Education.

Guzder, J. and Krishna, M. (1991), 'Sita-Shakti: Cultural Paradigms for Indian Women', *Transcultural Psychiatric Research Review*, 28, pp.257–301.

Harlan, L. and Courtwright, P.B. (1995), *From the Margins of Hindu Marriage*, Oxford: Oxford University Press.

Hoecklin, L. (1995), *Managing Cultural Differences*, Wokingham: Addison-Wesley.

Hofstede, G. (1980), *Culture's Consequences*, Newbury Park: Sage.

Jain, M. (1994), 'Change amidst Continuity', *India Today*, 15 July.

Kâğitçibaşi, Ç. (1996), *Family and Human Development Across Cultures: A View from the Other Side*, Mahwah, New Jersey: Lawrence Erlbaum.

Kakar, S. (1978), *The Inner World*, Delhi: Oxford University Press.

——, (1989), *Intimate Relations*, New Delhi: Penguin.

Kapur, P. (1979), 'Women in Modern India', in M.S. Das and P.D. Bardis (eds), *The Family in Asia*, London: George Allen & Unwin.

Karve, I. (1953), *Kinship Organisation in India*, Deccan College Monograph Series no. 11, Madras: G S Press.

Khare, R.S. (1976), *The Hindu Hearth and Home*, New Delhi: Vikas.

Kiernan, K. (1989), 'The Family: Formation and Fission', in H. Joshi (ed.), *The Changing Population of Britain*, Oxford: Blackwell.

Lannoy, R. (1975, 1971), *The Speaking Tree*, Oxford: Oxford University Press.

Lazar, R. (1979), 'Asian Family and Society: A Theoretical Overview', in M.S. Das and P.D. Bardis (eds), *The Family in Asia*, London: George Allen & Unwin.

LeVine, R.A. (1990), 'Infant Environments in Psychoanalysis: A Cross-Cultural View', in J.W. Stigler, R.A. Shweder and G. Herdt (eds), *Cultural Psychology*, Cambridge: Cambridge University Press.

Liddle, J. and Joshi, R. (1986), *Daughters of Independence*, London: Zed Books Ltd.

Markus, H. and Kitayama, S. (1991), 'Culture and Self: Implications for Cognition, Emotion and Motivation', *Psychological Review*, 98, pp.224–53.

Mehta, R. (1976), 'From Purdah to Modernity', in B.R. Nanda (ed.), *Indian Women*, New Delhi: Vikas.

Mies, M. (1980), *Indian Women and Patriarchy*, New Delhi: Concept (cited in Liddle and Joshi 1986).

Miller, J.G. (1984), 'Culture and the Development of Everyday Social Explanation', *Journal of Personality and Social Psychology*, 46, pp.961–78.

Mines, M. (1988), 'Conceptualising the Person: Hierarchical Society and Individual Autonomy in India', *American Anthropologist*, 90, pp.568–79.

Mitter, S.S. (1991), *Dharma's Daughters*, New Brunswik: Rutgers University Press.

Moore, H.L. (1988), *Feminism and Anthropology*, Oxford: Polity.

Nabar, V. (1995), *Caste As Woman*, New Delhi: Penguin.

Nanda, S. (1991), *Cultural Anthropology*, Belmont: Wadsworth.

Padmanabhan, M. (1995), 'Stains' in R. Advani, I. Hutnik, M. Kesavan and D. Kumar (eds), *Civil Lines 2: New Writing from India*, Delhi: Ravi Dayal.

Paris, J. and Guzder, J. (1989), 'The Poisoned Nest: Dynamic Aspects of Exogamous Marriage', *Journal of the American Academy of Psychoanalysis*, 17 (3), pp.493–500.

Prakasa, V.V. and Rao, V.N. (1979), 'Arranged Marriages: An Assessment of the Attitudes of the College Students in India', in G. Kurian (ed.), *Cross-Cultural Perspectives of Mate-Selection and Marriage*, Westport: Greenwood Press.

Raheja, G.G. and Gold, A.G. (1994), *Listen to the Heron's Words*, Berkeley: University of California Press.

Ramanujan, A. (1983), 'The Indian Oedipus', in L. Edmonds and A. Dundes (eds), *Oedipus: A Folklore Casebook*, New York: Garland.

Reibstein, J. and Richards, M. (1992), *Sexual Arrangements*, London: Heinemann.

Ribbens, J. (1994), *Mothers and Their Children*, London: Sage.

Roland, A. (1988), *In Search of Self in India and Japan*, Princeton: Princeton University Press.

Sandborg, K. (1993), 'Malay Dress Symbolism', in V. Broch-Due, I. Rudie and T. Bleie (eds), *Carved Flesh/Cast Selves*, Oxford: Berg.

Sciama, L. (1993), 'The Problem of Privacy in Mediterranean Anthropology', in S. Ardener (ed.), *Women and Space*, Oxford: Berg.

Sen, A. (1990), 'Gender and Cooperative Conflicts', in I. Tinker (ed.), *Persistent Inequalities: Women and World Development*, New York: Oxford University Press.

Seymour, S. (1983), 'Household Structure and Status and Expressions of Affect in India, *Ethos*, 11(4), pp.263–77.

Shah, A.M. (1974), *The Household Dimension of the Family in India*, Berkeley: University of California Press.

Sharma, U. (1986), *Women's Work, Class, and the Urban Household*, London: Tavistock.

Shweder, R.A. and Bourne, E. (1982), 'Does the Concept of the Person Vary Cross-Culturally?' in A.J. Marsella and G. White (eds), *Cultural Conceptions of Mental Health and Therapy*, Dordrecht: Reidel.

——, Jensen, L.A. and Goldstein, W.M. (1995), 'Who Sleeps by Whom Revisited: A Method for Extracting the Moral Goods Implicit in Practice', in J.J. Goodnow, P. Miller and F. Kessel (eds), *Cultural Practices as Context for Development*, San Francisco: Jossey Bass.

Sinha, D. and Tripathi, R.C. (1994), 'Individualism in a Collectivist Culture: A Case of Coexistence of Opposites', in U. Kim, H.C. Triandis, Ç. Kâğitçibaşi, S.-C. Choi and G. Yoon (eds), *Individualism and Collectivism*, Thousand Oaks: Sage.

Sissons Joshi, M. and MacLean, M. (1997), 'Maternal Expectations of Child Development in India, Japan and England', *Journal of Cross-Cultural Psychology*, 28 (2), pp.219–34.

Standing, H. (1991), *Dependence and Autonomy*, London: Routledge.

Taylor, S.E. (1995), *Health Psychology*, 3rd edition, New York: McGraw Hill.

Trawick, M. (1990), 'The Ideology of Love in a Tamil Village', in O.M. Lynch (ed.), *Divine Passions*, Berkeley: University of California Press.

Tysoe, M. (1992), *Love Isn't Quite Enough*, London: Fontana.

Varenne, H. (1996), 'Love and Liberty: The Contemporary American Family', in A. Burguiere et al. (eds), *A History of the Family*, Oxford: Polity.

Vatuk, S. (1990), 'To be a Burden on Others', in O.M. Lynch (ed.), *Divine Passions*, Berkeley: University of California Press.

Warnes, A.M. (1986), 'The Residential Mobility Histories of Parents and Children, and Relationships to Proximity and Social Integration', *Environment and Planning*, 18, pp.1581–94.

Wilson, A. (1978), *Finding a Voice*, London: Virago.

Acknowledgements

We would like to thank our informants (not listed to preserve their anonymity) and the following for their stimulating and useful comments on an earlier draft of this chapter – Hella Adler, Aparna Basu, Carol Dyhouse, Jaswant Guzder, Geoff Hawthorn, Joy Hendry, Dharma Kumar, Radha Kumar, Begum Maitra, Chris McDonaugh, Alok Rai, Jane Ribbens and Jenny Shaw.

11

Gender Identity and Gender Role Patterns in Cross-Cultural Marriages: The Japanese–Danish Case[1]

Kirsten Refsing

Male–female conversation is always cross-cultural communication.

(Tannen 1986: 109)

Introduction

The above quotation from Deborah Tannen is important to bear in mind when studying marriages between partners of different nationalities. Communication problems are not only about having different mother tongues; many communication problems are gender-related and common to most, if not all, marriages. In the final analysis, all marriages may be said to be cross-cultural in that they bring together the different cultural worlds and experiences of men and women. However, since men and women were traditionally assigned complementary gender roles within a specific culture, a man and a woman who have grown up in the same cultural surroundings will generally have a common model for understanding their separate roles in the marriage, which may help them overlook (or overcome) the communication difficulties caused by gender differences.[2] Where these models are undergoing change, the communication difficulties may, of course, be exacerbated.

Gender complementarity is not necessarily present in cross-cultural marriages, since partners may come together from two cultures with very different perceptions of male and female gender roles. When this is the case, the success of the marriage will depend on the satisfactory negotiation of a new kind of gender comple-mentarity acceptable to both partners. Both may be required to adjust their concepts of selfhood and identity, and the question of which spouse will have to make the largest concessions is not only influenced by the gender or the personal characteristics of the spouses, but also to a large extent by the demands made and the options offered by the socio-cultural environment in which the couple has chosen to live.

In the following, I shall look at how the partners in Japanese–Danish marriages in Denmark perceive their own gender and identity, and how the lifestyle and living conditions in Denmark influence the range of choices available to the couple when they try to establish a viable power and gender relation pattern for their marriage. This chapter is based on twenty-six interviews carried out in Denmark between 1993 and 1994. The interviewees were Danish and Japanese men and women, from a wide range of class and educational backgrounds, who were either currently intermarried or who had previously been. Ages ranged from twenty-five to sixty-five, and the duration of the marriages at the time of the interview from two years to twenty-eight years. Interviews were carried out in Danish, Japanese, or English, and in a few instances even a mixture of these languages. In some cases I interviewed the spouses together, in other cases separately. Each interview was based on an interview guide containing questions about the personal life history of each interviewee, the history of their married life, and their views on a variety of topics such as gender, cultural identity, religion, politics, cultural differences and similarities, child rearing, and life style. Each interview lasted between ninety minutes and six hours, with an average length of 2–3 hours. All interviews were taped and later transcribed. Although all my interviewees were living in Denmark at the time, some had lived for a period in Japan, and a few had lived in countries that were foreign to both spouses.

The Nature of Culture

Gender is a socio-cultural construct and gender identity is acquired largely sub-consciously by each individual through continuous, lifelong interactions with others within the same socio-cultural environment. Like other fundamental dimensions of culture, gender tends to be understood both collectively and by the individual as *nature* rather than *culture*. We tend to experience our own perceptions of gender and gender roles as the only possible and acceptable ones, and individuals who refuse to conform to the dominant gender role patterns (e.g. homosexuals or feminists) are considered by many to be 'unnatural'. Likewise, other cultures which subscribe to a radically different gender role pattern will often be considered either 'backward' or 'unnatural'. Societies where women have been emancipated will look upon strictly patriarchal societies as 'backward', and patriarchal cultures will see emancipated women as 'unnatural females' who have deserted their 'natural destiny'.

If we accept as a basic tenet that no culture has a monopoly on being 'natural', we must also recognize that all models for gender-role distribution are culturally determined and that no roles assigned to men or women warrant the term 'natural'. This basic premise, however, does not necessarily lead to 'cultural relativism', i.e. the attitude that since we all possess arbitrarily different cultures nobody has the right to condemn or judge any manifestation of any other culture: 'If you let me have my culture in peace, I will let you have your culture in peace.' Cultural relativists would say that European and American feminists should not object to African mothers choosing to have their two-year-old daughters circumcised on kitchen tables in Paris, nor to Turkish fathers who marry off their European-born and educated fourteen-year-old girls to illiterate farmers from remote villages in Turkey.

Cultures do not remain isolated and left to their own devices in today's world. All sorts of mobility across borders repeatedly forces contacts between cultures, and these contacts are not always free of conflict or mutual dislike, even though they may cause people to readjust their concepts of what is 'natural'. Cross-cultural marriages are just one instance of cultural contact in which a philosophy of 'live and let live' can hardly work. In such marriages two cultures must coexist under one roof, and many issues which might not come to the surface in monocultural marriages become subject to negotiation. One such issue is gender identity and gender roles.

Personal versus Collective Identity

Before I go on to discuss my empirical material on Japanese–Danish marriages, I shall touch briefly upon the concept of identity. This is a somewhat ambiguous and elastic term, since it can have two opposite meanings, namely that of 'sameness' (i.e. of being identical to others in a group), and that of 'distinctiveness' (i.e. self-sameness as distinct from others, cf. Erikson 1980: 109). These two meanings may in turn be applied to individuals (personal identity) as well as to groups (collective identity) (Jacobson-Widding 1983: 13; see also Breger, Shibata and Waldren, this volume).

Personal identity is often perceived by the individual as distinct from the collective identity, but in fact this personal sense of identity is strongly interrelated with and dependent upon the collective identity of the group or groups to which the individual belongs. Feelings of an inner, personal self depend vitally on the sharing of a collective identity with others, and the better the personal identity 'fits' (Jacobson-Widding 1983: 14) with the identity of the group or groups of which one is a member, the stronger it seems to be (see Khatib-Chahidi et al., this volume). If circumstances (such as entering into a cross-cultural marriage) force people to move out of one group and into another with a different collective identity, their personal identities no longer 'fit' very well, and therefore become threatened. People who experience a discrepancy between their inner identity and the collective identity of the surrounding group will experience an identity crisis: a loss of the inner self, which is no longer regularly reinforced by the immediate surroundings. (This group can, of course, be part-defined by shared cultural practices, class-based lifestyles, and so on.)

This experience was brought up by several of my Japanese informants, and it appears to be a common – though in most cases temporary – problem for the cross-culturally married partner who has moved into the culture of his or her spouse. The psychological problems involved in adapting to life in a foreign country are seen as considerable by my interviewees. Few of them had met with anything but friendly acceptance in Denmark, but some complained that this easy acceptance of them as 'just people' felt like a put-down.

> I wonder why the Danes have so little curiosity. They meet me and they know that I come from Japan, but they never ask me anything about myself or my background. It's as if I didn't exist before I came here.

> (Japanese woman in her fifties)

The need to establish a new identity because the old one did not count any more was mentioned by several of the Japanese people I interviewed. For some it had led to a crisis point, where they came close to deserting their marriages and going back to Japan. Others had found comfort in Japanese friends in Denmark, or in returning to Japan for short periods to gather strength. Since all the Japanese I talked to had – at least so far – eventually opted for staying in Denmark, they represent the more successful outcomes of the struggle to define a viable identity as a compromise between their culture of origin and their new, adopted culture. But in most cases this was seen as a problem which placed a potentially destructive strain on the cross-cultural marriage. In some cases, the Danish spouses showed a great deal of understanding and tolerance towards their partners' struggle, but in other cases they appeared unconcerned or even impatient with their spouses' failure to behave in a 'Danish' manner. The following excerpts from an interview with a young couple may illustrate the latter attitude. The exchange took place after the wife recounted in some detail how unhappy she had been during the first year of their marriage, because her husband was very busy, and she did not know what to do with herself and almost decided to go back to Japan.

Interviewer (to husband): How do you react when your wife is homesick for Japan?
Husband: Well . . . (laughs)
Interviewer: Do you feel that you understand her homesickness?
Husband: Of course, of course. But now we've been married for quite a while and lived here, so . . . It was worse

before. We also have a number of friends now who are Japanese–Danish couples, so it is not so . . . (to his wife) What do you think?

Wife: No it isn't – I don't feel like that anymore.

Husband: No, this is your home now. Of course you may be homesick for your mom and things like that. That's different, isn't it. That's hardly . . . Well, you can phone her now and then, but . . . that's quite expensive.

Later in the interview, the following exchange took place:

Interviewer: Did you have language problems in the beginning?

Husband: That shouldn't be in the past tense! We still have problems all the time. I guess most languages have unfinished sentences, and if my wife doesn't pay a lot of attention to what's going on in my head, she can't follow me. Things like that are always annoying – you have half a conversation, really. But no answer.

Interviewer (to wife): Are you able to say what you want to say in your husband's language?

Wife: There are things I can't express as clearly as I wish. But it's more of a problem to catch what my husband says. If I'm tired and can't concentrate, I listen to him, and I understand almost all the words, but I miss a few. Then I try to guess what he was asking and come up with a suitable answer. But then it turns out that he was asking something quite different. And then he gets very upset and agitated . . .. Maybe in his own language he doesn't have to concentrate all the time, but is able to listen with half an ear and still understand . . .. When I'm tired I also sometimes use a wrong word. The other day I wanted to say 'Why', but ended up saying 'How' instead. Then my husband thinks that I'm totally hopeless. But in my head I thought 'Why', it was just my mouth saying 'How', you see.

Husband: But 'How' and 'Why' are two quite different things! I don't quite remember the situation, but when things like that happen, I can't help thinking 'Oh my God, do we have to start all over again?'

Wife:	But you may be tired sometimes, too. When you're in a good mood, you understand me even if I make small mistakes. But when you're very impatient, you won't make allowances for such small mistakes. Then I must suddenly speak one hundred per cent correctly.

The solution to the identity problem rarely lies in trying to identify completely with the new culture, but rather in working out a compromise between the old and the new identities. Such a compromise may be more or less hard to achieve, depending on how far one ends up deviating from the original definition of personal identity. As we shall see in the following, there are large differences in the degree of accommodation required of Danish and Japanese intermarried wives and husbands, especially when it comes to gender identity and gender roles.

Gender Roles in Denmark and Japan

Besides being dependent upon the stage one has reached in one's life cycle, gender identity is furthermore liable to continuous reconstructions and amendments in accordance with changes occurring in the surrounding society. Also, there are differences between, for example, city and countryside, and between different social classes. Bearing all these reservations in mind, I shall, nevertheless, try to map out in the following some salient features of Japanese and Danish constructions of gender identity in order to provide some background for readers who are less familiar with one or both of these countries. In so doing, I may appear to present gender identities as rather more fixed and absolute than is really the case, and for this I apologize.

Gender identities are shaped by history, socialization, education, family system, class and other socio-cultural conditions. Historically, both Denmark and Japan have – not surprisingly – relegated women to a position subordinate to that of men, and the arguments for doing so have been much the same, namely that women are weaker and less intelligent than men, and if allowed to get out of control, they may even possibly be dangerous! However, if we look at the more recent history of the two societies, remarkable differences between them have emerged.

Since the late 1960s, there has been a concentrated effort in Denmark towards creating equality between the genders, and this has been largely successful. Men and women have the same formal opportunities for education and for having a career, and although men still hold the majority of top positions and well-paid jobs, women are gradually making their presence felt in all areas of society. Being a full-time housewife is now an exceedingly rare role for the younger generations of women in Denmark. Women have jobs outside the home, and if they do not, it is because the unemployment rate is generally high, and not because they do not want a paid occupation. Male chauvinist attitudes towards women still exist of course, but men with the audacity to voice such opinions in public are few and far between.

Japan, too, has moved towards an upgrading of women's position after the Second World War. Women are strongly represented in the labour market, but in lower positions and with much lower earning potential than men. As Robert Smith has put it: '. . . it is no exaggeration to say that while most women at one time or another in their lives hold down a *job*, it is still exceedingly rare for a women to pursue a *career* outside the home' (Smith 1987: 14). The support system for working mothers is poor in terms of paid pregnancy and maternity leave, guarantees for returning to the same job afterwards, proper childcare facilities, and paid leave when children are ill, so it is still the common choice for Japanese women to stop working during the years of child-bearing and rearing. Furthermore, since this is what both society and employers expect them to do, few employers are willing to take the trouble to educate their young female staff on a par with young male staff. The prevailing attitude that working mothers are guilty of fostering delinquent children, and unhappy and poorly maintained spouses, puts further pressure on women to give up their careers for the sake of their families. Women who return to the labour market when their children are older find themselves in badly paid, menial jobs with little or no job security.

It is therefore no surprise that the prevailing gender identities fostered in these two cultures turn out different: many Japanese women primarily identify themselves with the concept of 'good wives and wise mothers'. They see themselves primarily as caretakers, and they are encouraged to strive for the ideals of mildness (*yasashisa*), stoicism (*gaman*), consideration of others (*omoiyari*) and other 'traditional' female virtues. (These ideals were first actively propagated through the Meiji government ideology of motherhood from the 1880s: although they have older, Confucian associations, they do not seem to have been used so prominently in Japan before the Meiji era.) Japanese women often marry late because marriage tends to be perceived as a loss of freedom, and when they marry, they look for a good provider rather than for a partner with whom to share their lives. The Japanese saying, '[a good husband is one who is] healthy and away from home' (*joobu de rusu*) aptly expresses the attitude held by many Japanese wives towards their husbands.

In contrast, most Danish women are brought up to believe that anything a man can do, a woman can do just as well. Motherhood is the only thing that distinguishes the genders, but apart from actually bearing the child, official ideology has it that a father can fulfil the parental role equally well as the mother. Household tasks are no longer supposed to be gender specific and many couples share them on a more or less equal basis. Marriage is entered into for love, and not for practical reasons – even though it may turn out to be a practical arrangement as well. Ideals for young Danish women are independence, the ability to support oneself, and the successful pursuit of one's personal goals in life.

Looking at the male gender role, we find that Japanese men are raised to be good providers in a harsh world, and in return they feel that it is their birthright to have women support them in this, first their mothers, later their wives. They find it shameful to be caught doing household chores, and they are encouraged to live up to ideals of manliness, dedication to work, and strength of spirit (*seishin*). It is likely that these ideals of 'manliness' stem historically from the general patriarchal systems prevalent in all Japanese classes, despite their different codes, but are nowadays probably more influenced by portrayals of 'manliness' in the media and advertising. Their primary preoccupation is with their work, and they often feel more comfortable in the company of male colleagues than at home with their families.

Compared to Japanese men, Danish men have more trouble with their conventional gender role as main breadwinners and are often said to be going through an identity crisis brought on by the changing role of Danish women. Many feel that they are oscillating between a 'traditional' male image of strength and dominance, and a new one of sensitivity and empathy. The male role model in Denmark has changed from the 'macho' man of the 1950s and 1960s, through the so-called soft man of the 1970s, who could even go so far as to knit his own sweaters, and again to the 'new man' of the 1980s and 1990s, who tries to combine 'old-fashioned manliness' with the ability to be a good companion for his wife and a loving father towards his children.

Gender is a relational concept, and male and female gender identities within a specific culture ideally fit into each other like pieces in a puzzle. When a person marries out, the pieces of the puzzle no longer fit snugly together, but often collide in a variety of ways during the process of trying to organize family life. Below, I shall try to give an impression of how my interviewees viewed this question.

Views on Gender Roles among Danish–Japanese Couples

In Japanese–Danish marriages the initial differences are considerable, and when asked about gender roles in Denmark and Japan, most of my interviewees displayed rather negative feelings, especially about Japanese female gender role characteristics. Japanese housewives and mothers were seen by both Danish and Japanese women of the younger generation as subordinate, isolated and dependent. Danish women (and a few of the younger Japanese husbands) also mentioned that they saw young Japanese women as incredibly childish, always giggling.

I think there's a fundamental difference between Japanese and Danish women. I wouldn't say that they're oppressed, but the overall pattern is so different. In the beginning I got very annoyed – for example the first time I visited Japan and saw young women of my own age starting to giggle uninhibitedly over something. And the movements – like they were all in knots. I don't think it's because they're oppressed. Rather it's a cultural pattern which they're comfortable with. But I wouldn't be comfortable if I had to behave like that.

(Danish woman in her early thirties)

The younger generation of Japanese and Danish men did not often express any opinion on the subject of women's position, although they nodded agreement to some of their wives' comments, but older Danish men[3] did not hesitate to revel in their good luck in marrying an oriental woman and thus not having to contend with a 'selfish', 'independent', and 'outspoken' Danish wife (see also Breger, this volume, on stereotypes of 'oriental' women). One older Danish husband, who had met his wife when he was a sailor in his youth, said:

I think Japanese women know more about being a woman. Really, Danish women are more independent. They demand that their husbands do half of the housework. What kind of a marriage is that? I've never had that problem.

A similar attitude may be found among younger Danish men who import brides from other Asian countries such as Thailand or the Philippines, but it seemed to be totally absent among those men of the younger generation who had married Japanese women. On the contrary, there were cases where the Danish husband actually brought pressure to bear on his Japanese wife to learn Danish and have a career, and to be more assertive both in and outside of the marriage. One such husband said to his wife during the interview:

Well, at least you've gotten better at getting angry!

(Danish man about thirty years old)

And his wife replied:

Yes, I guess I show my anger more. I was told that if I never showed anger, the Danes would think that I was stupid. Then I'd just appear to be one of those Asian wives who can't oppose their husbands.

(Japanese woman in her late twenties)

There were cases, especially among the younger couples, in which the Japanese partner had – at least on the surface – given up most of the characteristics of Japanese gender identity and was doing his or her best to be almost more Danish than the Danes. Many of the Japanese wives had managed to find full-time jobs outside the home, whereas this seemed to be much more difficult for the Japanese husbands, many of whom exhibited a pattern of periods of unemployment interspersed with various temporary jobs. This left them time to do their equal share – if not more – of household chores and childcare. Even though most of them expressed contentment with this situation, one should not overlook the fact that there are structural conditions in the Danish labour market which limit the degree of employment choice for foreigners who settle down to live in Denmark. The official unemployment rate in Denmark passed the 10 per cent mark several years ago, and this means that foreign *men* in particular experience great difficulty in securing jobs, unless they have either a Danish education or special skills to distinguish them from their unemployed Danish rivals. Language problems are in part to blame for this, but it is also coupled with the fact that many Danish employers will choose a Danish applicant for a job rather than a foreigner whom they think might well have cultural traits which would interfere with their adaptability to a Danish workplace.

Japanese women who marry Danish men may also experience some difficulty in overcoming the language barrier and finding employment, but generally they can at least find jobs with Japanese firms in Denmark or in Japanese restaurants. Japanese men employed by Japanese firms are usually posted to Denmark by the Japanese head office (as the upper management); there seems to be far less resistance to employing women as local support staff than men. For a number of the Japanese women, their jobs in Japanese firms served as a springboard for finding similar employment in Danish firms or organizations.

For the Japanese men the absence of steady employment outside the home seriously impeded their chances of preserving the older conventional male gender identity of main breadwinners, and most of the Japanese men who did a large share of the household tasks said that they had begun doing so during a period when they were unemployed. Their Danish wives usually did not find their gender identity challenged by being the main breadwinners of the family, but most of them reported that they did in fact adapt in various ways to their husbands' expectations, even when it was perceived as going against what Danish women would normally tolerate in a marriage. One young Danish wife said:

In Japan I'd probably be seen as a terrible wife, but according to Danish standards I don't think that I'm all that bad. I think I've adapted rather well, and after all it would be a pity for my husband if I'd been a typical Danish wife.

(Danish woman in her mid-twenties)

Asked about what she thought was required for a cross-cultural marriage to succeed, the same woman later said:

> You have to give something of yourself. There may be some areas where you'd not be so generous if your husband were Danish, but sometimes you just have to say: 'OK, I'll do it because it'll make him happy . . .' or something like that.

Another wife said:

> Many times in our life together, I've compromised on issues where a Danish girl would normally not compromise. She might find it really silly and very unreasonable. But I think that my husband is bending corners for my sake, so if there are some things which mean a lot to him, I don't mind doing them. And I refuse to think of it in terms of female oppression.
>
> (Danish woman in her early thirties)

The Japanese wives with full-time jobs outside the home generally expected a lot less from their Danish husbands than a Danish wife would. And in most cases the husbands readily fell into routines that confirmed the expectations of their wives, even though the same husbands held the firmly expressed opinion that the fact that their wives were Japanese and not Danish made no difference at all. One Danish husband, the father of several children, described how he had gradually slipped into a work routine which was not very different from that of a Japanese company employee, and how this had resulted in his wife taking over more and more household chores in spite of the fact that she herself held a demanding full-time job. Another Danish husband said that the last thing he wanted was a submissive Japanese wife, so he had taken great pains to coach her in Danish and help her start a career. Nevertheless, when they had a baby, he readily accepted leaving everything concerning the baby to her. At the time of the interview, he was enjoying the short paternity leave granted to fathers in Denmark when a new child is born, but instead of spending time with the baby, he was using his leave to redecorate the kitchen. He put it this way:

> You know, even though I have this childcare leave, I sort of lack the natural qualifications for taking care of the baby when he's unhappy. And as you can see, my wife is deeply in love with him. It's hard to intrude into that relationship . . .
>
> (Danish man in his early thirties)

If we view Danish–Japanese marriages on a scale where one end is represented by a very conservative and patriarchal gender role pattern, and the other by a more 'modern' type of marriage between two equal partners (sometimes described by critics in Denmark as 'a family of two fathers'), we may say that the traditional marriage which clearly demarcates gender roles fits the gender identity of the Japanese woman best, with least conflicts of expectations. It can also work very well for Danish men who – as I pointed out above – have become somewhat ambiguous about their gender identity in recent years. Actually, this type of marriage was seen as satisfactory by both Japanese women and Danish men. The Japanese women got more help and support than they would have received from Japanese husbands, so even though they had to deal with both an outside job and the job of being a housewife, they considered themselves lucky. If they had married Japanese men they might not have had to stay in the labour market, but most of the women were happy with their outside employment, and they found it a definite plus that their Danish husbands encouraged them in this instead of vetoing it as a Japanese husband might well have done. And the Danish husbands considered themselves lucky for having wives who not only contributed as breadwinners like Danish wives, but also took the brunt of responsibility for everything concerning family and home with no complaints.

In the marriages where the husband was Japanese and the wife Danish, the marriage style would be positioned more towards the 'modern' end of the scale. Here the Japanese men had been forced to accept a considerable drop in status and a shared responsibility for daily chores. They had furthermore accepted that their wives could take part in society on an equal footing with them – or even with a status higher than their own. Such a marriage fits well with the gender identity of Danish women, but although it clashed violently with the gender identity of Japanese men, the very fact of the men leaving their home ground and committing themselves to life in Denmark had put them in a position, socially and economically, where they had no choice but to accept this reduced role. This was easier if the original reason for leaving Japan and marrying a foreigner was based on a rejection of the prevalent conventional roles available for men in Japanese society. In fact, quite a few of my male Japanese interviewees expressed disgust at what they called 'workaholic Japanese men'. Still, it probably comes as no surprise that divorce rates for Japanese men married to Danish women were significantly higher than the rates for Japanese women married to Danish men. In the fourteen-year period from 1979 to 1993, the number of registered weddings in Denmark between Danish men and Japanese women was sixty, and the number of registered divorces in the same period was thirty-six. This is only slightly higher than the divorce rates for monocultural Danish marriages. For Japanese men married to Danish women the corresponding numbers were thirty-four weddings and thirty-three divorces (Statistical Office of Denmark).

Concluding Remarks

Recapitulating what has been said so far, we may see that for Danish–Japanese marriages in Denmark the gender identity of the wife appeared to dominate in determining the gender-role distribution in the marriage. The gender identity of the Danish wives was generally unchallenged by having husbands doing household tasks, while they themselves became the main breadwinners. And most characteristics of the Japanese women's gender identity were appreciated by their Danish husbands who, although they did not encourage submissiveness, still enjoyed the freedom of not having too many demands made on them in the family. The ambiguity of the Danish male gender identity thus allowed for adaptation to both older gender role distinction and current role-sharing types of marriage. Consequently, the only group whose gender identity was seriously challenged among the Japanese–Danish couples in Denmark was the Japanese men.

If we look at the conditions for Japanese–Danish couples living in Japan we again find that in marriages between Danish men and Japanese women, the gender identities of the two are not likely to be seriously threatened. The gender identity of the Danish man does not hinge upon his being employed in a steady job, and even if it did, he might still have a better chance of finding employment in Japan than his Japanese counterpart has in Denmark. His Japanese wife will see advantages in being married to a man who is more considerate and less domineering than a Japanese man might be, especially since this might very well be her main reason for marrying him in the first place.

In marriages between Japanese men and Danish women in Japan, the man will have to conform to a Japanese style workplace, and this means that he will work long hours and spend time after work socializing with male colleagues. He will therefore be forced to leave everything to do with home and family to his wife. This situation will not fundamentally challenge his gender identity, but it is likely to create serious conflicts with his Danish wife. She, for her part, will find it extremely difficult to adapt to a lifestyle which in her opinion reduces her to 'a mere housewife'.[4] I have spoken with a number of Danish women who moved with their Japanese husbands to Japan, but who gave up after a few years and came back divorced. Also among the Danish wives living in Denmark there is unanimous agreement that they do not want to live for prolonged periods in Japan. Most of them have visited Japan with their husbands for some months or weeks, and although they liked the country and the people there, this experience convinced them that they would not be able to live there permanently. I shall present just one typical quote:

> The most difficult thing about living in Japan is the position of their women. I can't accept for instance that in my husband's family the women don't eat

together with the men. I want to sit down and talk, not to bustle around doing small favours for everybody.

(Danish woman in her early thirties)

To sum up, we may say that Danish female gender identity has no place in contemporary Japanese society, and that male Japanese gender identity cannot survive intact in Danish society. This puts a great strain upon those Japanese–Danish marriages in which the man is Japanese and the woman Danish. Marriages between a Danish man and a Japanese woman, on the other hand, stand a far better chance of dealing successfully with cultural discrepancies in the perceptions of male and female identities.

Notes

1. This chapter is a revised version of a paper which was presented at a conference on ethnic diversity in Macau in November 1993.
2. Of course this only holds true in more or less static societies. In societies where power relations between men and women are shifting and traditional gender roles are in the process of being redefined, gender role complementarity, too, will break down and temporarily lead to an increase in marital problems and rising divorce rates.
3. I have interviewed only one couple of the older generation in which the husband was Japanese and the wife Danish, and since this was a rather unconventional couple, the views of this specific marriage combination in the older generation cannot be adequately presented here. The scarcity of Japanese man–Danish woman combinations among the older couples is probably due to the fact that international mobility between Denmark and Japan in the 1950s and early 1960s consisted mainly of Danish men who travelled to the East as sailors or in connection with other work. Not many Japanese men came the other way, and the mobility of women was considerably lower then than now. The late 1960s brought a lot of young 'backpack travellers' who went around the world at just the age where relationships that might lead to marriage were formed with the opposite sex. Most of the first travellers were men, but the movement went to and from both Denmark and Japan. Recently, international student exchanges have further increased the opportunities for falling in love with and marrying a partner from another culture.
4. This outlook she may well share with a rising number of younger Japanese women who are ambitious for a career and who do not relish the thought of resigning themselves to the role of wife and mother.

References

Benson, S. (1981), *Ambiguous Identity – Interracial Families in London*, Cambridge: Cambridge University Press.

Blood, R. (1967), *Love Match and Arranged Marriage. A Tokyo–Detroit Comparison*, New York: The Free Press.

Broch, T., Krarup, K., Larsen, P.K. and Rieper, O. (eds) (1987), *Kvalitative Metoder i Dansk Samfundsforskning* (Qualitative Methods in Danish Sociology), Copenhagen: Nyt fra Samfundsvidenskaberne, 50.

Condon, C. and Saitoo, M. (eds) (1974), *Intercultural Encounters with Japan*, Tokyo: Simul Press.

Erikson, E.H. (1980, 1959), *Identity and the Life Cycle. A Re-issue*, New York: Norton and Company.

Hardach-Pinke, I. (1988), *Interkulturelle Lebenswelten – Deutsch-Japanische Ehen in Japan*, Frankfurt and New York: Campus.

Imamura, A. (1987), *Urban Japanese Housewives. At Home and in the Community*, Honolulu: University of Hawaii Press.

Itamoto Y. (1990), *Ueddinguberu ga kikitakute* (Wishing for the Sound of Wedding Bells), Tokyo: Shin Nippon shuppansha.

Jacobson-Widding, A. (1983), 'Introduction', in A. Jacobson-Widding (ed.), *Identity: Personal and Socio-cultural. A Symposium*, Uppsala: Uppsala Studies in Cultural Anthropology.

Kokusai kekkon handobukku. Gaikokujin to kekkon shitara . . . (Handbook of International Marriages. If one marries a foreigner . . .) (1987), Comp. by Kokusai kekkon o kangaeru kai, Tokyo: Meiseki shoten.

Kvale, S. (1987), 'Interpretation of the Qualitative Research Interview', in F.J. van Zuuren, F.J. Wertz, B. Mook (eds), *Advances in Qualitative Psychology: Themes and Variations*, Lisse: Swets & Zeitlinger.

——, (1987), 'Validity in the Qualitative Research Interview', in *Interviewet som Forskningsmetode (The Interview as Research Method)*, Aarhus: Psykologisk Skriftserie, 12/1, pp.68–104.

Lam, A. (1992), *Women and Japanese Management. Discrimination and Reform*, London: Routledge.

Lebra, T.S. (1981), 'Japanese Women in Male Dominant Careers: Cultural Barriers and Accommodation for Sex-Role Transcendence', in *Ethnology*, XX, 4, pp.291–306.

——, (1984), *Japanese Women: Constraint and Fulfillment*, Honolulu: University of Hawaii Press.

Mayer, E. (1985), *Love and Tradition. Marriage between Jews and Christians*, New York and London: Plenum Press.

Miyabara, Y. (1992), ''Kiri no Rondon. Kokusai kekkon daiichi-goo wa naze hitoku sareta' (In London's Fog. Why was the First International Marriage Kept a Secret?), in *Asahi Shinbun Weekly, AERA*, 5, 37, pp.30–3.

Mouer, R. and Sugimoto, Y. (1981), *Japanese Society: Stereotypes and Realities*, Melbourne: Japanese Studies Centre.

Nitta, F. (1988), 'Kokusai kekkon: Trends in Intercultural Marriage in Japan', *International Journal of Intercultural Relations*, 12, pp.205–32.

Oosawa, C. (1989), *Bairingaru fuamiri – kokusai kekkon no tsumatachi* (Bilingual Family – the Wives of International Marriages), Tokyo: Chikuma shobo.

Refsing, K. (1990), 'Kæreste, Hustru og Moder' (Girlfriend, Wife and Mother), in K. Refsing et al. (eds), *Gode Hustruer og Vise Mødre. Facetter af Kvindeliv i Japan* (Good Wives and Wise Mothers. Aspects of Women's Lives in Japan), Copenhagen: Rhodos.

——, (1995), 'The Discourse on Cultural Differences in Danish-Japanese Marriages', in S. Clausen, R. Starrs and A. Wedell-Wedellsborg (eds), *Cultural Encounters: China, Japan and the West*, Aarhus: Aarhus University Press.

Setouchi, H. (ed.) (1989), *Kokusai kekkon no reimei: Jinbutsu kindai josei-shi* (The Dawn of International Marriages. Biographical History of Women in the Modern Period), Tokyo: Kodansha.

Shukuya K. (1988), *Ajia kara kita hanayome, mukaeru gawa no ronri* (Brides from Asia, the Logic of the Recipient Side), Tokyo: Meiseki shoten.

Smith, R. (1983), *Japanese Society: Tradition, Self and the Social Order*, Cambridge: Cambridge University Press.

——, (1987), 'Gender Inequality in Contemporary Japan', *Journal of Asian Studies*, no.1, pp.1–25.

Spradley, J.P. (1979), *The Ethnographic Interview*, Fort Worth: Holt, Rhinehard and Winston Inc.

Sugimoto, Y. and Mouer, R. (1986), *Images of Japanese Society: a Study in the Structure of Social Reality*, London: Kegan Paul International.

——, (eds) (1989), *Constructs for Understanding Japan*, London and New York: Kegan Paul International.

Tannen, D. (1986), *That's Not What I Meant*, New York: Ballantine.

——, (1992, 1990), *Kvindesnak og Mands Tale* (trans. from *You Just Don't Understand*), Copenhagen: Munksgaards Forlag.

Thompson, L. (1993), 'Conceptualizing Gender in Marriage: The Case of Marital Care', *Journal of Marriage and the Family*, 55, August, pp.557–69.

Yamada R., Sawaki T., Minami T., Sumida H. (eds) (1990), *Wakariyasui kokusai kekkon to hoo* (International Marriages and the Law Made Easy), Tokyo: Yuuhikaku ribure.

Wagatsuma H. (1973), 'Some Problems of Interracial Marriage for the Japanese', in I.R. Stuart and L.E. Abt (eds), *Interracial Marriage: Expectations and Realities*, New York: Van Nostrand Reinhold.

Zavalloni, M. (1983), 'Ego-ecology: The Study of the Interaction between Social and Personal Identities', in A. Jacobson-Widding (ed.), *Identity: Personal and Socio-cultural. A Symposium*, Uppsala: Uppsala Studies in Cultural Anthropology.

12

Not all Issues are Black or White: Some Voices from the Offspring of Cross-Cultural Marriages

Audrey Maxwell

Although this volume focuses on intermarriage, it seems appropriate to include some voices of children of such marriages – which are becoming more numerous because of the expansion of worldwide contacts within the 'global village'. This chapter is not an in-depth study of a representative sample, but rather intends to recognize that cross-cultural marriages produce consequences for their progeny. Such children face ambiguous loyalties and difficult choices in their life encounters. Nevertheless, though media coverage tends to highlight their problems rather than their advantages, the offspring who spoke to me indicated clearly that they felt there are many rewarding features deriving from their cultural inheritances. It is encouraging that, though having no claim to representativeness, these accounts at least all end on a positive note.

In 1995 I interviewed eight such 'children' (aged between eighteen and thirty-four), reached through networking among people connected, in one way or another, with the University of Oxford. The respondents are middle class, well educated and articulate. I encouraged them to talk of their life histories using open-ended, unstructured, tape-recorded interviews. The accent was on their own thoughts and how they see their world.

Most of those to whom I talked had thought implicitly or explicitly about their experiences and how to cope with associated problems. As a child of very mixed descent myself, I found their discussion of self-identity and social placement of particular interest. One of them seemed to glide effortlessly between her varied cultural contexts, while others seem to have sometimes experienced difficulty when asking themselves 'where do I belong?'. Some, but not all, reported experiencing problems in being accepted, or wanting to be accepted, by one or other of the cultural groups to which they were affiliated by kinship, due to cultural attitudes and practices within the family group. In contexts where Black or Third World consciousness was high, they had had to face the possibility of accusations of 'betrayal' by Blacks when articulating their whiteness. But some also had to combat being stigmatized and made to feel inferior in White contexts, due to deeply embedded stereotypical expectations and categorizations (see also Shibata and Breger, this volume). For my respondents, physical characteristics (such as skin colour) denoting obvious difference from the majority seem to be important in identity questions (cf. Spickard 1989 on the politicization of colour). As a result, friendships with non-kin peer groups have often assumed great importance and marriage partners were sometimes found outside their birth communities.

Attitudes to gender relations were also mentioned as important, especially for the women interviewed. They also affected family relations and identifications.

Moreover, as the case-studies show, changes occurred for some as they matured, as perceptions and experiences varied significantly, or their place of residence or other circumstances changed, while, as explained below, political events sometimes had dramatic impact.

Class and socio-economic status were also significant factors. The more affluent respondents who were in prestigious, fee-paying schools generally had positive experiences whilst those in state schools did not.

A sense of exclusion from either side can occur for in-between individuals, depending on geographical, social and political context, age phase, peer pressure and family relationships. Choosing an identity and group affiliation therefore depends on a variety of experiences and on her or his phase in the life cycle, as the following autobiographical studies, loosely grouped under headings, exemplify.

Race and Belonging

Avi (34)

Avi's father is from Trinidad and black, whilst her mother is English and white. Her father met her mother, a nurse, whilst he was studying to be a doctor at Cambridge. Avi, the eldest of three children, was born in England.

Avi was taken to Trinidad as a toddler. Returning to England at seven years old, she attended primary school for six months. The only Afro-Caribbean mixed-race child in the class, she was placed next to a retarded girl who latched on to her since Avi was kind to her. This was her only friend because she was ostracized and teased constantly by others. She was called names, was unhappy and longed to be white.

> I was incredibly unhappy and I was more unhappy because nobody believed what went on. My mother didn't believe it. I was called 'toffee apple', that was their favourite nickname. I was called 'fat mouth' and teased constantly. I think I only became conscious of race when I was six or seven years old and went to

that school and was teased. I wanted to be white. I remember I used to wet my hair to make it straight. I used to purse my lips so that they didn't look so fat.

Avi returned to Trinidad where she had most of her schooling. She re-crossed the Atlantic to England when seventeen to attend university. She gained a good degree from Cambridge, a D.Phil. from Oxford, and an MA in Library and Information Studies. She states strongly that at university her performance as a student was judged solely on academic ability. However, racism invaded her social life and very few white persons had any interest in being friends. After two boyfriends expressed reluctance to be seen with her in public, she dated only black men. However, after leaving university she dated a white Englishman who had lived in Africa and, later still, she married another Englishman. They now have a baby daughter who, like her father, is white.

Colour again is an issue when it comes to making friends and being accepted in the neighbourhood. In North London, where she still lives, Avi was made to feel definitely unwelcome in a number of groups she tried to join. She felt she was looked upon as being different, an outsider. No one attempted to get to know her well enough to find out whether she fitted in. She felt they had looked on the surface and had classified her in their minds. For instance, they were surprised when they discovered she had a doctorate, for the stereotypical West Indian is not well educated. One of the groups disbanded shortly after she joined and the organizer clearly told her it was because of her. Whenever they met in the street this woman made strange remarks about Avi's daughter. Avi's baby is white with fair hair but the remarks indicated that the woman thought she was dark. 'I think this woman was looking at something that wasn't there; because she saw me as different, she had to see my baby as different as well. And that was a clue as to why I was seen as different and alienated from this group.'

Avi once worked in the British Council and now works in the Civil Service in the Ministry of Defence. As a result of efforts to recruit people from every sector of society, there are many ethnic minorities in the public service. She believes, however, that she would have more difficulty getting work in the private sector. She has tried to enter that sector and has never got past the interview stage. At work now, she has no problems with her colleagues but thinks it an obstacle to be female and black when it comes to promotion. Despite being vastly over-qualified for her job and having excellent reports, after seven years she has had no promotion. That gender and colour seem to be a handicap to promotion seems a justifiable observation, although she has no tangible proof to back this.

Avi notes that in the Caribbean there seem to be fewer rigid stereotypes determining who can be included in cultural definitions of the 'collective self', and this is possibly because of a long tradition of cultural mixing.[1] She says her English mother adapted easily to Trinidad, to her father's family and to the lifestyle. Her mother and father both come from Methodist backgrounds. Her mother, a committed Christian, found it easy to fit in with the church congregation (see also Shibata and Yamani, this volume, on how religion can be the basis of unity in mixed marriages). As for herself, Avi comments that she found two different types of attitude to colour. Her older relatives in Trinidad congratulated her on having a fair skin and less kinky hair. For them, marrying a white man was considered a way of 'whitening' and bettering oneself. On the other hand, according to the 'Black consciousness' of her adolescent contemporaries, stress on her identification with her White half would have been condemned as political betrayal. At this stage then, she identified with her black father and her West Indian roots. So here we see how the colour factor, and the current political attitudes of her peers, influenced her definition of herself from her childhood experience in England to her adolescent experience in Trinidad. Later, time, experience, and education led to further changes.

Many of Avi's negative experiences as a mixed-race person are certainly to do with colour. Even now she reports that she experiences difficulties at work and in her neighbourhood because she is perceived as different. Nevertheless, she has now come to accept her mixed ethnicity as an enriching part of her strong sense of self.

> I think I've got the best of both worlds. Particularly because I have been brought up in the Caribbean where people are not so hung up about race as they are here and I've been able to see both sides. I value both sides of my heritage. I'm not ashamed of the White and I'm not ashamed of the Black. I'm equally Black to White, I'm half and half . . . Any doubts I've had in the past I've overcome them now . . . I think it is an advantage to look what you are. I look like I'm mixed race . . . it is quite obvious . . . they accept you or they don't accept you. I'm a bit more concerned for my daughter. She is quarter black and she looks white. She may have slightly more problems with people who at a later date find out she is mixed . . . I'm glad I look like what I am and I think that the way forward in combating racism is that there ought to be more mixed marriages.

Far from seeing her mixed race and culture as something negative, something marginalizing, Avi now feels very balanced and optimistic.

Jack (32)

Jack was born in Leicester, England. His biological mother is English, his biological father an African-American in the US Air Force. He was adopted as a baby by another African-American air-man and his American (Creole) wife, and brought up in California. As a young child, moving from one Air Force base to another, being part of an incorporated family in a closed community, he had positive experiences. There were a number of other mixed-race offspring and there was acceptance and a sense of belonging. This could partly be due to the cosmopolitan character of the group and the lack of regional identity, or it may have been due to pride, elitism and the community spirit in the Air Force.

When he was nine his family moved and settled in southern California and there he began to experience racism (see Alex-Assensoh and Assensoh, this volume). He was bullied by both Black and White children, because he was in-between, not a member of either polarized category. Jack notes that his difficulties had partly to do 'with the reality of America itself, in that it does not know how to deal with people who are mulatto, because it brings up the whole baggage of relationships between Blacks and Whites for over two hundred years, an uncomfortable subject to this day. People react out of that, out of guilt and fear.'

When his family moved to northern California there was far less open expression of racial hostility. However, when attending State schools at secondary level, he was subject to a certain degree of harassment from both sides: being seen as not belonging to either Blacks or Whites because he was brown skinned and spoke differently from either group. However, he also experienced positive attitudes. He was popular and sought after by White American females who were attracted by the exotic, handsome, Other (see Rattansi 1992: 27; also Kohn, this volume).

Jack tended to identify with Black American culture because his family clearly did so, although his speech and skin colour made him atypical. Total acceptance by his adoptive family and their network proved very helpful. His mother, though Creole, considers herself Black, yet she totally accepts Jack's Black and Whiteness. She does not consider him a traitor in affirming his White half. His mother's positive affirmation of him has helped, as has his own ability to find acceptance and respect amongst both Black and White communities. Another important factor in increasing his self-confidence was that his biological mother sought him out when he was on a short-term mission in Washington and reassured him that he had not been unwanted. Rather, she had given him away as a baby because she put his interests first: she had reckoned that he would encounter problems growing up as a mixed-race child in Leicester and that he would have more opportunities living with his adoptive parents. His adoptive father, coming from the ghetto area where the Los Angeles riots took place, had extricated himself from his situation by joining the Air Force and rising to the highest rank of NCO, and this job, along with his, and his wife's, personalities had enabled them to rise to middle-class status. This has contributed quite a lot towards Jack's own confident attitude.

Jack attended Stanford University, where he began to see his mixed-race background as positive. His strong sense of self and social consciousness was further developed when he got involved in Christian mission work in an urban priority area of Washington DC. Religion and middle-class affluence probably helped develop his self-esteem. He saw the advantage of being able to identify with both camps. He also saw that it was important to have a sense of a whole, complete, self – without trying to please both sides. This was difficult but he has achieved it through growth and experience.

At university, he was helped by not feeling alienated but accepted by the more privileged strata of society. His studies in International Relations, looking specially at relations between rich and poor, increased his understanding. So, although there was a part of him that hated the rejection he would get from some Whites, as well as from some Blacks, he was able to transcend this and

> to come to grips with it and have a complete sense of self-worth – well, just being glad in the way God has made me, being happy with both parts of my life, being Black and White. That I didn't have to wear a different hat on different occasions according to the different types of people I was with in order to please them. At that point I began to have a sort of peace about who I was, that I could be a whole, integrated, self in any context.

After Stanford, Jack attended Fuller Theological Seminary and whilst there came to England for a summer school where he met his Dutch wife-to-be in Oxford. Later Jack took a further degree in divinity at Princeton, and worked in Phila-delphia. He spent three years working in Holland, where he encountered few negative experiences. At Oxford University too, the experience has been on the whole positive. At least there were no overt or obvious negative experiences – except for one, when a shopkeeper wrongfully accused him of stealing, and made remarks stereotyping Americans. In fact, he does have a sense of his Englishness, whilst affirming his Black American background also.

Jack has thought deeply about the increasingly multi-cultural nature of society. He considers that the experiences of offspring of cross-cultural marriages, with their deeper understanding and flexibility, could make a positive contribution to toleration.

From the above two case-studies, it seems that respondents sometimes felt marginalized in both cultural communities to which they had kin ties. Avi in her English primary school suffered racism because of her darker complexion and wanted to be white; in Trinidad, in adolescence, ashamed of her White half she affirmed her Blackness. Being coloured continued to be disadvantageous in certain contexts in England as an adult. Jack suffered racism in California from both Black and White schoolfellows who perceived his difference. Maturity, education and other experiences have helped both Avi and Jack to handle both sides of their families, and to achieve a balanced sense of identity.

Politics and Gender

Shan (23) and Raj (21)

The perceptions and attitudes of the next two people considered have been affected by their complicated situation. Shan and her brother Raj have an Indian father and a Sri Lankan mother. Shan was born in England and Raj in India. The father comes from an upper-class, elitist Parsee family, but was educated in England. The mother is Christian and mixed race, having a Tamil father and Burgher (Anglo-Asian) mother. These cultural backgrounds went unremarked in India, because of the presence of many Asians from different regions. The early upbringing of both children was in Bombay, but when Shan was fifteen and Raj thirteen the family moved to England and their later education was continued in Oxford. The differences in the two cultures where they lived – first as children in India, and then as adolescents and young adults in England – was the significant cross-cultural dimension. Their parents, though stemming from two different Asian communities, shared the same academic, English-speaking milieu, whereas the children had absorbed the culture of Bombay, and spoke Hindi and Marathi as well as English.

The culture of middle-class Oxford was acceptable and familiar to both parents, who had been to University there. But for the children the set-up was unfamiliar and difficult and they felt unaccepted. Both suffered from racism. They were called names, received derogotary remarks and were shunned or ignored. This happened both at school and outside school. These negative encounters were due to their being brown with obvious Asian looks. Shan states

> After coming to England my experiences of racism were very clear, very clear cut . . . As soon as I was in school they called me names, everything from a 'Bloody Paki', 'Black bitch', 'Black bastard' to 'dirty' and other nasty things. That has continued, not only in school, but in the streets, in shops, . . . and in buses people don't sit next to you. And now I can say, as a teacher, that in school I've had White girls say I was just a Black bitch and I've heard Afro-Caribbean girls saying I was neither here nor there, neither this nor that, and I have no right to talk . . . In Coventry in an Asian area, Punjabi people, old women, look at me with complete disgust when I walk down the street holding hands with, as they perceive it, my White boyfriend. I've had people spitting at me, throwing things at me, but I think that must be the experience of lots of people who are not from mixed race, but are black or brown (Cf. Rattansi 1992: 21,33,34).

The gender factor is also important in Shan's experience. There is no doubt that her negative experiences in England were worse than her brother's. Yet she feels she has got something positive out of coming to England by becoming aware of how much gender rules life in India and how much one had to compromise as a woman there:

> I never was so aware of how little freedom I had – whether it was to make a movement in the street, wear certain types of clothing, speak loudly or softly, hold someone's hand – as I was after I had been in England . . . I mean, I almost feel like my whole body becomes cramped when I get to India. I walk in a certain way, I talk softly, I do my hair in a certain way. Certainly, I found as a woman it has been much more empowering being for a while in England. Not because England is an empowering place for women but because India is such a disempowering place for them.

The change from India to England was helpful for her because 'I was not subject to the same scrutinies that English women have; my body is not looked at with the same gaze by White men. I'm just Black to them. In a sense my race freed me from my gender.' Her perception is that most Englishmen do not have the same expectations of her that they do of White women. Whether it means marginalization or not, it gives her freedom to behave naturally. In India she finds the scrutiny of men horrible and asserts that sexual harassment in India is an ongoing outrage on a grand scale, although women are ashamed to speak about it.

At university, although she felt respected for her academic ability, Shan considered that being a mixed-race Asian woman could be a burden. She found herself becoming more assertive in order to contradict stereotypical expectations: 'I found myself being forced by people's views of me as a Black woman to change my behaviour. I talked more than I would otherwise. I was more aggressive in certain situations', she says, 'to demonstrate that Asian women were individuals'.[2] In India, when women differed from the expected norm of the quiet submissive woman it had to do with class, power and education, not race.

Shan's mixed-race inheritance and mixed cultural background has led her to experience two different forms of exclusion: because of race in one society and gender in another. Therefore, she says 'I'm critical of identity politics which are exclusive, which are built on foundations which cannot be made common; for example: identity politics which excludes people of one colour or one religion or one gender or anything which excludes people completely.'

Shan has parents, grandparents and maternal relatives who are politically aware and articulate. She and Raj are likewise politically active. The Gulf War, which started soon after she got into university, was a critical event in her consciousness. 'It really had an immense effect on me because it showed me first hand what the Western countries could do to the Third World whensoever they chose, without any opposition, without being stopped. I felt terrifically strongly about the injustice of it.' She was incensed by the apathy of people around her who could go on leading their everyday lives unaffected, even condoning the action of the country killing people in their name. 'It made me aware' she asserts, 'of the creating of consensus in the war against the "dirty Iraqis". If anything it consolidated my sense of being an outsider, being always on the other side; being always critical of Western society and what it does to the Third World.' She also became aware of how unstable friendships were. To her, friendships were to a large extent dependent on political perception and she felt angered that many were unwilling to take responsibility for what their government was doing. This perception is important because, for a person of mixed race and culture, the community of friends is especially significant.

Shan considers that one of the positive outcomes of being a mixed-race child and living in two different cultures is that she has been forced 'to go out and build a community of my own'. Unlike those brought up in one society who usually tend to adhere to friends in the community of upbringing, Shan has been willing to lose people, to challenge tradition and to act independently. She could not depend on a birth community nor crave support from older persons here. When she needed to affirm her Indian identity in England she couldn't find anyone to identify with, because Indians saw her as different. On the other hand, acceptance in some Asian communities in England was conditional upon willingness to compromise her behaviour and identity. This difficulty in being accepted, with all her differences, was experienced in India too. The community of friends which she built up, therefore, was very important for maintaining who she was, the person whom she was seeking to be.

Shan's brother, Raj, has just completed his B.Sc. honours, as did Shan. He received a first-class degree and is now studying to be a teacher. In India, Raj states, he never consciously considered his mother as Sri Lankan. Contact with his father's relatives, a small elitist Parsee community, was frequent but not intimate:

I never felt that that side of my family was a major part of my identity. I should say my identity then was shaped more by the individuals my parents were. Partly also by my mother's side of the family, I would say, and partly by school, and partly by the things that I did as a child which had no relation to the family.

Although Raj seldom saw his mother's relatives he felt an affinity toward them. However, Sri Lanka was not known intimately, nor did they speak Sinhalese or Tamil. Thus Raj's most significant others were the ones he grew up with. 'I felt genuinely at home with the particular little subculture of my school and the people around. We spoke to each other in a kind of degraded Hindi which was effectively my main language apart from English – not in Tamil, Gujarati or Marathi as it should have been.' He was a little different to his schoolmates, he perceived, because English was his first language and books were important in his home. No rejection or negativity was experienced in Bombay.

In England, Raj completed his secondary education at the same state school as his sister:

> It was, of course, an extreme shock. Everything about being in England, in Oxford, was a complete shock . . . I felt it was a very violent school, not just in a physical sense, but there was a lot of mental bullying, some of which I was subject to more than others and which led me to hate it.

The other pupils and Raj had nothing in common, such as an interest in pop groups, music stars or football. 'I had nothing to relate to as a starting point for relationships.' The culture gap was a big reason for his unhappiness.

Raj goes on to say that 'Racist abuse was very prevalent, but I would say that that affected me less than a general form of ostracism.' He was shunned because of his different accent, his colour and because he was seen as Asian. Behaviour learnt in India, such as standing when talking to a teacher, made them laugh at him. In the fifth form he started adapting and made some friends. 'The change took place entirely by my adapting. No one was ever challenged to understand me.' Dominant cultures expect minorities to change and become acculturated. But though he was never close to them, Raj began to relate to some fellow pupils. He felt he could now fit into British as well as Indian society. However, this led to contradictions; he couldn't communicate the British side of himself to people in India or even to his family. 'I could never communicate the change which had taken place or which had to take place for me to be able to survive.'

Raj, Shan and their family lived in university accommodation. The postgraduate community, although more 'civilized and academic' than school, was not particularly friendly. Raj's father, unlike the rest of the family, had his set of friends and his own world of academic discourse. Raj found that he could communicate better with his sister and mother, both of whom were also experiencing their own traumas. He then began to perceive his mother as more Sri Lankan and recognize his Sri Lankan heritage, but he says the affinities he had were 'far more to do with the particular kind of individuals involved, than the communities involved'.

Raj had only white friends at school in Oxford. He never consciously attempted to make friends with Asians or Afro-Caribbeans, probably because he did not think of himself as Indian. Towards the end of his fifth-form year he began to see himself more broadly as Asian, as defined by British society. This realization of difference made it easier for him to relate to others. 'My identification was with any Third World people or any exploited people . . . I would say it was a positive thing, this change.'

At London University overt right-wing politics and a strong masculine culture (which he rejected) were more obvious than racism. Gender issues did affect his attitudes. He was critical of his father's male chauvinistic attitudes and the assumptions his father made within the home of being waited on and being the centre of attention. As for himself, Raj admits that females found him attractive even at school. One embarrassed him by going down on her knees in the playground and asking him out. At university he had begun to adjust and with conscious efforts made friends with persons from different communities, White, Afro-Caribbean, Asian and mixed. His present partner is English and White. 'I think ultimately a growing political awareness was much more important than what I saw as my ethnic background.'

In India he had been aware of injustice at a micro-level, of men against women, rich against poor. In Britain at this stage he became starkly aware of the unequal relationships between First and Third Worlds. The Gulf War highlighted this for him as it did for his sister. He says it was 'a major, very important experience in terms of my politicization'. He felt a deep anger at what he saw was another kind of racism, different from direct personal affront; one that was dangerous, costing people's lives. He saw how propaganda was used to shape people's attitudes and was appalled at assumptions made by nice people about Iraq and the Third World – how cheaply they held the lives of people over there! His views of British society were significantly affected by these events and his identification with the exploited strengthened. Those he kept as friends were coloured by his politics rather than his ethnic background.

Raj considers mixed-race or cross-cultural unions to be positive events. The movements in some Afro-Caribbean groups and Asian communities towards 'a kind of ethnic nationalism which particularly targeted people in mixed-race relationships', he sees as 'a uniformly negative thing, a sign of Black male control over Black women'. Sometimes, he thinks, people extend one unfortunate individual experience so as to generalize about total communities. Also, where people are unaware of sexism as a dynamic, they respond by viewing every problem from a racist angle. He considers marginalization to be a problem of the communities involved rather than of the individuals affected, and therefore thinks that the answer lies in the education of these communities.

Sheriff (21)

Sheriff's father is an Iraqi businessman from a wealthy, middle-class family, while his mother is Irish, from a strict, Catholic, working-class family living in England. The parents first met in Liverpool. Sheriff has spent most of his life in London except for three years in California. During his early childhood his parents ran a successful restaurant in London. In the USA they lived in an upper-class area in the San Fernando Valley, and were wealthy. Although they were not affluent after their return, he and his two younger siblings attended private schools. At university he obtained a good honours degree in philosophy. He is now studying to be a teacher.

Sheriff, his brother and sister were perceived as White by others because they had pale complexions, therefore they did not suffer from racism from white people. His first recollection is of living in London among a multi-racial population on a Council Estate in Chelsea. Similarly, the catchment area of the private, upper-middle-class primary school he attended had children from several cultures. Many were diplomats' children. 'We liked the fact that there were children from several other cultures. That made us feel at home.' In retrospect Sheriff sees that there may have been some racist encounters which he did not recognize as such when young or of which he has suppressed recall. 'Only recently I've started to discover ways in which I might have experienced racism as a child and not known it, and ways in which I wanted to suppress it as well.' At his less upper-class secondary school with a high Asian intake, he was more aware of racism, though not acutely affected himself. Sheriff says 'It wasn't a kind of coincidence that all my friends were of mixed race or were completely black . . . My name was the giveaway really and wherever it came up we were perceived as Other and it came up right throughout my schooling.' However, compared with the previous respondents the negative aspect was minimal.

Sheriff's family relationships and his mixed cultural background played an important part in his life-experience and perceptions. He was aware of his mother's feelings. She had five sisters and two brothers. The sisters all married foreigners. Sheriff says 'they all married out which indicates a pattern . . . connected to their upbringing, I think. Their father was very bigoted and narrow minded and they've all had that tendency to break away and marry into a different culture . . . My mum was very rebellious . . . My dad represented a larger world and I think he represented some kind of social mobility, to move up a bit' (cf. Merton 1941: 361–74). The assumptions and expectations revolving round vague stereotypes could be functioning here (see Kohn, this volume); the father possibly seen as an 'exotic other', a prince from the 'Arabian Nights', for the poor working-class mother, who defied her father's objections to her liaising with a Muslim. The relationship did not have difficulties on religious grounds because neither his father nor his family were strict Muslims. There was interaction with the families of each parent, especially the mother's Irish siblings and their families. They also knew the father's two brothers and sister, who eventually married Iraqis. The main cultural influence on the Arab side came through the restaurant; through the food, music, language spoken, and through the working personnel and their Arab clientele. In the three years that Sheriff spent in America (1982–5) he did not experience racism but felt a sense of isolation and culture shock, a lack of community.

The gender factor came out strongly in Sheriff's experience, as well, he reports, as in that of his siblings. This applied to difficulties not only in the relationship between his parents, but also to his father's sexist behaviour towards his sister. The gender dimension was tied also to the clash of cultural notions, perhaps of expectations about women and the woman's place in the home. Sheriff says

> As a child I wanted to repress or suppress my Arab side because I only saw the bad side of Arabic culture . . . I didn't want to identify with it . . . My mum brought us up single-handed. Even though we had lots of money he never gave any money to her. She did all the cooking and cleaning, later also the business side of things. There never was any question of him doing anything. He was an alcoholic so he was incredibly verbally abusive and also physically abusive as well, though not in front of me.

Sheriff had a close relationship with his Irish mother and was protective towards her. He hated his father's oppressive behaviour towards her and his sister.

Male dominance was evident in the Arab guests, customers and workers in the restaurant. His mother, excluded from this circle, associated with her sister whose Egyptian husband also worked in the restaurant; her brothers gave some support. At this period Sheriff, identifying with everything non-Arabic, suggested that his parents separate.

At London University, despite efforts to make white friends, Sheriff gravitated towards mixed-race people because they shared a common sense of unease and insecurity, even though middle class. 'I see them as being more open minded in many respects than the white children.'

Sheriff has now changed his politically conservative opinions. His interest in Iraq, Iran and Islam is because of his father. 'The most politicizing influence I had was the Gulf War . . . the dehumanizing way the Iraqis were spoken of . . . as rats. This I couldn't take, and actually having to go to school which was one hundred per cent behind the Gulf War and beating the war drums every day.' He went to great lengths to watch the news, and read all he could about it. The way things were written angered him.

> The way the whole thing was described . . . the way the Iraqis were not people, made me speak out at school. I organized a debate at school in which we won, saying the war was unjust . . . That had one of the biggest effects on me, in terms of my identity as well, and then after I went to university. Before that I would never have identified as Black in the political sense of the word. I always viewed myself as White, and I understand why I did it, because my experiences weren't as bad as, say, an Afro-Caribbean's and also some Asians . . . but nonetheless I identify as Black now. I think there were connections and similar experiences. They don't have to be to the same degree always in order to relate to other people, virtually all my best friends are other ethnics. One of my best

friends is Pakistani and of course my partner now is Asian. So I very much identify with that and feel a real sense of having had the world opened to me.

Sheriff's words state clearly how his experience, his friends and world events shaped his thoughts, perceptions and identification. He considers his present identity positive because of his identification with the Third World and the possibility of doing something to help.

Sheriff reflects on the various ways he regarded himself and says 'I've never felt really British. I've felt Irish, which is distinctly not British, and I've felt Iraqi. So I identified with both these things at different parts of my life.' Also his closeness to his mother made him articulate his Irish culture as a young person. He says 'I think, now, my identity tends more towards Iraqi and Black.' His mother, who always retained her Irish identity though living all her life in England, cannot accept the change in him:

I think one thing my mum finds difficult to accept these days is me identifying as Asian or mixed race. She doesn't understand that even though I've experienced some bad things in Arab culture, I wanted to keep links with Arab culture. My brother particularly, too . . . He's closer to my dad . . . She does not want to accept this. When we were kids we accepted our mum's culture. We never initiated bringing Arab culture home. But now me and my brother feel a connection with that and my mum can't take that, and she kicked us out for that – which was completely unjust.

Meanwhile, Sheriff's sister has negative reactions to anything Arabic because of her father's abuse, though she has many black and mixed-race friends. Sheriff's father has expressed explicitly his racist attitudes toward Afro-Caribbeans and Asians. When the children were younger he did not mind his son dating girls from these cultures, but Sheriff is certain that his father would object to his marrying his present Asian partner. The father adamantly forbade Sheriff's sister having black boyfriends. She eventually ran away from home. Sheriff comments on how much more difficult it is for a female than a male to be black or of mixed race. He says that he has seen this for himself with regard to people's behaviour and attitudes towards his partner and other girls.

Despite the negative factors Sheriff has experienced lately, he still sees the positive side.

Having mixed-race parents has given me an interest in those cultures which has a snowballing effect which creates an interest in other cultures as well. It has also helped me to relate to people from other cultures, especially if they are in similar situations . . . So I think it is very positive. It has given me an interest in struggles round the world, being politicized and identifying myself as Black, fighting things, anti-racist and Black struggles, and feeling differently about things in this country, feeling less apathetic than I would have, feeling kind of White.

He also feels positive about his own partnership. He is glad that he has witnessed people discriminating against his partner and others. He says 'I think it is positive, me having had the background I've had and then gravitating towards people who feel similarly concerned about change.' Life experience clearly changes his perceptions of the world, the way he identifies himself and his priorities for action.

Class Similarities

Gavin (18) and John (21)
Lack of any distinguishing physical features, including colour, seem important in the construction of identity for the next two respondents, the brothers Gavin and John. Their Iranian mother has lived in several European countries and speaks fluent French and English, but still consciously accesses her Iranian culture. The father is English and also well educated. Both parents are from upper-class back-grounds. The brothers both look English and act English. In everyone's perception, including their own, they are English. They live now in rural Oxfordshire but both boys, besides travelling widely, have lived abroad in Malaysia, Hong-Kong and Romania following their father's postings. Both were educated in prestigious English fee-paying boarding schools. The older one is now completing university whilst the younger one has taken a year out prior to university. Thus their con-sciousness is upper-class English. Neither has received any racist remarks or negative attitudes, either at school, from their village community or from society at large.

Both boys have obviously benefited from the cultural and personal input from the Iranian side, their mother's socialization, and through their maternal grand-parents who have made lengthy visits every year. Their mother's sister, her husband and children, plus friends, are often house guests and give them experience of Iranian extended family life. Listening to Persian history, stories, anecdotes and music extends this cultural dimension. On their father's side, except for occasional contact with their father's mother who died several years ago, his sister and some cousins, they have little interaction. The father comes from a conservative, but not close-knit, English family. Both boys feel accepted by both maternal and paternal relatives. Gavin says that

Having been brought up in England and having visited Iran only once when I was very young, I think I feel very much English. This stems of course, very strongly, from my education. It has been solely English. I don't speak Iranian. Therefore, that shuts out a great deal of the Iranian side. However, I do understand certain bits of Iranian. Also, I think religion plays quite a large part in it. Being a Christian . . . never having visited a mosque, I don't know much about the Islamic side.

However, he is keen to know more about this part of his heritage. He is an enterprising young man and in his year out, after earning his way to New Zealand and working on a sheep farm, he intends to rectify this. 'I'm very keen to learn more about Iran and this is why I'm going to visit Iran on my year off. Having just scratched the surface, I'd like to go much deeper into it as well as go and see the physical things, the architecture, the mosques, etcetera.'

Both boys have been brought up Anglican Christians. The fact that their mother is a Muslim presents no difficulty. The younger lad of eighteen years seems more conscious of the positive aspects of his mixed heritage. 'I think I have an advantage over many people because I have the English culture and background. I can learn from that and at the same time I can learn from the Iranian side. It gives me a broader perpective on life as a whole.' Despite his not speaking Persian, his upbringing and contact with maternal relatives and friends has fired his interest in and wish for a deeper knowledge of Iran. John too, found the familiarity with extended family life a distinct advantage in helping to cope with living in Gambia during his year out. John says he has not thought much about questions of identity: 'I think I feel mainly English. I'm aware that there are other sides to my identity.' What he says about his peers at school and university also accords with his brother's impressions that they have been broad minded and not racist. He believes that others who were black were not subject to racism at school either, or at least he didn't perceive or recognize any problem. The school environment, relatively protected from the outside world, could have affected their perceptions, but the quality of education and high expectations of mores and behaviour could account for the absence of racism.

Switching Identities

As we have seen from Sheriff's experience, identities can change. It is possible to move between two distinct identities according to context and place in the life cycle, and to one's perceptions of one's reference group and the felt need to fit in with it. Here we may listen to Sarah's voice as she adopts an ultra-English way of speech or a Sri Lankan accent as she deems is required. She feels a strong sense of belonging in Sri Lanka amongst her relatives; but equally she is proud to be a 'maid of Kent'. She chooses to be what she calls 'chameleon-like'.

Sarah (19)

Sarah has a story similar to that of Gavin and John in some ways. It also has some interesting differences. Sarah's mother is Sri Lankan; light-skinned, she also came from elite mixed parents. Sarah's father, born and bred in Britain, has Swedish and Scottish antecedents. Sarah's parents met at the University of Oxford and married despite objections from her father's family. Her father, Sarah says, is the epitome of a distinguished, elegant, English gentleman, her mother is ladylike and equally clever. The family live in Sevenoaks in the stockbroker belt. She remembers that as a child she and her mother were conspicuous as the only foreign-looking persons in their small town. People turned to stare at them, possibly not because of their colour but, understandably, because her mother wore a sari. There were no negative comments or behaviour of any sort towards them that she remembers. In fact, she has never experienced any racism in Sevenoaks, or understood it as such, if it occurred.

Like Gavin and John, Sarah attended prestigious, elite private schools, at both primary and secondary level. Like them she has a light-coloured skin. She did not experience any racism at school. Only once has she felt uncomfortable – when changing for swimming, a child asked her whether the dirt was difficult to remove. With a child's instinct to fit in and not appear different, she said she took pains to speak English with the same accent as her school friends. 'But when I was a Brownie, it was a great issue because in my Brownie pack there were girls from working-class backgrounds, as also in the Brownie pack which would share the Brownie camp. They would gang up on me and call me a Paki. They were very spiteful, pulled the ears off my soft toys, and things like this, because I was Other.' Interestingly, she associates racism with class. The only other time Sarah's mixed background had caused aggravation was when trying to catch a bus in London where she was subjected to racist name-calling such as 'Paki bitch'. Although her skin could be described as creamy, she had acquired a considerable summer tan at the time of this incident. Although some children identified her as 'Paki', given all the other signals and symbols she carries with her, she can be seen as White and English. In fact, whilst in England, she claims her British identity. At Somerville College, Oxford, her British friends do not see her as different, since she speaks and acts as an English lady. As at school, her experience has been unproblematic (see Brah 1992).

When in Sri Lanka, however, Sarah articulates her Sri Lankan identity. 'I think I see myself belonging to both very strongly, but I am who I'm with. When in Sri Lanka I speak differently. I do have the same Sri Lankan accent as my aunts have.' She is clever at adapting to either environment and takes pains to do so. She says that it isn't from her father she gets her feelings for England and

It isn't from him I've got the way I speak, which is much more extreme than my father's. I think it's a part of trying to be English. It is part of my chameleon instinct to fit in with wherever I am. In the same way as I said that in Sri Lanka I had this Sri Lankan accent, here, I have a very, very English accent. So much so, that a friend of mine, turned round and used me as an example of absolute Englishness, which I had to spend a great deal of time saying I wasn't . . . I'm not. Yet as soon as I opened my mouth I betrayed myself as an English lady, I hope.

Sarah feels accepted by both parents' families so that she can choose to identify with whichever group she is with. She says that when she is in Sri Lanka she fits in, she is familiar with everything and knows her background through her mother's stories. However, she probably fits in only with her particular class. She has met about sixty members of her mother's family and was not only accepted but congratulated by a respected Kandyan relative on looking Kandyan. 'I feel very, very strongly that I belong to them.' With regard to Britain, however, she states

I don't think I identify with England, Britain. I identify with my county, not my country. Being Kentish, being a maid of Kent, is very, very important to me. I've lived in Kent all my life. I love it in a way I love no other part of England or Europe. The only place for which I have a comparable affection in terms of landscape is Sri Lanka. I'm a girl of the Weald. I live at the foot of Pilgrim's Way and the landscape there is the absolute picture of England.

As Sarah speaks, her accent becomes very upper-class English, adding conviction to her self-perceptions. She goes on to say later, after expressing her great appreciation of her England, that 'In a sense, I do feel some identification but I don't feel the intense patriotism I see in some people.' This statement modifies Sarah's previous one, placing county in opposition to country. Most often sentiments for locality nourish sentiments for one's country.

Sarah expresses the ambiguity of her mixed culture more than any other interviewee (see Benson 1981), but it is not a negative experience, it is more a switching of identity, her acknowledged chameleon quality. This could be due in part to personality or to the particular phase of life she is at and could change with time and growth. Sarah sees both the advantage and the disadvantage in being of mixed race and culture. 'Being this mixture is much more interesting, more individual than being exactly like everybody else is. Yet at the same time I see myself as not fitting in anywhere exactly, because I'm always ever so slightly outside.' In the last analysis she finds it positive because she is adaptable and says 'I call myself "Eurasian" because it is the simplest way to explain. I don't belong to one place, I belong to all of them.'

Conclusion

The few, relatively economically privileged, cases we have to consider here clearly show how many variables – such as colour, class, education, gender, place of residence, family attitudes and political events – all intertwine in different permutations and are of varying significance. Religion did not seem a problem – it was, in two cases, a help.

The anecdotes related here suggest that people change through time. It would be interesting to find out how these respondents, ten or fifteen years on, change their perceptions. Will they accept established views of power structures, become more and more a part of the establishment, and challenge assumptions less, because of the need to advance their careers? Will they work to change the attitudes from which they themselves suffered? Or might they and/or their peers become racist if their own offspring were to consider marrying someone with different coloured skin? Will their children agree that their mixed heritage is a blessing?

Despite the problems encountered, these respondents evaluate as an asset their mixed inheritances – and an interesting factor is that several were not merely dual inheritances but they were multi-stranded. They felt that to be a mixed-culture person is more interesting, gives more flexibility and a broader outlook and interest in other cultures. A mixed heritage can foster an ability to cross cultures, to understand and relate to others, empathize with the exploited and sufferings of the Third World, and may contribute toward combating racism.

The respondents here almost give the impression that they see people of mixed blood as a growing constituency with the potential for acting as an important moral force. Offspring of mixed marriages whose experiences have already necessitated having to come to grips with questions of citizenship, belonging and identity, have much to contribute.

Notes

1. See Alibhai-Brown and Montague 1992: 53–65, especially pp.61–5. Lord Tony Gifford expresses similar views choosing Jamaica in preference to England to live with his Jamaican wife. See also Shibata, this volume.
2. A common predicate of racism, 'you can't tell the difference, they all look the same'.

References

Alibhai-Brown, Y. and Montague, A. (1992), *The Colour of Love*, London: Virago.

Barth, F. (1969), *Ethnic Groups and Boundaries: The Social Organization of Cultural Difference*, London: George Allen and Unwin.

Benson, S. (1981), *Ambiguous Ethnicity*, Cambridge: Cambridge University Press.

Brah, A. (1992), 'Difference, Diversity and Differentiation', in J. Donald and A. Rattansi (eds), *Race, Culture and Difference*, London: Sage Publications in association with the Open University.

Fanon, F. (1986), *Black Skin, White Masks*, London: Pluto Press.

Gilroy, P. (1987), *There Ain't no Black in the Union Jack: The Cultural Politics of Race and Nation*, London: Hutchinson.

Hall, S. (1990), 'Cultural Identity and Diaspora', in J. Rutherford (ed.), *Identity, Community, Culture, Difference*, London: Lawrence and Wishart.

——, (1992), 'New Ethnicities', in J. Donald and A. Rattansi (eds), *Race, Culture and Difference*, London: Sage Publications in association with the Open University.

Merton, R. (1941), 'Intermarriage and the Social Structure', in *Psychiatry*, 4, 3, August.

Rattansi, A. (1992), 'Changing the Subject: Racism, Culture and Education', in J. Donald and A. Rattansi (eds), *Race, Culture and Difference*, London: Sage Publications in association with the Open University.

Rutherford, J. (1990), 'A Place called Home: Identity and the Cultural Politics of Difference', in J. Rutherford (ed.), *Identity, Community, Culture, Difference*, London: Lawrence and Wishart.

Solomos, J. and Back, L. (1996), *Racism and Society*, London and Basingstoke: Macmillan Press Ltd.

Spickard, P. (1989), *Mixed Blood. Intermarriage and Ethnic Identity in Twentieth Century America*, Madison: University of Wisconsin Press.

Thompson, B. and Tyagi, S. (1996) (eds), *Names we Call Home: Autobiography on Racial Identity*, New York and London: Routledge.

Index